SCIENCE FICTION,

Today and Tomorrow

A Discursive Symposium by

BEN BOVA

FREDERIK POHL

GEORGE ZEBROWSKI

FRANK HERBERT

THEODORE STURGEON

ALAN E. NOURSE

THOMAS N. SCORTIA

REGINALD BRETNOR

JAMES GUNN

ALEXEI AND CORY PANSHIN

POUL ANDERSON

HAL CLEMENT

ANNE MCCAFFREY

GORDON R. DICKSON

JACK WILLIAMSON

SCIENCE FICTION,
Today and Tomorrow

edited by
Reginald Bretnor

HARPER & ROW, PUBLISHERS
New York, Evanston,
San Francisco,
London

For Rosalie

SCIENCE FICTION, TODAY AND TOMORROW. Copyright © 1974 by Reginald Bretnor. All rights reserved. Printed in the United States of America. No part of this book may be used or reproduced in any manner whatsoever without written permission except in the case of brief quotations embodied in critical articles and reviews. For information address Harper & Row, Publishers, Inc., 10 East 53rd Street, New York, N.Y. 10022. Published simultaneously in Canada by Fitzhenry & Whiteside Limited, Toronto.

FIRST EDITION

Designed by Gloria Adelson

Library of Congress Cataloging in Publication Data

Bretnor, Reginald.
  Science fiction; today and tomorrow.
  Bibliography: p.
  1. Science fiction—Addresses, essays, lectures.
I. Title.
PN3448.S45B7   809,3'876   73–4142
ISBN 0–06–010467–8

CONTENTS

Introduction

It is now scarcely necessary (as it was when I assembled and edited *Modern Science Fiction: Its Meaning and Its Future* in 1953) to explain to any literate general readership why a book on science fiction should be written, for in the past few years the field has achieved the wide recognition then denied to it. However, because this sudden recognition has not meant sudden understanding, much remains unchanged. In the preface to *Modern Science Fiction,* I wrote about the book's purposes and my own:

> This is not the first book to deal with science fiction. It is, however, the first general survey of modern science fiction against the background of the world today. It is the first attempt to examine modern science fiction in its relation to contemporary literatures, contemporary human problems. Having taken the approach of the ecologist, rather than that of the anatomist, for its model, I have made no effort to confine its authors too rigidly to the defined limits of their subjects, or to inhibit their discussion of whatever matters they considered pertinent. Under these circumstances, naturally, I have allowed myself a similar degree of liberty in the writing of my own chapter.

Twenty years have passed, during which many more books on science fiction in its various aspects have appeared. Aside from that, everything in the statement applies equally to this new symposium, *Science Fiction, Today and Tomorrow*. It is an examination of science fiction in our contemporary world, which means of course that it looks at science fiction as a life process—something that has its sole existence in the minds of men, created by those minds out of their aspirations and imaginings, their passions and philosophies, influencing those minds for good or ill, and through them influencing and being influenced by that exterior world of which we are a part.

Today the world is vastly more complex, in many ways more puzzling, and to most thinking men far more perilous than the world of 1953. Besides, we have become very largely a mandarin society, where (except in the hard sciences) the steps taken toward status too often are equated with learning, status with wisdom, notoriety with stature, and platitudes with profundity. In such societies, which tend to manufacture literatures and speculations according to ever narrower "go/no-go" criteria, the creative mind is curbed from the beginning. When, in addition, the manufacture is on a mass basis, when literatures and speculations are contrived by fewer and fewer men to reach more and more people through mass news-entertainment media, those natural channels of interpersonal interchange and feedback that enrich a culture become spontaneously constricted (very much as they are deliberately constricted by totalitarian governments), and creative minds not only are constrained, but the chances for creative individuals to realize their potential can be nullified almost completely.

In my own chapter, I have discussed those aspects of this process which I consider vital to the future of science fiction, and indeed, to the future of the arts in general. I will say no more about them here. However, my concern with them has to a great extent determined the nature of this book. Even more than in 1953, I wanted to present as many fresh and vital views of our surrounding complexity as possible, not interpreted ritualistically, not forced into conformity with any rigid teleology, not carefully culled to display the fashions and pretensions of literary criticism, but marshaled to produce what can perhaps be described as a survey of *Science Fiction, Today and Tomorrow* from that broad perspective which science fiction has itself invented. Essentially, this meant that the imaginative scope, the creative talent, the vast variety of backgrounds in education and experience, and the almost limitless range of beliefs and hopes, ambitions and ideals, which have produced science fiction as we know it, should be harnessed to the task of its interpretation.

That is why all the contributors are writers well known in the field. That is why as individuals and as writers they are so diverse. That is why they were selected. The book was written to a prepared table of contents, from which we departed only very slightly as the text took shape. Alan Nourse, for instance, suggested his own subject of "Science Fiction and Man's Adaptation to Change," which I had not thought of, and Tom Scortia, by changing one word in the title of his chapter, made its meaning much clearer.

The book is, I think, a good and useful one. My major debt is, of course, to its authors, who brought it into being and who, in the majority of cases, gave it much more than was required, with an enthusiasm and a generosity far beyond what I had contracted. I am also indebted to Victoria Schochet and others on Harper & Row's editorial staff, first for their interest in the book, and then for their patience with its compiler. I am very grateful to Jacques Barzun and to Larry Niven for permission to quote from their published works, and to Richard J. Portal, Chief Reference Librarian at the Jackson County Public Library, for his prompt and always accurate answers to my many questions. Finally, I want to thank Carol Young, of Grants Pass, Oregon, who somehow puzzled out and typed the final manuscript.

REGINALD BRETNOR

Science Fiction
Today

Ben Bova

The Role of Science Fiction

The year 1972 was marked by publication of a controversial book, *The Limits to Growth*. This study of the world's future, done by a team of MIT scientists with the aid of computer "models" of the future of our society, was sponsored by an international organization called The Club of Rome. The study forecast a planetwide disaster unless humankind sharply limits its population growth and consumption of natural resources.

The MIT group worked out a technique for simulating certain aspects of the world's social and economic behavior, and the interrelationships among them. Thus the computer model could show how population grows when the death rate is kept low and the birthrate is unchecked, how consumption of natural resources is affected by increased population, how pollution stems from industrial output, etcetera. Putting all these factors together, the study showed that total disaster is waiting for humankind within a century.

According to the computer's model of the world, if we don't change our present style of growth-oriented society, and change it drastically, we will soon use up all the available natural resources, and produce so much pollution and overpopulation that the entire world society will collapse. Resources will run out. Food and industrial production will tumble. The death rate will climb out of sight. Mass starvation, war, pestilence—all shown on clear, inexorable-looking graphs, straight from the computer's print-out.

The graphs show that the curves representing population, industrial production, farm output, and natural resources all peak early in the twenty-first century, then collapse. Super-disaster. And it's all very real, if you grant a few critical assumptions.

The MIT study evoked immediate howls of protest and delight. Some said the book was a mathematically accurate forecast of a doom that we must work hard to avert. Others said it was a grab bag of poor assumptions and unwarranted straight-line extrapolations. As of this moment, the debate rages on. And the clock is ticking.

Most people were caught by surprise when the book came out. Many refused to believe that disaster is possible, probable, inevitable—if we don't change our mode of running Spaceship Earth. But science fiction people were neither surprised nor outraged. The study was really old news to them. They'd been making their own "models" of tomorrow and testing them all their lives.

(Incidentally, several science fictionists—including Arthur C. Clarke—immediately pointed out that the MIT scientists automatically assumed that the earth is a closed system. The MIT team didn't consider that humankind now has the ability to draw natural resources from elsewhere in the solar system. This is perhaps the major flaw in the MIT study.)

What the scientists attempted with their computer model is very much like the thing that science fiction writers and readers have been doing for decades (or centuries, if you want to define the works of earlier writers as science fiction). Instead of using a computer to "model" a future world society, science fiction writers have used their human imaginations. This gives the writers some enormous advantages.

One of the advantages is flexibility.

Science fiction writers are not in the business of predicting *the* future. They do something much more important. They try to show the many possible futures that lie open to us. If the history of the human race can be thought of as an enormous migration through time, with thousands of millions of people wandering through the centuries, then the writers of science fiction are the scouts, the explorers, the adventurers who send back stories that warn of the harsh desert up ahead, or tales that dazzle us with reports of the beautiful mountains that lie just over the horizon.

For there is not simply *a* future, a time to come that's preordained and inexorable. Our future is built, bit by bit, minute by minute, by the actions of human beings. One vital role of science fiction is to show what kinds of future might result from certain kinds of human actions.

Have you ever stood on a flat, sandy beach, at the edge of the water, and watched the little wavelets that play at your feet? After the breakers have dumped their energy and the water rushes as far up the beach as it can, there's a crisscross pattern of wavelets that mottle the beach. If the sun's at the proper angle, you can clearly see what physicists call *interference patterns*. The wavelets interact with one another, sometimes adding together to form a stronger wave, sometimes canceling each other to form a blank spot in the pattern.

The myriads of ideas that parade across the pages of science fiction magazines and books each month form such a pattern in the minds of readers and writers. Some ideas get reinforced, added to, strengthened by repetition and enlargement. Other ideas get canceled, fall out of favor, are found lacking in one way or another. Thus, for more than a generation now, science fiction people have been worrying about problems such as pollution, nuclear warfare, overpopulation, genetic manipulation, runaway technology, thought control, and other threats that burst on the general public as shocking surprises.

Other potential problems have been examined and dropped. Today there are few stories about invisible men seized by dreams of power. Or plagues of "space germs" infecting Earth. When Michael Crichton's *Andromeda Strain* became a vastly popular book and movie, most science fiction people groaned. "But it's an old idea!" they chorused, meaning that it's no longer a valid idea: the problem does not and probably will not exist. But this old idea was shatteringly new and exciting to the general public.

To communicate the ideas, the fears and hopes, the shape and feel of all the infinite possible futures, science fiction writers lean heavily on another of their advantages: the art of fiction.

For while a scientist's job has largely ended when he's reduced his data to tabular or graph form, the work of a science fiction writer is just beginning. His task is to convey the human story: the scientific basis for the possible future of his story is merely the background. Perhaps "merely" is too limiting a word. Much of science fiction consists of precious little except the background, the basic idea, the gimmick. But the best of science fiction, the stories that make a lasting impact on generations of readers, are stories about *people*. The people may be nonhuman. They may be robots or other types of machines. But they will be people, in the sense that human readers can feel for them, share their joys and sorrows, their dangers and their ultimate successes.

The art of fiction has not changed much since prehistoric times, mainly because man's nervous system and the culture he's built out of it have not basically changed.

From the earliest Biblical times, through Homer to Shakespeare, Goethe, and right down to today's commercial fiction industry, the formula for telling a powerful story has remained the same: create a strong character, a person of great strengths, capable of deep emotions and decisive action. Give him a weakness. Set him in conflict with another powerful character—or perhaps with nature. Let this exterior conflict be the mirror of the protagonist's own interior conflict, the clash of his desires, his own strength against his own weakness. And there you have a story. Whether it's Abraham offering his only son to God, or Paris bringing ruin to Troy over a woman, or Hamlet and Claudius playing their deadly game, Faust seeking the world's knowledge and power, Gully Foyle, D. D. Harriman, Montag the Fireman, Michael Valentine Smith, Muad'Dib—the stories that stand out in the minds of the readers are those that are made incandescent by characters—people—who are unforgettable.

To show other worlds, to describe possible future societies and the problems lurking ahead, is not enough. The writer of science fiction *must show how these worlds and these futures affect human beings.* And something much more important: *he must show how human beings can and do literally create these future worlds.* For our future is largely in our own hands. It doesn't come blindly rolling out of the heavens; it is the joint product of the actions of billions of human beings. This is a point that's easily forgotten in the rush of headlines and the hectic badgering of everyday life. But it's a point that science fiction makes constantly: the future belongs to us—whatever it is. We make it, our actions shape tomorrow. We have the brains and guts to build paradise (or at least try). Tragedy is when we fail, and the greatest crime of all is when we fail even to try.

Thus science fiction stands as a bridge between science and art, between the engineers of technology and the poets of humanity. Never has such a bridge been more desperately needed.

Writing in the British journal *New Scientist,* the famed poet and historian Robert Graves said in 1972, "Technology is now warring openly against the crafts, and science covertly against poetry."

What Graves is expressing is the fear that many people have: technology has already allowed machines to replace human muscle power; now it seems that machines such as electronic computers might replace human brainpower. And he goes even further, pointing a shaking finger at science as the wellspring of technology, and criticizing science on the mystical grounds that science works only in our usual four dimensions of space/time, while truly human endeavors such as poetry have a power that scientists can't recognize "because, at its most intense [poetry] works in the Fifth Dimension, independent of time."

Graves explains that poetry is usually the product of intuitive thinking, and grants that some mathematical theories have also sprung from intuition. Then he says, "Yet scientists would dismiss a similar process . . . as 'illogical.' "

Apparently Graves sees scientists as a sober, plodding phalanx of soulless thinking machines, never making a step that hasn't been carefully thought out in advance. He should try working with a few scientists, or even reading James D. Watson's *The Double Helix*.

As a historian, Graves should be aware that James Clerk Maxwell's brilliant insight about electromagnetism—the guess that visible light is only one small slice of the spectrum of electromagnetic energy, a guess that forms the basis for electronics technology—was an intuitive leap into the unknown. Maxwell had precious little evidence to back up his guess. The evidence came later. Max Planck's original concept of the quantum theory was also mainly intuition. The list of wild jumps of intuition made by these supposedly stolid, humorless scientists is long indeed.

Scientists are human beings! They are just as human, intuitive, and emotional as anyone else. But most people don't realize this. They don't know scientists, any more than they know much about science.

C. P. Snow pointed out two decades ago that there is a gap between the Two Cultures, and Graves's remarks show that the gap is widening into a painful chasm. Graves is a scholar who should know better. He's justly renowned for his work in ancient mythology, where he's combined his gifts of poetry and historical research in a truly original and beautiful way.

But he doesn't seem to understand that scientists do precisely the same thing. Because he doesn't understand scientists.

Since the prehistoric days of tribal shamans, most people have held a highly ambivalent attitude toward the medicine man-astrologer-wizard-scientist. On the one hand they envied his abilities and sought to use his power for their own gain. On the other hand, they feared his power, hated his seeming superiority, and knew damned well that he was in league with dark forces of evil.

There has been little change in this double-edged attitude over the centuries. Today most people still tend to hold scientists in awe. After all, scientists have brought us nuclear weapons, modern medicines, space flight, and underarm deodorants.

Yet at the same time, we see scientists derided as fuzzy-brained eggheads or as coldly ruthless, emotionless makers of monsters. Scientists are a minority group, and like most minorities they're largely hidden from the public's sight, tucked away in ghettos —laboratories, campuses, field sites out in the desert or on Pacific atolls.

Before the public can understand and appreciate what science can and cannot do, the people must get to see and understand the scientists themselves. Get to know their work, their aims, their dreams, and their fears.

A possible answer to this problem of humanizing science and scientists comes from the field in which Graves made his major contribution: mythology.

Joseph Campbell, professor of literature at Sarah Lawrence College, has spent a good deal of his life studying humankind's mythology and writing books on the subject, such as the four-volume *The Masks of God*, and *Hero with a Thousand Faces*. He has pointed out that modern man has no real mythology to turn to. The old myths are dead, and no new mythology has arisen to take their place.

And man needs a mythology, Campbell insists, to give a sort of emotional meaning and stability to the world in which he lives. Myths are a sort of codification on an emotional level of man's attitudes toward life, death, and the whole vast and sometimes frightening universe.

An example. Almost every primitive culture has a Prometheus myth. In our Western culture, the Greek version is the one most quoted. Prometheus was a demigod who saw man as a weak, starving, freezing creature, barely able to survive among the animals of the fields and woods. Taking pity on man, Prometheus stole fire from the heavens and gave it to man, at the cost of a horrible punishment to himself. But man, with fire, became master of the Earth and even a challenge to the gods.

A typical myth, fantastic in detail yet absolutely correct in spirit. One of man's early ancestors "discovered" fire about half a million years ago, according to anthropological evidence. Most likely these primitive *Homo erectus* creatures saw lightning turn shrubbery into flame; hence the legend of the gift from the heavens. Before fire, our ancestors were merely another marginal anthropoid, most of whom died out. With fire, we've become the dominant species on this planet.

The Prometheus myth "explains" this titanic event in terms that primitive people can understand and accept. The myth gives an emotional underpinning to the bald facts, ties reality into an all-encompassing structure that explains both the known and the incomprehensible parts of man's experience.

Much of today's emotion-charged, slightly irrational urge toward astrology and the occult is really a groping for a new mythology, a mythology that can explain the modern world on a gut level to people who are frightened that they're too small and weak to cope with this universe.

Joseph Campbell's work has shown that there are at least four major functions that any mythology must accomplish.

First: a mythology must induce a feeling of awe and majesty in people. This is what science fictionists call "a sense of wonder."

Second: a mythology must define and uphold a system of the universe, a pattern of self-consistent explanation for both the known and incomprehensible parts of man's existence. A modern mythology would have a ready-made system of the universe in the continuously expanding body of knowledge that we call science.

Third: a mythology must usually support the social establishment. For example, what we today call Greek mythology apparently originated with the Achaean conquerors of the earlier Mycenaean civilization. Zeus was a barbarian sky god who conquered the local deities of the matriarchal Mycenaean agricultural cities. Most of the lovely legends about Zeus's romantic entanglements with local goddesses are explanations of the barbarian, patriarchal people overwhelming the farmers' matriarchies.

Fourth: a mythology must serve as an emotional crutch to help the individual member of society through the inevitable crises of life, such as the transition from childhood into adulthood, the adjustments of the individual to his society, the inescapable prospect of death.

Science fiction, when it's at its very best, serves the functions of a modern mythology.

Certainly science fiction tries to induce a sense of wonder about the physical universe and man's own interior private universe. Science fiction depends heavily on known scientific understanding as the basic underpinning of a universal order. Science fiction does not tend to support a given political establishment, but on a deeper level it almost invariably backs the basic tenet of Western civilization: that is, the concept that the individual man is worth more than the organization—whatever it may be—and that nothing is more important than human freedom.

Whether or not science fiction helps people through emotional crises is more difficult to tell, and probably the only remaining test to the genre's claim to mythological stature. It is interesting that science fiction has a huge readership among the young, the adolescents who are trying to figure out their own individual places in the universe. And how many science fiction stories about superheroes and time travel and interstellar flights are really an attempt to deny the inevitability of death?

On this emotional level, science fiction can—and does—serve the functions of mythology. On a more cerebral level, science fiction helps to explain what science and scientists are all about to the non-scientists. It is no accident that several hundred universities and public schools are now offering science fiction courses and discovering that these classes are a meeting ground for the scientist-engineers and the humanists. Science *and* fiction. Reason *and* emotion.

Science fiction can also blend reason with emotion in another way: to show the true beauty and grandeur of the universe, whether it's a galaxy full of stars or a drop of water teeming with delicate, invisible life.

How many young students have been "turned on" to science by reading science fiction? Most of the men who have walked on the Moon's surface trace their careers back to early readings in science fiction. For, in addition to examining the problems of the future, science fiction opens the door to the widest of all possible worlds. The bone chess cities of Ray Bradbury's Mars, the galaxy-spanning adventures of E. E. Smith, the quietly ex-tra-ordinary pastorals that Zenna Henderson writes, Asimov's robots, Dickson's droll aliens—the canvas available to science fictionists is as wide as the universe and as long as time itself. And by showing this marvelous, varied, puzzling, colorful uni-verse—and humanity's role in it—science fiction stories give their readers the kind of excitement that simply does not exist elsewhere.

And there's more. By showing the wonders of the physical universe, science fiction also tends to show the beauty of this system of thought that is called science.

The essence of the scientific attitude is that the human mind can succeed in understanding the universe. By taking thought, men can move mountains—and have. In this sense, science is an utterly humanistic pursuit, the glorification of human intel-lect over the puzzling, chaotic, and often frightening darkness of ignorance.

Much of science fiction celebrates this spirit. Although there are plenty of science fiction stories that warn of the dangers of science and technology—the Frankenstein, dystopia stories—there are even more that look to science and technology for the leverage by which human beings can move the world. Even in the dystopia stories, where the basic message is usually, "There are some things that man was not meant to know, Doctor," there is still an aura of striving, an attempt to achieve greatness. Very few science fiction stories picture humanity as a passive species, allowing the tidal forces of nature to flow unperturbed. The heroes of science fiction stories—the gods of the new myth-ology—struggle manfully against the darkness, whether it's geo-logical doom for the whole planet or the evil of grasping politi-cians. They may not always win, these Kimball Kinnisons and Charlie Gordons and James Retiefs. But they always *try*.

This attitude may stem from science fiction's long ghetto existence in the pulp magazines. But it is very much the same attitude that motivates scientists. As Einstein once said, when struggling with a particularly difficult problem in theoretical physics, "God may be subtle, but He isn't perverse." The prob-lem may be tough, unsolvable even; but men still try, through the application of human thought.

That's what is behind this elusive quality that science fictionists call "the sense of wonder." When a Larry Niven hero detours his spaceship so that he can take a look at the complex beauty of the double star Beta Lyrae, when James Blish creates a detailed and marvelous world of intelligent creatures of microscopic size whose world is a tiny pond, when A. E. van Vogt's time traveler swings across the aeons to trigger the creation of the universe—the sense of wonder inspired in the reader is twofold. First is the sheer stupendous audacity of the writer in attempting to create such exciting settings, and getting away with it! But at a deeper, perhaps unconscious, level is the thrill of realizing that the human mind can reach this far, can encompass such ideas, can both produce and appreciate such beauty.

Understanding and appreciation: two more words that help define the role of science fiction.

But perhaps the most important aspect of science fiction's role in the modern world is summed up in a single word: *change.*

After all, science fiction is the literature of change. Each and every story preaches from the same gospel: tomorrow will be different from today, violently different perhaps.

For aeons, humankind accepted and expected that tomorrow would be very much the same as today. Change was something to worry over, to consult priests and oracles about, to fear and dread. Today we talk about "future shock" and long for the Good Old Days when everything was known and in its proper place.

Science fiction very clearly shows that changes—whether good or bad—are an inherent part of the universe. Resistance to change is an archaic, and nowadays dangerous, habit of thought. The world will change. It is changing constantly. Humanity's most fruitful course of action is to determine how to shape these changes, how to influence them and produce an environment where the changes that occur are those we want.

Again, in this attitude, science fiction mirrors science itself. Lewis M. Branscomb, former director of the National Bureau of Standards, has said:

Technology has brought us changes, most of which we should welcome, rather than reject. Wealth is the least important of these changes. Of greater importance is change itself. Those young humanists who think themselves revolutionaries are nothing compared to technology.

Perhaps this is the ultimate role of science fiction: to act as an interpreter of science to humanity. This is a two-edged weapon, of course. It is necessary to warn as well as evangelize. Science can kill as well as create; technology can deaden the human spirit or lift it to the farthermost corners of our imaginations. Only knowledgeable people can wisely decide how to use science and technology for humankind's benefit. In the end, this is the ultimate role of all art: to show ourselves to ourselves, to help us to understand our own humanity.

Science fiction, with its tremendous world view, with all of time and space to play with, gives its adherents a view that spans galaxies and aeons, a breadth of vision that exposes provincialism and prejudice for the petty concepts that they are. This is the world view that a modern mythology must have.

And this is what makes science fiction so much fun.

Ben Bova

Ben Bova is editor of *Analog Science Fiction-Science Fact* magazine, the most widely read and influential science fiction magazine in the world. He succeeded the late John W. Campbell, Jr., in this post in 1971.

A prolific writer of science fiction and science fact himself, Bova has also been a working newspaperman, an aerospace executive, and a writer of teaching films. As Manager of Marketing for Avco Everett Research Laboratory, in Massachusetts, he has worked with leading scientists in advanced research fields such as high-power lasers, magnetohydrodynamics (MHD), plasma physics, and artificial hearts. Prior to joining Avco, he wrote motion-picture scripts for the Physical Sciences Study Committee, working with the MIT Physics Department and Nobel Laureates from many universities. Earlier, he was a technical editor on Project VANGUARD with the Martin Co. in Baltimore. He also worked on several newspapers and magazines in the Philadelphia area.

Bova has lectured on topics ranging from the history of science fiction to the future of America's cities. His audiences have ranged from junior high students to the New York Academy of Sciences. He was born in Philadelphia, where he attended Temple University and received a degree in journalism.

His short stories and science articles have appeared in all the major science fiction magazines, as well as the *Smithsonian Magazine*, the *IEEE Spectrum*, and many other technical journals. His book, *The Fourth State of Matter* was honored as one of the top one hundred science books of the year, in 1971, by the American Library Association. *Starflight and Other Improbabilities* was selected as a Junior Literary Guild book in 1973.

SCIENCE FICTION

The Star Conquerors, 1959 (Winston Co.)
Star Watchman, 1964 (Holt, Rinehart & Winston)
The Weathermakers, 1967 (Holt, Rinehart & Winston)
Out of the Sun, 1968 (Holt, Rinehart & Winston)

The Dueling Machine, 1969 (Holt, Rinehart & Winston)
Escape, 1970 (Holt, Rinehart & Winston)
Exiled From Earth, 1971 (Dutton)
THX 1138, 1971 (Paperback Library); with George Lucas
The Many Worlds of SF, 1971 (Dutton), editor
Flight of Exiles, 1972 (Dutton)
As On a Darkling Plain, 1972 (Walker)
SFWA Hall of Fame, Vol. II 1973 (Doubleday), editor
The Winds of Altair, 1973 (Dutton)

SCIENCE FACT

The Milky Way Galaxy, 1961 (Holt, Rinehart & Winston)
Giants of the Animal World, 1962 (Whitman)
Reptiles Since the World Began, 1964 (Whitman)
The Uses of Space, 1965 (Holt, Rinehart & Winston)
In Quest of Quasars, 1970 (Crowell)
Planets, Life and LGM, 1970 (Addison)
The Fourth State of Matter, 1971 (St. Martin's)
The Amazing Laser, 1972 (Westminster)
The New Astronomies, 1972 (St. Martin's)
Man Changes the Weather, 1973 (Addison)
Starflight and Other Improbabilities, 1973 (Westminster)

Frederik Pohl

The Publishing of Science Fiction

Although science fiction exists in many forms—film, television, radio, the graphic arts, and the think tanks—and, in fact, one writer defines *science fiction* as a method of looking at the world, still when most of us use the term science fiction we mean to describe some story that, in some form or another, we have read.

In order for a story to be read by any sizable number of people, it has to be published.

The basic fact that one must realize about the publishing business is that it is a business. It happens to be a business that is devoted to the preservation and circulation of an art form, namely writing. Nevertheless publishing itself is not an art, and like every other business it is basically concerned with earning a profit. There are exceptions. Some kinds of publishing companies are subsidized (university presses, denominational presses, and the like), and a few are run as hobbies—most of these latter are small, although from time to time the odd Texas oil millionaire will buy himself a book firm or a magazine to get rid of some of his surplus cash. But by and large publishers who do not show a profit do not survive. Once one gets this fact firmly in mind, a lot of questions that come up about the publishing of science fiction resolve themselves pretty quickly: "Why isn't sf published in weekly magazines on slick paper with four-color illustrations?" Because whoever tried it would lose his shirt, that's why. (Hugo Gernsback did try something like it, around 1950, and did in fact lose a packet. It was called *Science Fiction Plus.*)

There are two main genera of publishing: books (defined as anything that does not bear a date) and periodicals (newspapers and magazines).

For much of the active part of the history of science fiction, its principal medium of publication was the magazine. This is no longer true: as I write this, there are only about eight English-language sf magazines in the world, and most of them are struggling bimonthlies in imminent danger of collapse, or use a lot of reprints, or dilute the sf with fantasy. And there was a time, prior to 1926, when there was no such thing as a specialist sf magazine at all. Science fiction did appear, rather a lot of it. Wells's stories appeared in all the big slicks and in book form. Doyle, Burroughs, and the dozen or two lesser-known sf writers operating in those antediluvian days also appeared in general magazines, or in adventure pulps, or in book form only. But the real birth of science fiction as a specialized genre or category (you use the first term if you are a literary critic, the other if you are a publisher) occurred in April 1926, with the first issue of *Amazing Stories.*

It was incredibly cheap to publish a magazine in those days, and incredibly easy to get it put out on the newsstands where customers could buy it. Hugo Gernsback, who published that first sf magazine, once wrote an editorial complaining about the bitter fact that out of every one hundred copies he had printed, as many as twenty might never get sold. He urged the readers to subscribe, or to reserve their copies in advance at their corner newsstand, thus permitting the dealers to order exactly as many as they could sell and avoid that shameful twenty percent waste. Modern publishers who happen to come across that fifty-year-old editorial will either laugh or weep. An eighty percent sale is an impossible dream today. Fifty percent is close to the industry average, which means that, by and large, every time a customer buys a copy of an sf magazine or paperback, he is paying for two of them: the one he takes home to read, and the one that the wholesaler strips of the cover (to return for a refund of what he paid for it) and puts through a shredding machine, without ever displaying it on a newsstand at all.

But in those days before inflation, before The War, before even the Great Depression, paper was cheap, printing was cheap and not yet unionized, writers were cheap enough, too. The word rates that writers were paid were low; well, they are still pretty low, but in those days the check a writer got from an sf magazine was all he had any real hope of ever seeing for that particular story, while now it is usually only the first installment of a much larger sum that will be realized from various book editions. Since *Amazing Stories* was the only sf magazine there was, it was in a good position to set its rates at whatever Hugo Gernsback thought appropriate, and he was not known as a big spender on writers. Most of the stories *Amazing* published in its first few years were reprints, picked up for whatever the copyright owners would accept or for nothing at all. H. G. Wells, Jules Verne, Fitz-James O'Brien with his *Diamond Lens,* and a dozen other writers turned up in *Amazing* with stories ranging from a decade to half a century or more in age. Even when the magazine bought original and previously unpublished work, its rates were not high. Fletcher Pratt, in Paris with his bride, Inga Marie Stephens Pratt, trying to keep ahead of the concierge and the *bistro* proprietors, wrote some forty thousand words called *A Voice Across the Years* and sold it for $250. More fortunate writers, closer at hand and better able to haggle, might get a cent a word and occasionally even a little more, but usually even that was not paid until the story had been published—at least a few months, sometimes a year or more after the story was accepted.

But the magazine was succeeding, and other publishers could see that it was succeeding. In 1929 and 1930 other magazines began to appear. Gernsback, who had lost control of *Amazing Stories* in the stock disasters of 1929, came back with a new company and two new sf magazines, *Air Wonder Stories* and *Science Wonder Stories,* soon to be merged into just plain *Won-*

der Stories. The pulp chain publishing house of Clayton started an sf title to add to their Westerns and air-war magazines, called *Astounding Stories.*

Those were the "Big Three" sf magazines. They had incredibly high survival rates. Their outward forms changed, to be sure; but still *Wonder,* sold to a different publisher and rechristened *Thrilling Wonder Stories,* survived World War II, and that was the shortest-lived of the lot. Both *Amazing* and *Astounding* as of this writing still survive. (*Astounding* is now called *Analog Science Fact and Fiction,* but it is, as anyone knows, the same magazine.)

The magazines did not, however, maintain perfect health. The real world kept battering at them. For one thing, there was a Depression. This need not have been fatal in itself, and wasn't; magazines are traditionally thought of as a depression business, because the people who can't afford a new car or a nightclub can often manage the price of a magazine to read and lose themselves in, night after night. Even so, by the mid-thirties both *Amazing* and *Wonder* were down to every-other-month publication, and tottering at that.

Astounding, after some shaky times around 1933, seemed to be doing better than either of its competitors, but *Astounding* had an advantage neither of the others possessed. The Clayton company, which had started it, had gone up in smoke, and after a hiatus the magazine had been taken over by Street and Smith.

Street and Smith was a giant. It owned a whole building of its own—rather a rickety old barn, on Seventh Avenue just above Fourteenth Street, to be sure, with elevators that were controlled by tugging on ropes and "no smoking" signs all over, since the place was a firetrap. But still it was its own building, populated by the staffs of dozens of successful pulp magazines in all categories.

Street and Smith's bigness was *Astounding*'s opportunity. There are distinct scale advantages in publishing magazines. A big company can afford things a small company can't. It can hire roadmen, as many as a hundred or more of them, going around to all of the wholesalers and many of the retail dealers in the country, selling them on ordering the magazines their company publishes, making sure that once placed they are given proper display, checking to see that they go to the right outlets at the right times (college towns are seasonally good in the winter; beach resorts are seasonally good in the summer; someone has to know this and take the trouble to adjust the dealers' orders accordingly).

A big company can afford an art department and a production department. It can buy printing and paper more cheaply in bulk than the fellow who has only a single magazine, a few thousand pounds of paper at a time. Above all, it can afford an advertising department, and even can attract (or in those days, could attract) advertisers. In advertising, scale is all-important. Advertising is placed through advertising agencies, which generally speaking get a commission of fifteen percent of the cost of the ads they place, from which they are supposed to pay the costs of preparing the ads and earn a profit. They simply cannot afford to place cheap ads. The agencies of the '30s might well have been happy to spend two thousand dollars or so of their clients' money to place an ad in all the Street and Smith pulps. They would not be willing to spend fifty dollars of their clients' money for the same ad in a single issue of, say, *Amazing Stories*. Each ad might be exactly as much trouble and expense as the other to prepare, but on one their commission would be $450 and on the other—$7.50.

So for these reasons and others (not forgetting two able and energetic editors, F. Orlin Tremaine and John W. Campbell), *Astounding* delivered a tidy profit to its owners every month while *Amazing* and *Wonder* were having trouble meeting their printing bills.

Both *Amazing* and *Wonder* found themselves cutting corners and trying curious expedients to survive. The first and easiest thing to do was to cut their expenses, which they did— as much as they could. Where they couldn't cut prices, they gave themselves operating-capital loans by paying their bills as slowly as they possibly could. They paid their writers "on publication"—sometimes not even then. My own first sale, I remember, was to *Amazing Stories*. It was a poem; I wrote it in 1935, it was accepted in 1936, it was published in 1937—and it was paid for in 1938. That is not a record. There are writers who got paid far more slowly and, as recently as a few years ago, some who still had not been paid, more than thirty years later.

Wonder Stories tried the experiment of starting the first large-scale science fiction fan club, the Science Fiction League, as a promotion device. It was their hope that they would be able to enroll thousands of members, all of whom would buy every copy of the club's official organ, which of course was *Wonder Stories*. Their expectations were not realized. Many of the members bought the magazine more or less regularly. But more importantly they invented science fiction fandom, which now can turn out more people for a single weekend convention than the SFL ever managed to sign up. It was through the SFL that local clubs got their first major impetus in forming and staying alive, and from them came everything else.

In this same burgeoning era of the late '20s and the whole decade of the '30s, a certain amount of science fiction was still being published in book form.

It was almost never labeled science fiction. That term was reserved to the pulp magazines and, in fact, most of them even called it by other names—"science fantasy," or "stories of super-science," or Gernsback's private, pet coinage, "scientifiction," abbreviated "stf." But science fiction the books were, and some of them were of high quality: S. Fowler Wright with *The World Below;* W. Olaf Stapledon with *Last and First Men* and others, originating in England and being reprinted in the United States; a series of first-rate juveniles by Carl H. Claudy in the United States, and so forth. There were not a great many of them, and no book publishing house ever considered anything like a science fiction "line," as they had mystery lines, romance lines, Western lines, and so on. But they did come out, a trickle every year, eagerly snapped up by the fans and, except for a few blockbusters like Aldous Huxley's *Brave New World,* generally ignored by the rest of the human race.

They did not sell very well, but that was not particularly important. Most books don't sell very well, and in those days they sold even worse than they do now. But they were also cheap to produce. A novel that sold a thousand copies at a list price of two dollars or so would just about pay its printing bills; the author would not get much, but at least he would taste a couple of hundred dollars for his trouble. Most publishers stayed in business because their sales departments had carefully kept their contracts bright with "buyers"—not the cash customers who bought books to read, but those persons charged with buying books wholesale for libraries, bookstores, rental libraries, and so on. A good sales department made a prosperous publisher. And now and then one book out of ten or twenty would have a quality about it that made people like it and talk about it, and then reorders would come in voluntarily and it would go back to press and everybody would make money. Even the writer.

But that did not often happen with science fiction in those days.

So by the end of the '30s, the science fiction publishing world consisted of a handful of spottily successful magazines and an even smaller output of books—plus one other thing.

The other thing was a vigorously boiling body of fan activity. The fans had begun to publish their own magazines to fill in the dry weeks between the times when the new issues of *Astounding, Amazing,* and *Wonder* came out.

These amateur magazines are still with us; they are called "fanzines." In the '30s that term had not yet been invented. They were called "fan mags" when they were called anything at all, and they existed in uncountable numbers. Uncountable because no one ever knew, from one day to the next, how many of them there were. Some fan or club would stir itself into activity and borrow a mimeograph machine, and they would put out one issue, or twenty, as long as momentum held out. Probably six fan mags were announced for every one that really appeared. Most were mimeographed, one or two professionally printed or offset, quite a few hectographed (making use of a process that involved flat trays of jelly, remorselessly curling pages, and hideously purple-stained fingers for everyone involved), or even carbon-copied. Mostly what they contained were comments on the stories in the professional magazines, or news of fan activities, or gossip or debate; but many of them printed amateur stories and amateur art. This was generally pretty poor stuff, particularly the fiction, but C. M. Kornbluth, Donald A. Wollheim, Ray Bradbury, Hannes Bok, and a hundred other latterly successful sf writers and artists got their start that way. (I was one of them.)

Two other developments were occurring in the late thirties. One was that prosperity was beginning to sneak back, a little at a time. There was more money around than there had been. All kinds of money, including risk capital for starting marginal new publishing ventures. The other was that *Astounding* had a bright new editor, John W. Campbell, still in his twenties and full of ideas, energy, and obstinacy. He was using those things to change the whole nature of science fiction, finding and developing new writers, distributing plot ideas and story elements to every writer who would listen, propagandizing for "the kind of story that might be a contemporary novel—in a twenty-fifth-century magazine" and, in general, turning science fiction into a tool for exploring alternative futures. Campbell was a remarkable man. In a field dominated by idiosyncratic and able editors, he was the best of them all. He succeeded in all his aims.

And all of a sudden there was a science fiction boom. Was it the change in the kind of stories Campbell was printing? The stirrings of prosperity? The burgeoning of fandom, with its recruitment of new talent graduating every year out of the fan mags into professional activity?

It may have been any, or all of them, but something was happening. *Thrilling Wonder Stories* brought out a companion magazine, *Startling Stories,* and then another, *Captain Future.* Hugo Gernsback, having sold off *Wonder* but anxious to get back in the game, started *Future* and *Science Fiction Quarterly.* F. Orlin Tremaine (who had been replaced by Campbell on *Astounding,* and then departed Street and Smith entirely) came back with a magazine of his own called *Comet.* A small company with an editor named Robert O. Erisman started a couple of magazines; so did another, with an editor named Malcolm Reiss. I became editor of two new magazines, *Astonishing Stories* and *Super Science Stories.* Donald A. Wollheim found a publisher to give him a couple of magazines called

Stirring Science Stories and *Cosmic Stories*. About all anyone seemed to need to start a new sf magazine was a title, and clearly it didn't even have to be a good one. Before one knew what was happening the three shaky magazines had multiplied themselves five-fold, into fifteen and more.

Rates were low, so were salaries, so were profits. I had a budget, I remember, of $405 with which to buy fifty thousand words of fiction, a full-color oil painting for the cover, and all the black-and-white interior illustrations I wanted. Wollheim had no story budget at all most of the time; he had to get stories given to him for nothing. Even the leaders—*Astounding, Thrilling, Wonder, Planet*—rarely passed a penny a word for the stories they bought. But they were coming out, and they were selling.

Unfortunately, the times were against them. In 1941 the United States entered World War II, and it became immediately apparent that this was going to be a tough war to fight. Civilian enterprises had to give way to the war effort. Gasoline was rationed. Householders were enjoined to save fats in tin cans for recycling, on the threat of not having any of either in the future if they didn't cooperate. And publishers found paper both expensive and hard to get.

Like wheat under a scythe, the magazines were chopped down. Only a handful survived the shortages and priorities of the war.

But when the war ended, something new began to happen in the publishing of science fiction. Major trade book publishers began to experiment with books that not only were sf, but were clearly labeled as such.

The first pioneers were Random House and Crown Publishers, each with an enormous omnium-gatherum anthology of sf: *Adventures in Time and Space*, edited by Raymond J. Healy and J. Francis McComas, from Random House; *A Treasury of Science Fiction*, edited by Groff Conklin, from Crown.

They were tremendous books. Each contained the equivalent of eight or nine issues of an sf magazine in wordage, and the quality was high: after all, the editors had the cream of twenty years of sf magazine publishing to choose from. The books made money. They were even critical successes, which meant that they were noticed by reviewers who had never noticed anything with the words "science fiction" on it before. The book trade discovered there was a whole new category whose existence they had not even suspected, to join the categories of mysteries and Westerns, et al.

The response of the trade publishers to this development was neither quick nor strong. After all, every one of them had been spending the whole war making up dream lists of books to publish the minute paper became freely available again. They were all very busy turning those dreams into reality, and the sf phenomenon had to wait.

But fans noticed. And some of them knew enough about printing and publishing, or thought they did, to start their own little specialist publishing companies. It didn't take much; they could sell through the mail, directly to their fellow fans, enough copies to take the chill off publishing a book, and a few bookstores began to order copies for stock.

Martin Greenberg and David A. Kyle founded Gnome Press. Erle Korshak in Chicago started Shasta Publishers. Lloyd Eshbach in Pennsylvania began publishing books as Fantasy Press. And so on, Arkham House, Prime Press, F.P.C.I.—the books began to come out. Some had the look of homemade jobs. Others were as handsome as anything from Knopf or Viking. It didn't much matter. Each book was an event, blessed with lavish publicity in the science fiction magazines. The editors were tickled pink, being themselves fans, to see their kind of stories receiving the imprimatur of publication between hard covers (and it did not seem to occur to any of them that they were contributing to their long-range extinction).

The new publishers operated out of their homes. They had no overhead. They did not really care if they made much of a profit or not, most of them. They did not need a big sale to stay in business: fifteen hundred or two thousand copies sold of a book would meet their bills and leave them enough cash in hand to bring out another. And the authors, most of whom had never fantasied a world in which any publisher anywhere would publish any of their stories in book form, were easy about advances and royalties. Often enough they did not even ask for the former, and signed whatever the publisher put before them about the latter. They had written the stories in the first place for whatever price John Campbell or Leo Margulies would pay, six hundred dollars or so for a sixty-thousand-word novel. Those checks had long been cashed and spent. Anything the stories brought in was found money.

And the books did sell, surprisingly well considering how little any of the publishers knew about sales staffs and credit ratings. It was not long before the big trade publishers noticed what was happening and decided to move in.

I was a literary agent at the time, and this was a most enjoyable development for me. The first two major publishing companies to get their feet wet in sf as a category were Doubleday and Simon and Schuster. I was personally involved in both. In the time-honored publishing tradition, I let them pick my brains about sf, and they let me sell them books, and all of us were happy as could be.

The boss editor at Simon and Schuster in those days of the late 1940s was a marvelously personable and persuasive man named Jack Goodman. He had no difficulty bending sf writers and agents to his will. Not that any of us minded. Having science fiction published by so prestigious a company as S and S was already so heady a triumph that money, royalties, and other contract terms seemed pretty irrelevant to the central joy of the event. Goodman took a particular interest in the work of Jack Williamson, caused him to splice together two short novels from *Astounding* under the the collective title of *The Humanoids*, and did well enough with it to go on to bring out six or eight science fiction books a year.

Doubleday's editorial hierarchy then included Walter I. Bradbury, and the new sf program became his to administer. He began with a novel, *The Big Eye*, purchased from an out-of-the-field commercial writer named Max Ehrlich, but quickly swung around to concentrate on the established sf magazine writers, particularly Isaac Asimov. Asimov's first book was a short novel that had been written for, and rejected by, *Thrilling Wonder Stories*. Expanded and retitled *Pebble in the Sky*, it was a success that encouraged Doubleday to continue the line and Asimov to continue writing books. (As of the end of 1972 his total had reached more than 130 titles, 50 of them published by Doubleday.)

A number of smaller publishers began to join the giants, and by 1950 there were half a dozen regular trade publishers in the sf field, plus the half dozen more specialist fan presses, and all were thriving.

These were hard-cover publishers; the paperback houses were yet to be heard from.

Some of the larger and more daring houses had already begun to get their feet wet. Pocket Books had published *The Pocket Book of Science Fiction* almost a decade earlier. New American Library had begun to sign up some of the hard-cover books for paperbound reprint. Bantam Books had published one anthology, *Shot in the Dark*, edited by Judith Merril, and was showing signs of interest in more. But no paperback house had actually begun a "line" of science fiction.

Then Ian Ballantine, who had been president of Bantam Books, left that company to open up shop on his own as Ballantine Books. Ballantine was (and is) an enterprising and original soul, and was willing to take a chance on science fiction on a continuing basis. The first two books he bought were both from me, as it happens—*Star Science Fiction*, first of a series of anthologies of original science fiction stories, which I edited; and a novel that C. M. Kornbluth and I had written for *Galaxy*, where it was published under the title of *Gravy Planet*. Somewhat revised and slightly shorter, it appeared in simultaneous hard- and soft-cover editions from Ballantine as *The Space Merchants*.

Some of the magazine editors, who had been gung-ho for the new fad of hard-cover science fiction book publishing, looked askance at seeing the books come out in paperback form. They felt that the paperbacks represented serious competition where it counted, in the marketplace. It took nearly twenty years for their worst fears to be realized, but they were right.

Paperbound books reach much the same market as magazines. They are on sale in the same candy stores, drugstores, bus terminals, airports, and hotel lobbies; they are distributed through the same national distributing concerns. But they are intrinsically easier and therefore cheaper to distribute than magazines, in that they do not have an official off-sale date. Magazines stay on sale only for the period of issue. Your December issue of *Analog* is no longer a salable commodity on January 1st. The paperbound book that comes out on the same day can still be sold the following month, or the following year, or any time at all—at least, up to the point where it becomes so thumbed and shopworn that it has to be returned for decency's sake. Or, more likely, the dealer wants it out of the way to make room for new stock. The competition for newsstand space is ferocious, and even paperbacks have grave trouble in staying on sale long enough to reach their optimum audience; but at least they do not have a self-imposed termination date, as magazines do.

By 1953 Ballantine had a lock on nearly every major sf writer as far as his paperbound book rights were concerned: Arthur C. Clarke, Ray Bradbury, Robert Sheckley, John Wyndham, and a dozen others. As other companies came into the field they had to be content with the books Ballantine had somehow overlooked, or had not wanted in the first place. Some, even so, were markedly successful, particularly Ace Books which, under the editorship of Donald A. Wollheim, quarried out a highly successful list of primarily adventure sf books—they are sometimes called "space opera." But Ballantine was first and even now, more than two decades later, it retains a list that includes more acknowledged sf classics—the books that are taught in the college courses and go back to print year after year—than any other paperback house.

In spite of this new competition, the magazines were enjoying a new and even more high-flying boom than ever before. The old magazines were multiplying themselves—*Amazing* was publishing the thickest issues ever seen, rebinding them to sell as quarterlies and bringing out companion magazines. New ones were appearing. The publishers of *Ellery Queen's Mystery Magazine,* feeling the need to expand their list to get some of those scale economies working for them, listened to Anthony

Boucher and J. Francis McComas's suggestion and tried a "one-shot" (i.e., a magazine that may or may not ever have a second issue, depending on how well the first issue sells) called *The Magazine of Fantasy*. It sold; they tried it quarterly, then bimonthly, then brought it out every month under the expanded title of *The Magazine of Fantasy and Science Fiction*, or *F&SF* for short. In upstate New York, a publisher named James Quinn tried his luck with *If* (still surviving, though under its second subsequent set of owners), and an Italian publishing company that had made a pile of *lire* out of confession comics in Europe decided that the same thing would work in the United States. It didn't, as it happened; but they were also looking for scale economies, and so they elected to publish three or four additional magazines, more or less at random. One of them happened to be science fiction, and is the only survivor of the firm. It was called *Galaxy* and, under its brilliant editor H. L. Gold, did in the 1950s almost a repeat performance of what John Campbell had done in the '30s and '40s in attracting new writers and reviving old ones, and imposing a new and more literate personality on sf.

By the middle of the 1950s the number of existing American sf magazines had reached an all-time high—some thirty-eight separate titles, including a few that were marginal in that they dabbled in other fields than sf (*Weird Tales*, for example).

Then three things happened almost at the same time, and all three of them were bad for sf magazines.

The first was a disaster that smote all magazines, and it had to do with distribution.

Magazine (and paperback book) publishers do not ordinarily send their publications directly to your corner newsstand. They use a system of distribution which has survived essentially unchanged since Frank Munsey got his start a century or so ago. The publisher sells the whole edition of his magazine at about half the cover price to a national distributor. The national distributor breaks up the edition and sells it, fifty or five hundred or several thousand copies at a clip (as many as he can, depending on what the market is for that particular magazine) to the six hundred or so local wholesalers who divided up the United

States. The local wholesalers put that magazine, along with all the other magazines and paperbound books and odds and ends they handle, on their trucks, and send them around to the local newsstands. The newsstand puts them on sale. Each of these people takes a piece of the fifty percent or so that is the difference between the cover price and what the publisher gets for it in the first place; and each of them has the privilege of returning all unsold copies to the place they got them from for full refund.

What happened in the 1950s was that the big old American News Company, first and largest of the national distributors, was taken over in a stock raid. Some canny investors had noticed that the cash value of the real estate and other properties ANC owned was a lot more than the aggregate value of the stock. So they bought up the stock and liquidated the company. They made a fortune in capital gains, but in the process they put ANC out of the business of distributing magazines.

The worst part of it was that ANC had a unique position among national distributors. It was so large that it maintained its own entire network of local wholesalers around the country. All of the other national distributors combined (they were collectively called "the independents") shared the same parallel network. When ANC folded, all of its local wholesalers folded with them, and every independent wholesaler in the country became an instant monopolist. Costs went up. Services went down. All magazines were hurt, and many of them folded.

The second event also affected all magazines; it was called television. What TV meant to magazines was unwelcome competition for the advertising dollar. More and more advertising money poured into the boob tube, and much of it came right out of the budgets that had once been allocated to buying space in periodicals.

Those two things affected all magazines—and still do. The third event was of peculiar importance to the sf magazines, and it was Sputnik. No one had guessed that that first puny venture of man into space would have a disastrous effect on sf publishing, but it did. The little steel basketball the Russians coaxed into orbit turned much sf into reality, and apparently readers began finding in their daily newspapers what they had once had to buy sf magazines to read about. (It seems probable that something similar occurred after the first atomic bomb at Hiroshima, but it was obscured by the greater publishing disaster of paper rationing and postwar upheaval.)

If editors and publishers had expected any effect at all from the explosion of man into space it was a hopefully beneficial one. They acted that way, almost all of them, scheduling articles on the space program and switching the main themes of their covers from Bug-Eyed Monsters to orbiting hardware. They probably would have been better off staying with the BEMs because, for a solid year after Sputnik, magazine circulations slid down and down. In the last few years of the '50s the mortality rate was terrific, and the decline has continued to this day. As of this writing (January 1973) there are only about four or five real magazines of sf alive in the United States today, and most of them are showing symptoms of unease.

There may have been one additional factor operating at the time of the great weed-out of sf magazines. It may even have been the most important one.

There simply were not enough good stories around to fill thirty-eight science fiction magazines. Even if there had been, there were not enough good editors to select them. Most of the great boom crop of the '50s consisted of terrible stories.

In an ideal world the effect of this would be that the bad magazines would die and the good ones flourish. It isn't an ideal world. Unfortunately, most casual readers of sf do not know one magazine from another; they do not even know one writer from another (a terrible truth most writers are reluctant to recognize), and so a bad story hurts everyone. With thirty-eight magazines in the field, the most one can expect is that the average reader will find himself in a bus terminal or a candy store, look for something to read, decide on an sf magazine, and pick up the one that looks most promising in some arcane way. (No one knows exactly what makes one package sell better than another, either.) If he reads it and enjoys it, he may pick up another sf magazine for the return trip on the bus. If he doesn't, perhaps he'll buy a newspaper or a mystery instead. The bad magazines turn marginal readers off to the good ones, and the trouble with turning off marginal readers is that there are so many of them. Maybe each one of them only buys one or two sf publications a year, but there are millions of them, and only some tens of thousands of dedicated almost-every-issue-of-everything addicts, and so if you lose the marginal readers you have lost most of your chance of making a profit.

Now it is 1973, and those are the three main channels for the publication of science fiction: the magazines, the hard-cover books, and the paperbacks.

There are others. For instance, there have always been science fiction comics, both in strip form in the daily newspapers and as comic magazines, back as far as Buck Rogers and the Big Little Books of the '30s. Science fiction does appear in general magazines. The stories in *Playboy* in particular are high in quality, and because *Playboy* pays ten or twenty times as much as any sf magazine does, they do attract some of the best writers in the field. And of course there are films, TV series, and other forms of dramatized science fiction. They are of varying merit, but they exist, and there are tens of thousands of people who consider themselves addicted to science fiction because of, say, *Star Trek* but have never bought a magazine or book.

Battered and bruised, the magazines still survive. Partly they keep going because of the dogged loyalty of their hard-core fans, perhaps even more because of the dogged loyalty of their publishers and editors, most of whom operate on hopes and fringe benefits more than on actual tangible dollars taken in. (In 1972 one science fiction magazine editor was eligible for welfare because his salary was so low. The case isn't typical—but it's scary.)

Would it matter if every science fiction magazine folded, as long as the books in paperback and hard-cover editions kept coming out?

It would probably matter a lot. It probably has seriously damaged the field already to have them in doubtful shape, if only because they are the time-honored, and also the easiest and best, vehicle for recruiting new writing and art talent to the field. To see how this works, just think of some reader—it could be yourself—out in, say, Sweetwater, Texas. You've read a lot of stories. At some point you think to yourself that you could write a story as good as some of the stories you see published. (That's what most of us did, at some time or another, and out of every hundred of us who thought this, perhaps one or two turned out to be at least partly right.) So you write a story.

Then what do you do with it?

If you have been in the habit of reading science fiction magazines, you have likely noticed that on the contents page there is an editor's name, and an address, and some wordage (perhaps only "We accept no responsibility for the return of unsolicited manuscripts") which suggests that they do, indeed, expect to have some people send them stories to consider. So you put your story in an envelope and mail it off to the magazine. If it is good the chances are it will be bought (if not by the first magazine, then by the second or nth), and you have become a "pro," are eligible to join the field's trade union, the Science Fiction Writers of America, and quickly find yourself in touch with all the other pros and their collective expertise. They will gladly share it with you. It is a friendly field. And so you are on your way.

But if there are no magazines, or they are so scant that they never show up in Sweetwater, what do you do with your story? Even if the books come your way, they are less inviting, and certainly less personal.

So very likely you do nothing at all with your story. One of the most famous of all sf stories, *The Skylark of Space*, languished in a desk drawer for seven years for that reason. Doc Smith wrote it because he wanted to, but since there was no science fiction magazine when he wrote it in 1919, he did little with it until *Amazing Stories* appeared in 1926.

This easy road to professional writing has become pretty hard going, and it has had its effects already. More and more of the new writers come into the field through personal contact of one sort or another—fandom primarily, but also sf conventions, clubs, writing courses, or the sheer happenstance of running into somebody well connected in the field. There is no way to estimate the loss, or to prove that there are dozens or hundreds of good new writers out there who simply have not happened to make connections. But it is probable that this is so.

To some extent, the gap is being filled by that unusual phenomenon of the sf field, quite unknown in most categories, the anthology of original stories.

These are much like magazines in most ways. An editor gets a contract with a book publishing house, hard-cover or soft, to provide them with seventy-five thousand words or so of new, previously unpublished science fiction stories. He writes or phones those authors he would like to have represented in it, and gets from them enough stories to make up his book. There are dozens of these volumes around. I was the editor of the first such series, the *Star Science Fiction* anthologies published by Ballantine beginning in 1953. Other major series since then have been Damon Knight's *Orbit* collections, Harlan Ellison's three *Dangerous Visions* books, a large number edited by Roger Elwood, and others. But there are few really new writers in any of them, and almost none who have spontaneously generated themselves in the way described above. Ellison prints a number of new writers, but most of them come out of the writing courses he teaches. The other editors rely almost entirely on established professionals.

Anthologies in general are an important feature of science fiction book publishing. It took book publishers a long time to believe that this could be so, for in most fields anthologies are traditional losers, but in sf they are no less popular than novels or single-author collections, and often sell better.

The sf anthologies come in all varieties. There are "theme" anthologies of all descriptions (a dozen sf stories all laid on the planet Mars, or *Great SF Stories About Doctors, A Treasury of Science Fiction Stories About Pussycats,* etc.) There are "best" anthologies; in 1972 there were five separate volumes, each purporting to contain the selected best stories of the year. And there are endless numbers of plain anthology anthologies, representing some individual editor's choice of stories he thinks customers may have missed and would like to read. When you consider how few new short sf stories are published each year (long ones are hard to fit in), and how many anthologies are waiting to gulp them up, you can see duplication is common. A good sf story may be defined as one that has appeared in a minimum of five anthologies. Some stories have appeared in fifty. (This is not an exaggeration; my own story, *The Midas Plague,* has appeared in thirty-five.)

Altogether, science fiction is a respectable fraction of the total publishing industry. In the United States it is probably the most successful category, beating out mysteries (traditionally the most successful line) by a fair margin and infinitely outdistancing Westerns, war stories, romance stories, and Gothics, year in and year out.

It is hard to put numbers to the phenomenon, but here are some estimates which, if not wholly reliable, probably come close to what happens in an average year:

All science fiction magazines combined (including those sf stories which appear in other magazines) probably publish in the aggregate some two-and-a-half to three million words a year, for which they pay authors somewhere between seventy-five and a hundred thousand dollars. Of the stories in magazines, about half of them in numbers of stories are shorts (up to six thousand words), a little more than a quarter are intermediate-length novelettes and novellas (six thousand to twenty-five thousand words), and the remainder are novels, most of them ranging from fifty thousand to seventy-five thousand words. In terms of total wordage in the magazines, the percentages are probably about fifteen percent in short stories, thirty-five percent in the intermediate lengths, and fifty percent or better in novels.

The book publishers combined publish at least ninety percent of the stories that have first appeared in the magazines in one form or another. It is a very rare novel that manages to appear in a magazine and yet avoids coming out as a book, and the shorter pieces are also almost always given book publication either in anthologies or as one-author collections. In addition, the book publishers bring out a much larger volume of new work, principally in the form of novels. The four principal companies specializing in science fiction books—Ballantine, Doubleday, Ace, and DAW Books—aggregate more than six million words of first-book publication a year, probably two-thirds of which has been written especially for them. Smaller publishers, in the aggregate, add another million words or more.

In all, there are at least ten to twelve million words of new adult science fiction appearing each year in the United States. If one counts juveniles and such peripheral books as *Fail-Safe* or *The Andromeda Strain,* the total may exceed fifteen million words.

As was true during the magazine boom of the mid-1950s, there may be a quality-control problem here: there do not appear to be enough good stories being written to fill all those blank pages. Certainly there are a lot of bad books being published. But there are also a good many excellent ones, and every year a few which are superb; and at least as of this writing the industry appears healthy.

Although hard-cover and paperback publishers compete for the same writers and the same stories, and there is not much to choose between them in the quality of what they publish, there are significant differences between the two fields.

To a large degree, the hard-cover publishers are parasitic on the paperbacks. Few hard-cover science fiction publishers would find their lines profitable if they could not count on selling most of the books they publish to paperback houses for reprint; and they share in the income received from this source with the author. (Usually fifty-fifty, although more and more a few writers have been able to get a better percentage split.)

A typical hard-cover science fiction book brings its author a $2,000 advance against royalties, sells for $4.95 or so retail, earns him therefore not quite 50¢ on each copy sold, and therefore must sell four thousand copies to pay back his advance. Typically, four thousand is roughly what most sf books do sell. This same four-thousand-copy sale is, again roughly, just about enough to cover the publisher's payment to the author, cost of printing and paper, payrolls, office rent, overhead, advertising expense (if any), free lunches for the agents, and general hidden costs of all kinds. If either writer or publisher want more than this bare-bones existence, they have to look toward additional sales of some kind.

The basic sources of additional sales are: book club; foreign and translation editions; and paperbound book reprint.

Book clubs have not been greatly interested in science fiction (although Doubleday has maintained a specialized outlet, called the Science Fiction Book Club, which distributes a dozen or more titles a year successfully enough). The major clubs, however, have used almost no science fiction.

Foreign and translation sales are much more common. At least half the sf books published in the United States do in fact ultimately come out again in at least one other country. Many of them do so over and over again. (The most successful science fiction book whose history I know well, *The Space Merchants*, has been translated into about forty languages, and in some countries has had six or eight separate editions over a period of twenty years.) Although the revenue from a single foreign sale is seldom as much as American publication, and may indeed be as little as fifty or one hundred dollars for the right to publish in one of the smaller countries, in the aggregate it can run to as much as the earnings from the American edition or more. This income the original American book publishers would generally like to share, to the extent of twenty-five percent or so.

The biggest source of dependable subsidiary rights income, for both writers and hard-cover publishers, is the American paperback reprint. A representative advance for a title is in the fifteen-hundred- to two-thousand-dollar range. But prices of five thousand, ten thousand dollars, and more are not uncommon, and some isolated titles have gone much higher. As far as they are able, the hard-cover publishers try to keep fifty percent of that sum. For most of the books they publish, the thousand dollars or so that is their share from the paperback sale, plus the additional several hundred or thousand dollars from other subsidiary sales (less the cost of maintaining a subsidiary rights department to make the sales for them in the first place, and agents' fees and so on where they exist), constitutes just about their entire profit on publishing the book.

Of course, the hard-cover publishers would like to make money on actually selling copies of the book itself, too. Their chance of doing so on the first printing of thirty-five hundred or five thousand copies is not very good, but if that sells out in a reasonable time they may well go back for additional printings.

This seems a simple thing to do, but in practice it doesn't happen as often as one would think. It is partly a matter of the velocity of sale—a book that the publisher can expect to sell at the rate of one thousand copies a year for two years may seem to him worth keeping in stock, while one that might sell three hundred fifty copies a year for ten years isn't. Hard-cover books are sold to bookstores by salesmen, before the bookstores sell them to the customers. The salesman for any one publishing company can be expected to keep just so many titles in mind. His time with any buyer is limited, and so the book that will sell over a period of years, but not very much in any one year, tends to get forgotten. (This is even more true in paperback publishing, and is why some of the famous sf titles that schools and individuals would happily go on buying year after year are often allowed to go out of print.)

Twice a year the hard-cover publishers count up the number of copies they have sold, multiply it by the royalty due the author on each copy (generally ten percent of the retail price on the first five thousand copies, up to fifteen percent thereafter), and send him a check for his earnings. If the book is selling reasonably rapidly, they will try to keep it in print.

If the book is a juvenile, they are often successful, partly because juveniles are blessed with a new audience of potential customers growing into the book-buying range every year, and partly because juveniles are not as frequently reprinted in paperback form.

Adult science fiction is not as likely to stay in print. (You may find it difficult to distinguish "adult" from "juvenile" sf, but the trade has no trouble—the books are marked one way or the other.) The publishers are eager to sell the paperback rights for a quick cash income. And once the book is available in paperback at 95¢ they consider the chance of selling further hard-cover copies at $4.95 to be too low to justify keeping the book alive.

The paperback publishers operate in much the same way, but

with a few important differences.

To begin with, they do not have the prospect of a paperbound reprint sale to sweeten their profits. They *are* the paperback reprinters. So the bulk of their income they must earn by selling actual physical books to actual real customers—not even to libraries or institutions (which find paperbacks too fragile to circulate very efficiently), but to individual readers.

There is also a fundamental difference in the way sales are counted and royalties are paid. Your hard-cover book is printed, and the publisher's salesmen go out to sell it. Every time they sell a copy they report it, and that sale gets added into your royalty statement so that, half-year by half-year, each statement should show at least a trickle of additional sales to the author. The additional sales may be small, and may even be wiped out by returns of unsold books for credit; but typically there will be a pattern of continuing sales and earnings for some time.

Paperback books, on the other hand, are "sold" outright as soon as they come off the press. An edition of one hundred thousand copies of a new science fiction paperback title is not placed on sale, it is simply shipped out directly from the printing plant, in batches of a few hundred or a thousand copies each (along with similar batches of every other book the publisher is bringing out that month), allocated to the various wholesalers all over the country who have agreed to accept such shipments from the publisher's national distributor.

So if you were to see the publishers' sales figures on your paperbound book the week after publication, you would be delighted to find that all one hundred thousand copies were "sold." Unfortunately, they do not stay sold. Within weeks, certainly within a month or two, the wholesalers begin to return the copies they do not expect to sell. Sometimes they will send back the whole book. More often they simply strip the covers off and return them for credit, destroying the rest of the book. (Much inventive technology has gone into designing machines which have no function but so to mutilate coverless paperbound books and magazines that they cannot be read!)

So a month after publication your publisher's records show you have sold only ninety thousand copies. Two months after publication, eighty thousand. And so on. By the time the cycle is complete (it takes about six months to reach the point where you can really feel secure in estimating how many copies will be returned, and you can still be surprised unpleasantly for another year), you find you have sold only forty thousand to sixty thousand copies.

A lot of writers do not understand this, and so they think something is funny when they get a July royalty statement that shows they have sold fewer copies than the January statement showed—but those are the facts of life.

An ugly aspect of the practice of returning paperback books' covers for full refund has turned up in recent years. Some underground genius (the word is that the Mafia has something to do with it) decided that as long as you could sell a single sheet of paper—the stripped-off cover—back to publishers for half a dollar or so, it would be profitable to print up covers yourself and, with the connivance of "legitimate" wholesalers, mail them in for a neat piece of change.

No one knows exactly how many of these counterfeit covers have been returned, but the number is undoubtedly in the millions. This is very unpleasant to paperback publishers, representing an out-of-pocket loss of perhaps ten thousand dollars or more on a single title. It is even worse for the writer, partly because these "returns" are deducted from his royalty earnings, but even more because they give a very false picture of the sale of his book and therefore have an effect on future editions as well. The publishers are trying all sorts of stratagems to to make their covers uncounterfeitable, and these work reasonably well, but of course add to the costs and annoyances of publishing.

If a paperback book does sell well, it is not impossible for the publisher to notice this fact and go back to press for more copies almost at once. It is, however, extremely unlikely, at least on the average sf book. Big blockbusting best sellers are watched carefully and great efforts are made to keep them in print, but this process is expensive. When the total expectancy of sale is only average, it is cheaper and simpler for the publisher to wait until the whole fifteen-month or eighteen-month cycle of release and returns is complete, and then to take the final sales figure as gospel. By then so much time has passed that the simplest way for the publisher to capitalize on the success of the book is to put a new cover on it and reissue it as though it were a brand-new title. (He might even want to change the title of it so as to confuse the customers into ordering again, as well as the whole-salers, but he can't because that has become against the law.)

Since by the time that happens the publisher is committed to a bunch of new titles, and since he may well feel that so much time has passed that the sales figures no longer represent the current market, there is an excellent chance that he will prefer to forget the whole thing.

So much for science fiction publishing as it is.

What of the future?

When I was an Air Force weatherman we were taught to plot isobars and sample the atmosphere with radiosondes and to make use of Bjerknes's air mass theory and the adiabatic lapse rate in order to predict what the weather was going to be; but most of the forecasts that we issued were made on the basis of what is sometimes called "The Persistence Theory of Meteorology." That is, you look out the window. If it is raining, you allow as how it will go on raining for a while. If it isn't, you predict that it won't.

This is not a bad way of predicting the close-range future of anything, and it is very likely the best way to look into the next few years of publishing. Large masses have a certain inertia; they change, but they seldom change rapidly. And publishing practices have immense inertia.

So it is likely that for the immediate future things will not change drastically. The magazines will remain in trouble. The hard-cover publishers will continue to live in large part off reprints. The paperback publishers will continue to suffer from fifty percent wastage of everything they print, and from slow, unreliable sales figures.

Yet things could change. It might only take one brilliant new editor coming along to change the shape of sf magazine publishing. If someone could find a new approach he might well build a loyal readership that would repeal the market laws and revivify the whole field, in spite of climbing costs and declining advertising revenues.

In book publishing, there is a very good chance of a useful new kind of sf book publishing emerging, intermediate between the hard-cover lines and the mass-market paperbacks.

There is a particular need for some mechanism that will permit a basic backlist of one hundred or so "classic" science fiction titles to remain in print year after year, if only so that the five hundred or so science fiction courses which are currently being given in the nation's colleges and high schools can order them for their students. This kind of publication is what is called the "quality paperback." These are physically a little bigger than the Ballantine or Ace mass-market books. They are usually printed on better paper, and their covers are typically less buckeye. Their editions are substantially smaller—ten thousand or twenty-five thousand instead of one hundred thousand. And they cost about twice as much as the mass-market books.

Their advantage is that each title can be stocked and sold on its own merits, as the titles on a mass-market list cannot. Instead of suffering a wastage of fifty percent on copies stripped and pulped, over a period of time each printing should approach a one hundred percent sale. There are technical and commercial problems involved that will take some solving, but the need and the market are there; it is probable that this will happen in some form in the fairly near future.

Further in the future there is an excellent (but not very immediate) prospect of "custom" publication.

This is a proposal made principally by a man named Eugene Leonard, who is in the business of designing systems approaches to communications problems. His notion is that when you want a book you pick up your telephone and dial in an order, whereupon your parlor teleduplicating machine starts printing a copy up for you. A system involving a screen like a closed-circuit TV set, plus a duplicating machine like a Xerox, could run off a three-hundred-page novel for you in a few minutes, just before duplicating your morning newspaper and after bringing you your morning mail. Clearly this would be more expensive per copy produced than conventional printing and binding, but it could amount to not much more than a penny a page to duplicate. And there would be zero wastage, since the copy of the book would not exist until you ordered it.

Microfilm and microfiche are interesting possibilities on the horizon. They have been on the horizon for so many years now that most people in publishing have begun to turn off their brains to the potential here, but just in the past few months some new developments have come along. There exists a new process which involves shrinking the size of each individual letter on a page, and printing other letters in the spaces thus left free, so that a single piece of film contains sixty-four or more pages of copy. A cheap and portable reading machine (probably smaller than a dispatch case and costing something like five dollars) separates out the characters that belong to any single page and reenlarges them so you can read them; so that you can sit in the bus with a few slides and a viewer and read a novel on the way to work. Once enough people have the viewers it will not be hard to manufacture and market microfilms. They would be substantially cheaper than regular books, and would have the further advantage of using up the forests at a markedly slower rate—not to mention saving the difficulty of getting rid of all those old books, magazines, and newspapers.

All of this, of course, assumes that an audience capable of assimilating the printed word will still exist.

That may be an untenable assumption, since TV already makes reading a minor skill for many people. It may well be that the future of communications will hardly involve the written word at all, and that TV, video and audio cassettes, and personal receivers for broadcast and closed-circuit programming will abolish publishing, as such, entirely.

But those developments are outside the scope of this chapter.

Frederik Pohl

Frederik Pohl, three-time Hugo winner, editor of some thirty science fiction anthologies and author and/or co-author of more than forty books, mostly fiction, is now acting as science fiction consultant at Bantam Books.

He has a broad and diversified background as a science fiction editor and writer. From 1960 through 1969 he was an editor at Galaxy Publishing Corp., publishers of *Galaxy* and *If* science fiction magazines. Since then he has devoted himself full time to writing.

He is the author, with C. M. Kornbluth, of *The Space Merchants* (1953) which has been translated into more than thirty languages. His most recent science fiction novel is *The Age of the Pussyfoot* (1970), and his latest nonfiction book is *Practical Politics* (1972), a handbook of the political process in America.

He also is the author of *The Case Against Tomorrow* (1957), and *Drunkard's Walk* (1960), and the editor of *Star Science Fiction Stories, The Expert Dreamers, Galaxy Reader,* and *Nightmare Age.*

For three years in a row (1966–68) Mr. Pohl was honored with the Hugo Award, given annually by the Science Fiction Convention. In 1972 he was designated the guest of honor at their annual convention. Several times he has represented the United States in International Science Fiction Conferences in Europe and South America.

A native of New York City, he has lived for the past twenty-two years in Red Bank, N.J., with his wife and family.

George Zebrowski

Science Fiction and the Visual Media

Science fiction film is mainly a story of failure on many fronts. Numerous critics, those who know science fiction and those who do not, have pointed this out for so long now that it has become a familiar point in many discussions of the subject. I would like, however, to avoid a parade of bad films or films which contain technical virtues of interest only to those willing to ignore the absence of everything else a good science fiction film should have to preserve their enthusiasm. Rather, I would like to explore those very fronts where science fiction film fails, and where it can succeed. So very often the different positions expressed about science fiction film suggest the pieces of a puzzle, a puzzle such that if only the pieces had been cut correctly, the picture would emerge.

The most general cause for hope, one which I would like to offer again, more clearly than I have encountered it to date and in the light of recent developments, is that there exists a real possibility for good science fiction cinema. Such a possibility in any field is always exciting. Yet so few realize that, as in written science fiction, science fiction film is an area where almost everything remains to be done. Then why has it not been done? There are financial and technical barriers, and I will present newly developed ways of overcoming them. To begin with very few have tried to do enough. Little has been done because it has not been tried. Generally, this problem afflicts all film. As a medium it seems to lack an aesthetic sufficiently flexible so as not to constrict very creative individuals, yet sufficiently authoritative to orient newcomers. Ironically, the dream-made-real medium breaks newcomers of their dreams. Things which they would like to do are labeled "unfilmic" or unfamiliar to audiences. Some of this is justified, but much of it is an expression of budgetary and technical restrictions. Motion-picture executives seek to guarantee the success of a film in advance, and to repeat it as often as possible. As a result the selection process for new projects is weighted against innovation. This is less true today, but one is surprised that given the obstacles, *anything* good has been done.

Science fiction film from 1950 to 1970 makes the above problems more acute and specialized. The past of science fiction cinema rarely suggests much that can be considered innovative today. Good science fiction films are individual, and cannot be repeated endlessly like the monster cycles. The serious science fiction film maker must depend on his own judgment, the resources of his studio, and his knowledge of written science fiction, in addition to his own cinematic skills and the abilities of his writers.

Here we come to our first big problem. John Baxter, author of *Science Fiction in the Cinema,* tells us that science fiction film is an intellectual impossibility. "With *2001: A Space Odyssey,*" he writes, "science fiction came as close as it could to an alliance with sf film. Whether by instinct or design, Kubrick and Clarke had found a plot device that combined the positive attitude of science fiction with the negative attitude of sf film. They had set the particularising mood of film in the visionary sweep of literature, the mythopoetic basis of sf film in the rigidly real world of Clarke's space fiction. But despite this superficial combination, the tension is still there. One doubts that it can ever be otherwise when too dissimilar fields, for better or worse, are nailed together."

Throughout his book, Baxter stresses that what is called

science fiction film is a primarily visual, sensuous medium which cannot express the science fictional *ideas* found in the written form. We should view sf film as a visual play of man's fears and symbols in the twentieth century. Written science fiction tries to be logical, abstract, and scientifically believable; while sf film is associative, immature, scientifically innaccurate and irrational. And it should not even try to be good science fiction because that is impossible.

Baxter directs our attention to the visual things in a large selection of examples from sf film. Much of what he points out about the visual elements of past sf films is revealing, managing to show things, which many of us had not noticed, about even the worst of the monster-mold sagas of the 1950s. But he puts himself in the position of the opera lover who must admit that the story of a particular work may be inane, while the music is a work of genius. In fact Baxter does admit this sort of thing a number of times, but manages to hold that it is not damaging at all to the concerns of a legitimate appreciation of science fiction cinema.

Naturally it would be as wrong to deny film its visual glories as it would be to deny opera its music. The novel quality of film is the visual experience, just as one of the important aspects of opera is the music. But a film is also theater drama, including sound and music; and opera has been known to be excellent theatrical drama, apart from its music. As a matter of historical record there have been intermediate states. Legitimate plays have been filmed, with the camera expanding audience awareness. Television programs are often an example of well-made plays, if uninspired, which are simply filmed. At least two operas, Purcell's *Dido and Aeneas* (baroque) and Berg's *Wozzeck* (modern), have been said to use music and action cinematically. It is not a question of reducing any one form to another, which is where much of the jealousy and confusion between, for example, films and novels originates. It is a matter of recognizing that all dramatic art does not spring out of a vacuum. Originalities of expression and content do advance beyond the media of the past—or much more accurately, new qualities appear. But it is not a mystery where film borrows and where it is new. Therefore, it becomes nonsense to deny science fiction film the capacity to embody sophisticated sf ideas on the screen as well as in the written form, just as it would be foolish to argue against the Greek dramatists, or Ibsen, Shaw, and others, that ideas cannot be made to work on the stage.

Film is not the drama of theater, but drama is an aspect of it, an aspect *uniquely* expanded by the camera. Film makes more demands on what has been written. The result is more than theater drama can do. But film remains drama and fiction to a degree. The problems of relationship between these things are not insoluble. What works well *written* is often not as good *spoken*. What goes well *shown* may not be well *written*. A good example of this last problem is *THX 1138,* a beautifully visual science fiction film released in 1971, which expressed a certain mood of pathos and defiance growing out of some well-known science fiction ideas. It was unremarkable in book form. Like *Fantastic Voyage,* the book was a novelization from the film, and did not require exceptional writing *to be an adequate verbal memento of the film.* As a work of written science fiction, it would have required a more ambitious approach in that medium to have been exceptional. For example, *A Clockwork Orange* by Anthony Burgess is a fine novel, but it suffers in the minds of those who have seen the film first and then read the novel trying to untangle Kubrick's images from those of the novelist. This cannot be helped except by understanding that a true novel is not a memento of whatever film has been made from it. *THX 1138* is primarily a film, and it took some courage on the part of George Lucas to make, because it presented futuristic ideas not universally familiar, though many sf writers and readers found them so.

Consider the problem of *ideas* in science fiction film more closely—assuming that they can be conveyed on the screen. The problem is very much like the one of ideas in written sf. Necessary ideas and backgrounds involving a future world, or any world significantly different from the present, tend to stop the progress of a story while the reader is made aware of what he has to know to understand the particular nature of the story, story problem, and final resolution. I am assuming here Theodore Sturgeon's view that a science fiction story is one which could not have taken place without the scientific idea (current science or extrapolated science—actually any relatively fantastic element) affecting the lives of persons (human or other) in the story. If the story is written in a scientific spirit of believability and serious concern about the future, it is a science fiction story; but if the fantastic element is intentionally left unexplained (and need not be explained), the story is a fantasy and need be only internally consistent. The common ground lies in the variety of fantastic element used.

The *information load* of a science fiction story has always been a problem because the work must also be a work of fiction, subject to the demands of good fiction. When the information is extensive, characters convey it to each other in conversation, which is sometimes legitimate dialogue and sometimes contrived. The author tells things to the reader, quoted information is placed in front of chapters; direct thoughts of characters are presented. When the needed information is scant and the story takes place near or during our times, the author can get in a few things at the beginning and let the reader assume others, as in a contemporary novel or story, where no one explains elevators or taxis. One reason why the monster films of the '50s are so easy is because all the viewer has to *know* is that there *is* a monster, and the story moves forward visually.

American science fiction, growing up as it did in the pulps, is defensive about ideas. They are something to be slipped into the story. The story action comes first, before characterization and style, or ideas. This is not difficult to understand if we remember that fiction is a *story* medium. A well-plotted story tends to survive even when everything else is minimal. Sf films inherited this traditional reluctance. A science fiction writer fears being called an essayist when he aims to be a writer of fiction, a maker of words, a purveyor of altered human experience and character. But he also fears having his ideas ridiculed for implausibility or scientific error. Science fiction is at once vulnerable from the side of the intellectual and the anti-intellectual.

But the root question to ask, one which will help us see the solution, is this: what are ideas—where are they found? And the answer is that *people* have ideas. Characters think them, say them, write them, *live* them at *all* levels of articulation. It is not everything they do, but it is enough to help us out of our problem in film and in written sf. The theater has always known this, as have European novelists. In science fiction, Robert Heinlein has known this from the start of his career, as did H. G. Wells. Heinlein's and Wells's characters always need to know what the reader needs to know as the story progresses. The first person subjectivity of Heinlein's characters enables them to relate to the reader on any level, intellectual as well as emotional. I'm not saying that other writers do not do this at all. I am saying that few authors have the self-assurance to practice ideas in fiction and make a seamless fabric out of the effort. Too many never get over the feeling that it is always a case of *slipping in the ideas.*

Sf film tries to leave them out. Sf writers who have worked in Hollywood tell the same story too often. They do a script which tries to be good drama, good fiction, and good science fiction—leaving the visual expression to the director and visual effects teams—and the result too often is a rewrite designed to reduce the whole thing to the primary emotions of love, hate, pleasure, pain and fear—above all fear and violence for their own sake. Everything deserves stimulation except the brain. In recent years we have seen human sexuality win its case in the cinema; one wonders, can the brain be far behind?

The infuriating fact is that often many efforts achieve beautiful visual results, things which are a contribution to the visual aspect of film, so much so that critics like John Baxter retreat into the visual as the only relevant point of discussion. The king has a great tan, which only helps emphasize that he has no clothes. Parallel attitudes in written science fiction are those which gravitate toward style, ideas, or action at the expense of other things. One might just as well insist on breathing by itself, hearing or tasting by itself. Even radio, which could imagine *anything* for its listeners, gave strong attention to other fictional virtues. Advanced gourmets insist on the total experience of a restaurant, from the decor to the excellence of the food. To be fair, all this is the inevitable result of different people being good at different things. But there is little excuse for being unaware of the problem on a critical level. Again, very few have made the effort to think about the problem very much, much less try to put the pieces together in a constructive way.

The amount of mystification present in much of the writing about film tends to discourage lucid thought with a flourish of technicalities and specialized knowledge. I have high admiration for those skilled in the aspects of preparing a film, and the highest regard for those who make the visual image itself real and individual before my eyes. I understand the tendency to be involved with what one does best. My point lies not with the improvement of the image maker's art—that is up to him—but with a specific answer to the problem of making a good science fiction film. We know that it can be done and should be done; we know that the specter of ideas as a problem can be put to rest, in the sense that Baxter raises it—as an inherently insoluble one. We know that the image makers are more than up to it, even in the realm of ideas. The art of montage, for example, can produce a sequence of images which can forcefully elicit thoughts and ideas, as well as feelings, from the viewer.

A good science fiction film must be made, therefore, with craftsmanlike attention to its dramatic and filmic possibilities— its fictional qualities (drama, character, conflict, resolution, etc.), its science fiction possibilities (*ideas* which must be *embodied* in characters *and* visual images).

Ironically, sf film should have some advantage over written sf, because it can show backgrounds and people living in them in a self-explanatory way. Strange, also, that films based on the lives of the great inventors and scientists, like Edison, Curie, and Pasteur, are not afraid to communicate ideas concerning what these people did. Why is it that sf film makers lack the confidence to do the same thing consistently in sf film? Does reality lend authority where imagination and extrapolation seem contrived?

All that can truthfully be concluded is that making a good sf film, much less a great one, is extremely difficult, no matter how easily the problem and solution are resolved on paper. The work demands conviction and familiarity with the things peculiar to science fiction on a level of working confidence, as well as filmic skill. It is a difficult but not impossible task, contrary to the thesis of John Baxter's book. Over-impressed with the difficulties and past successes, he shifts the debate away from the hard, demanding things, to the comfortable areas of existing achievement not peculiar to sf cinema, but characteristic of all cinema: visual skill. He diverts our attention away from what is possible and still remains to be done in sf film.

Part of the problem that conceptually mature science fiction has had in America exists in the problem of communicating ideas. Ultimately this kind of problem lies deeply embedded in the educational character of a people, which expresses itself in the popular attitudes toward intellectuals, scientists, and others who deal in ideas. These attitudes have been communicated to those who back films, and many sf films express these prejudices. The circle closes and new audiences learn these prejudices again.

But there are ways of entertaining the mind, even the popular one. Film makers ignore a number of things in the popular audience. People are *curious* (a self-educational quality), especially if they know they can find out. People are game players. They like to solve things. Television programs like *Mission Impossible* and *Hawaii Five-O*, crude as they are in many ways, are filled with complex ideas unpretentiously explained. For example, in one episode of *Hawaii Five-O* the viewer learned a few things about how agencies use computers in stock transactions; and the information was vital to the human problem and to the enjoyment of the program, as well as satisfying in itself. The computer was shown as a tool, a working aid to be used or misused by human beings, while in science fiction film it is often the monster come back in new garb to plague us. No one is against a menace, provided that it is not there only to have one, but is essential to the possibility being explored.

For example, *Colossus: The Forbin Project*, is really about the emergence of an artificial intelligence, a *person* in form different from us, in what should have been a tool with no subjectivity of its own. Its conflict with us is incidental to its education and growth. The beauty of the film is that it *shows* us the computer's daily life and gradual reaching out into the world as the human characters try to explain what is happening. It is vital that they find out (and the audience too) because Colossus does not see the difference between a peace that is *imposed* on the world, and one that is *chosen*, the difference between enforcing the right thing and having the world freely accept it. Given this misconception of the moral life (where did Colossus learn it?), it logically proceeds to use the means at its disposal to enforce it. This is not such a strange notion. Our concept of law says that we must have a government of laws, not men. Colossus resembles the idea of judgment and law enforcement made practically incorruptible and inexorable, much like the giant police robot in *The Day the Earth Stood Still* (1951), from the short story "Farewell to the Master" by Harry Bates. Gorth, like Colossus, will not wait for men to behave. He will make it impossible for them to misbehave—a guardian angel who would enforce certain limits much in the same way the natural world imposes limits on our lives, while we go on within it. This idea occurs in Asimov's robot stories, where the built-in Three Laws of Robotics resemble Kant's Categorical Imperative, or perhaps even Moses' Ten Commandments. But the interesting problem with Colossus and Gorth is that we cannot know, or guarantee, that they are like this or like many error-prone specimens of humanity. More likely, Colossus is our true child, logical from bad assumptions and inconsistent at the same time, while Gorth is the conservative's ideal solution to the governing of an imperfect man. What is delightful about both films is that their makers were not afraid to *show* a conflict of ideas and make them accessible through sf films, which are also genuine science fiction.

Films like these suggest the questions that sf film makers should always ask themselves. These are questions which show respect for the audience, especially for its capacity to understand *while viewing* a film. It should not be asked what will be familiar to the audience, or whether some science fiction sequence will be too technical, but rather how to *make it* comprehensible: logically, emotionally, dramatically, visually. One need not succeed on all levels with all people for them to know and appreciate the significance of what is happening. *2001: A Space Odyssey* is a wonderful example of this kind of success. So many people knew or sensed what was happening on some level—intuitive, emotional, intellectual, scientific—to some degree, that it put to shame the literal-minded critics who believe that *communication* runs only in certain explicit and univocal channels.

The audiences of *2001* are now ready for still better things in sf film. The lesson is that all film, including sf film, can and must educate its audiences to expect more, understand more next time. It must whet appetites, not feed the audience pablum. On television the pablum gets so bad so regularly that even mildly innovative programs are greeted with enthusiasm.

Sf film, like all film, then, can create its own demand for better film through itself. There will always be films which are visually meritorious, though poor in other ways. And we will have those who are drawn in this direction, crying that this is all there is to it, the summit of what film does and can ever do; the sound of the craftsman in love with his tools, fearful of revealing that the tools cannot do everything. And there is considerable truth in this, though we should be wary of saying how much. We are still in the honeymoon phase of the sf film maker's art. Many films are exercises of talent, compendiums of differing abilities, showing us bits and pieces which are the shadows of a whole work.

Those who undertake the making of sf films should do their homework, and understand the problems. They should view those few sf films which are reasonable successes by all the demands discussed. There are not many such films. The film maker should not be dominated by attitudes of "pure cinema," but simply be influenced by them. In those few cases where a science fiction writer was directly involved in the making of an sf film, the product came out weighted toward science fiction virtues—ideas expressed visually, through the spoken word, musically, the virtues of intelligence and coherence in regard to sf characters and events. Often the visual craftsman had more to bite into as a result. His ingenuity was challenged again and again by the content which he had to express.

The first great sf film, although its view of the future is quite simplistic, is Fritz Lang's *Metropolis*, an epic silent released in 1926. It is a flawed film, but one which genuinely works to express its ideas visually and dramatically. We know and see what ideas are in conflict. We see how the huge technology works, how it oppresses, and what the people think of it. *Metropolis* says everything it wants to say, but fails in credibility at the intellectual level. Its characters are puppets for its ideas. Its view of the future cannot be seriously held for social, economic, logical, and technological reasons. Its future is symbolic projection, not extrapolation, a grotesque nightmare only visually satisfying. More can be said of it as a social document of the times in which it was made than as real sf film. The special effects are still startlingly effective. The film is a technological gothic.

The first sf film to succeed on almost all counts is the Wells-Korda-Menzies *Things to Come* of 1936. Like almost all sf films, good and bad, it was overpraised or unfairly condemned, and continues so. Like the later *2001* its virtues are considerable.

It has a strong screen play, which is acted by giants, characters who speak out against each other and against their fate with classical passion. Its themes are lasting ones, despite the film's specifics. The anti-war sentiments are historic now in the light of the war that followed—especially in view of the Vietnam war, whose end was promised again and again much like the repeated promises of the Chief in Wells's film; the idea of man remaking the earth; the insistence on law *and* sanity; the love of reaching for the stars, of risking comfort for something creative in us; the sense of human waste and ignorance; the ascetic, apolitical superman, who is calm, saving his passion for the most worthy ends. All these things, which belong so clearly to what many of us who write and know science fiction think of as a worthwhile future, make the film a unique expression of general attitudes that surely belong in any good future.

But the film is rich in more than this. It rises to a special kind of brilliance, Baxter points out. He is on strong ground when he writes, "The most remarkable quality of *Things to Come* is the coherence and consistency of its design. Menzies may not have been a master of direction, but his sense of balance and mastery of what Eisenstein called "visual counterpoint" has never been better displayed than in this film. Concerned only in the most general way with textures and movements within the frame, Menzies puts his whole effort into the balance of his sets, the conflict between masses, and the choreography of matter. His designs fill the frame, both vertically and horizontally, while the use of the low angle sends individual groupings surging out at the audience." Baxter should say at this point that the film's design supports its ideas and theme; its visual side is integral with its science fiction content.

The sequence of special excellence is the final one at the reflecting telescope, as Cabal (played by Raymond Massey) and Passworthy (Edward Chapman) catch a fleeting glimpse of the space vehicle on its way to the moon. The scene is lighted from one side only, giving the character's faces a dark edge which contrasts well with the white telescope and dark, starry heavens. One could easily make a case for the explicit symbolism of man's backward and forward looking natures in the halfdarkened faces.

Passworthy asks, "If they don't come back—my son and your daughter—what of that, Cabal?"

"Then, presently, others will go."

"Oh, God, is there never to be any age of happiness? Is there never to be any rest?"

"Rest enough for the individual man—too much, and too soon, and we call it Death. But for Man no rest and no ending. . . . First this little planet with its winds and ways, and then all the laws of mind and matter that restrain him. Then the planets about him, and at last out across immensity to the stars. And when he has conquered all the deeps of space and all the mysteries of time, still he will be beginning."

"But . . . we're such little creatures. Poor humanity's so fragile, so weak. Little . . . little animals."

"Little animals. If we're not more than animals we must snatch each little scrap of happiness and live and suffer and pass,

mattering no more than all the other animals do or have done."
John Cabal points to the reflection of space in the mirror. "Is it
this—or that: all the universe or nothing? Which shall it be,
Passworthy? Which shall it be?"

Baxter writes, "Over this dialogue Bliss imposes a soft but
powerful melody, building with the intensity of Cabal's speech
until the full orchestra and choir surge up at the end with an
echo of his final question. . . . The final scene is a triumph of
music and image. The hard edged side lighting and almost
stylized close-ups of Massey's face, his impeccable delivery of
what is basically a technocratic credo and Bliss's profoundly
moving music combine to give it a unique quality of optimism
and dignity."

At this point Baxter again fails to complete the statement he
should have made about music and science fiction. Music has
always had the quality of transcendence and striving, qualities
directly associated with science fiction ideas. *Things to Come*
employed Sir Arthur Bliss, the English composer, to create a
serious score for the film. But it was Kubrick who fulfilled the
promise of serious music for sf film. He took the intuition, held
by many in science fiction, that the music already existed. He
took the work of serious composers and gave it new life in *2001:
A Space Odyssey*. The music in both films expresses what Baxter calls "the essential spirit of science fiction." It supports the
transcendent movement of ideas which belong to good science
fiction, generally the ideas of change and creativity.

Baxter grants that *Things to Come* is "rich in the essential
spirit of science fiction," but he continually makes hopelessly
vague attacks on the film. He uses condemnatory phrases like
"politically and sociologically specious," and sneers at the film
for advocating "a mild and undemanding happiness" in its view
of the future. He finds this future dull and unworkable, missing
the point that no blueprint or vision can ever be the actual
future.

What is important in the ideas department of *Things to Come*,
something which the thesis of Baxter's book prevents him from
approaching with any perceptive enterprise, is that Wells
wanted us to understand not his specifics, which belong to the

world of the film's story, but the general constructive attitudes —the idea that the future must be an object of creative concern, that futures are to be *made, invented,* not passively predicted. "The essential spirit of science fiction" with which Baxter credits the film has never stood for one party-line future. The dull utopia that Baxter complains about is far from static. It is itself being shaken up by the conflict over the creative space venture which is the film's finale. I need not point out that this conflict is a modern one, and still with us. As in the film, it is a challenge to further growth, one which strikes at out entire awareness of the earth as an island in the void. That the idea of space travel should be pitted against the reality of human welfare on earth, and in 1937, is proof that even in his old age Wells had an historical imagination of the first order. Even the much-ridiculed electric cannon which launches the space craft in the film, is a much more sophisticated invention than many know about. It is not a simple Vernian cannon, which would compress the astronauts into pulp when fired. It is a "graduated electric catapult" in the shape of a cannon within a cannon, which would accelerate the vehicle by stages. Both the U.S. and the Soviet Union have considered such economical ground-based and powered booster systems.

Wells could not sneer at "whole-wheat" utopias in a world where so much was lacking. He did have a sense of priorities in the full modern sense. Wells scholars are gradually freeing his name of the taint of technocracy and scientism which has been imposed on him by proponents of the "two cultures" myth. *Things to Come* is rich in ideas as well as being an excellent film. It demonstrates that ideas are an important part of good sf film, and that written sf is not hopelessly at odds with the film medium. Baxter fails to demonstrate the truth of his charges against Wells and the film. He merely states certain second-hand and untenable assertions which represent a superficial and antiquated view (from a critical-scholarly standpoint) of the historical Wells.

The interplay of ideas in the film can be demonstrated, even briefly. They show a unified movement without which the film's images would be diminished. The visual counterpoint is paralleled by a counterpoint of ideas. A tug of war goes on in the film between Wellsian social ideas and Vernian technological elements, between what Alexei Panshin defines as the didactic and romantic elements in science fiction. On the one hand there is a concern with the improvement of human life in practical material and engineering terms; and on the other hand there is a concern with the ineffable, the aesthetic, noble and transcendent. All these things are present in what we see and hear. In every scene the film expresses the intrusion of the unknown into the known and limited—the sort of thing which every now and then pushes our imaginations into new realms, and without which life would not be worth living. It is the attitude which Wells tried to harness to the remaking of the world. He did not have to succeed with the world, or be a perfect prophet with a workable scheme on the screen, to make this a great sf film —which it is because it does everything necessary to such a work.

Where *Things to Come* falls somewhat short is in its model work, which is inferior to *Metropolis*, though adequate. But for all its visual beauty *Metropolis* fails as *sf* film, though not entirely as *film*, because it says so little—not much more than something about how workers and factory owners should cooperate. The story and characters of *Metropolis* carry no conviction. At its most simplistic, *Things to Come* projects a sense of open possibility absent from *Metropolis*. *Things to Come* has a strong grasp on the polar opposites of safety and adventure, of boredom and novelty, of consolidation and innovation. Its finale is an archetype of great science fiction moments—in this case the moment when a future state of affairs is about to be surpassed by further progress.

Wells was a critic of progress, as Jack Williamson has pointed out in his study of Wells, not simply an advocate. In *Things to Come* we are made to feel dramatically, intellectually, and visually that the overall pattern of progress cannot be grasped in advance, except momentarily; and that beyond the attainment of social welfare lies the problem without end, the question of what makes living worthwhile: creative ventures of our own choice, made possible by the dull comfort of material welfare which Baxter scorns. This problem lies deeply in human nature, and is the source of pessimism about humanity. That Wells should present it to us alongside the outward looking dream of space travel, constitutes a vision of maturity, a turning away from the frustration of solipsism and despair, the diseased pessimism which World War II placed over his mental life like a shroud.

Other science fiction films which were good science fiction include *Destination Moon* (1950). It taught audiences about the reality of space travel (ironically a child of the war) and its problems. It taught them to expect accuracy in scientific details, as well as showing them the natural beauty of earth-moon space, as much an object for visual poetry as any part of nature. The film was made by George Pal, with the cooperation of Robert Heinlein. As with *Things to Come, Destination Moon* has the virtue of being well *spoken.* The characters speak with a moving, quiet dignity and authenticity, though on a lesser scale than in Wells's film. The element of the spoken work is one of the things that makes both films exceptional drama.

The Time Machine (1969), also by George Pal, is a well made adaptation of Wells's classic novel. As in the book the film clearly reflects Wells's fear of a comfortable utopia which will put us to sleep. The film has been called conventional, but it does capture Wells's technical wonders—the time machine itself—as well as his concern for mankind. Rod Taylor is perfect as the likeable time traveler. No one who is attentive to the film's all around virtues will come away disappointed. It may not be what it should have been, but it is good sf film—an almost nonexistent thing.

More recent examples give cause for hope. Good sf came to television regularly in the 1960s, and a few of the best examples of sf film were presented on the small screen. The finest examples were Harlan Ellison's "Soldier," and "Demon With a Glass Hand," both one hour episodes in the anthology series *The Outer Limits.*

"Soldier," a fascinating glimpse into the mind of a fighting man from the future lost in our present, becomes more meaningful during reruns, as we watch him trying to understand our world—where war is not the all embracing reality, even though we took a step in that direction during the 1960s. The film brilliantly gives us indirect glimpses into the terrible reality of the future world, where cats are bred to be intelligent spies, where super-weapons and inhuman war situations require human war robots, bred artificially, parentless devices of the state. The meticulous craftsmanship of this film is a wondrous thing to be seen, and more than once.

"Demon With a Glass Hand" is more fantastic, but an intriguing joy to watch and think about, again fulfilling that union of genuine science fiction ideas and brilliant film making. The idea of the title, a computer hand with five plug-in fingers, is a concept that can live brilliantly in a film or science fiction novel. The story was shot in an old iron-latticework office block, and gives the film a unique quality of brooding darkness.

Ellison later went on to write "The City at the Edge of Forever" for *Star Trek*. It was one of the few episodes which made its people live and suffer believably in a science fiction framework which genuinely pervaded the entire situation, and which provided both its human and science fiction resolution *at once*. Traditional by written sf standards, this episode was brought with conviction to the television screen.

In *Modern Science Fiction: Its Meaning and Its Future*, edited by Reginald Bretnor (1953), Don Fabun wrote: "In time we may see the modern literary form called science fiction legitimately married to novel and exciting techniques . . . written by craftsmen who are skilled at writing with real actors . . . just as today's better writers are skilled in turning out really fine stories for the printed page." He laments that the visual media's plasticity can be realized by few living writers.

The situation began to change by the late 1960s. *2001: A Space Odyssey*, made with the help of Arthur C. Clarke and directed by Stanley Kubrick (who confessed that he wanted to make the good sf film that everyone was always talking about), proved that a new audience for sf film had arrived.

2001 brought out clearly, through the reactions of audiences and critics, all the problems associated with sf film. It became obvious that the critic or viewer *chooses* to pay attention to one thing or another, and his assessment of a film depends on what elements he happens to value above others. But we have seen why sf film demands an attention to a variety of elements on the part of the film maker. And this same attention must also be demanded of the critic and viewer. Like the viewer the critic must learn to understand, not preconceive. The critic has no business watching a film casually or uncritically. An sf film, especially, demands more than facile reactions written in ignorance of what makes a good science fiction film.

2001 was full of science fiction ideas presented visually. The film did what no sf novel could do outside the imagination of a perfectly imaginative reader. It worked well for those who brought to it only minimal understanding of its backgrounds and concepts, as well as for those who knew science fiction. Like the other sf films which involved sf writers significantly, *2001* preserved much of its writer's character and concerns in its final form. The lesson is not that every sf writer will work well in film if given the chance, but that many surely will, for reasons which are not enigmatic. The same holds for directors who know sf. We are at the start of an innovative period in science fiction film.

A few examples of technical advances which will remove all the barriers between what the science fiction writer can imagine and what can be put on the screen with complete realism, include the so-called "Magicam" process, minisets, microphotography and video-tape techniques. Any set can now be built in miniature and live people can be projected into the sets with complete believability. This allows the instant changing of sets during shooting, as well as their construction and use for a fraction of previous costs. The use of video tape, involving the transfer of video-tape images to film, means that sf film—as well as all film—can be produced more flexibly and economically.

What this means for science fiction writers, for those who will or will not work in films, is that sf films will become more ambitious, moving closer to the use of genuine sf ideas on the screen. Filmed sf will have a chance of becoming more than the morality play of the monster cycles. It will become *science fiction film*, possessing the characteristics of both mediums.

The problem, we have seen, has been on the film maker's side, as well as on the side of the critics and audiences who *adapted* to the level of sf film in the past, confusing it with horror and fantasy stories. *Things To Come* was a financial failure and a critical target. Too much was suddenly required in the understanding of the new literary child called science fiction, and its filmic brother. The idea of menace in the form of a monster was more familiar than the country of the future.

Things changed after 1945. *Destination Moon* remains a victory. *The Day the Earth Stood Still* made audiences feel that there was something serious about science fiction. They saw that an alien could be more than *The Thing,* but perhaps a person. The idea of the future permeated the public awareness in the 1960s. The audience changed. Film makers learned more about sf films' potential from sf writers and the younger breed of film innovators. *2001,* more complex than *Things To Come,* became a financial success. It would have baffled the audiences of 1937. And maybe Wells also would have had some trouble with it. Film audiences and critics and film makers alike learned, to some degree, that sf cinema, like all film, is a cultivated taste where it is serious, a continuing process of enjoyment and widening awareness which should lead to an understanding of what its best creators intend, both in terms of good sf and what sf film requires as visual expression.

The successful creation of sf film will require a level of skill and creativity beyond all except those who deliberately set out to meet the challenge. If I am correct, and sf film making achieves an integrative, unified approach to its various aspects, then the resulting excellences are not ones I would want to miss. They may even be strong enough to convince me that fully half the life of science fiction in time to come will be in the visual media.

Acknowledgments: I would like to thank James E. Gunn, who discussed with me certain points made in this article. And Harlan Ellison for information concerning new film processes.

George Zebrowski

Born in 1945 in Villach, Austria, of Polish parents, George Zebrowski grew up in England, Manhattan, Miami, and the Bronx. He attended Harpur College, SUNY at Binghamton, where he studied philosophy. He brings much of his interest in the philosophy of science to this science fiction. He was Lecturer in Science Fiction at SUNY Binghamton in 1971, teaching a full credit course in the genre. He has also taken part in informal seminars on the future in the School of Advanced Technology, Center for Integrative Studies, SUNY at Binghamton, under John McHale. He is a speaker at colleges and universities, a member of the World Future Society and the Science Fiction Writers Speaker's Bureau. Since 1970 he has been the editor of the Bulletin of the Science Fiction Writers of America, the official publication of the SFWA. In 1971 his short story "Heathen God" was a Nebula Award Finalist for Best Short Story.

His short fiction has appeared in *If, The Magazine of Fantasy and Science Fiction,* and in original collections like *Infinity One, Three, Four* and *Five,* in *Strange Bedfellows* (Random House); and in forthcoming original collections from Doubleday, Trident Press, Aurora, Ballantine, Avon, Walker, Pyramid, and others. He has written science fiction for younger readers for Lerners Publications and Allyn & Bacon. He is a reviewer for the British *Vector,* the publication of the British Science Fiction Association (BSFA). He has been a full-time writer since 1970.

The Omega Point, 1972 (Ace)
Faster Than Light, (Harper & Row, forthcoming in 1974), co-edited with Jack Dann
Planet One: Tomorrow Today, (Unity, forthcoming in 1974)

Science Fiction,
Science,
and Modern Man

Frank Herbert

Science Fiction and a World in Crisis

Washington's Mount Olympus is a pile of dirt and rock with snow on its crown. I can see it out of my study window. It helps sometimes to look out at it and remind myself of Lao-tze's words:

> The soul may be a mere pretense.
> The mind makes very little sense.
> So let us value the appeal
> Of what we can taste and feel.

If you write science fiction in a crisis-ridden world, the value of the pragmatic reasserts itself regularly. You have to say to yourself: "As I see it . . . " We need to touch base on occasion the way Atlas had to touch the earth. If we don't, we lose an important contact and we may write sentences such as this one from NASA's Apollo 14 documentary:

> Astronauts Alan B. Shepard Jr. and Edgar D. Mitchell were climbing a steepening slope (on the moon); their maps indicated they were approaching their destination, the rim of Cone Crater where rocks may have remained unchanged *since time began.* *(Italics mine)*

Since time began?
You see it all around in crisis after crisis —how deeply we remain immersed in the Cartesian division between material

and mental. It is virtually impossible for anyone conditioned in a Western culture to think with any empirical directness about Infinity—about a universe without beginnings and without end, a universe of continual temporary conditions, one merging into another forever.

Time does not begin in such a universe. A beginning may be only the moment you notice something move against that background which ancient India called "the void."

I found it necessary to begin this way because of something that happened to me at a recent cocktail party. The setting was so common to our culture that it has become a cliché—and so was the tall, heavyset fellow with the bushy black beard who came up to me with a question often asked of science fiction writers.

"You science fiction guys have imagined every problem the world could face. What the hell do we do about this planet that's ready to come apart?"

It is to laugh, but bitterly.

With alcohol-induced clarity, the fellow had just realized that the end of the Vietnam war has changed very little in respect to a world balanced precariously on the edge of an explosive finale. The threat of ultimate war is still with us and just as potent as ever.

But I've thought about every problem, so. . . .

My God! Every problem? Not by a long shot on a rainy Monday. Otherwise I'd be out of work. In common with the rest of my fellows, I do not have the book of answers. Sorry. I do, however, know something about crises. They're the stuff of good stories. If you write fiction, you become fairly adept at solving unsolvable problems which (and this is crucial) you have first created that you may solve them entertainingly.

Straw men.

But every now and then, we hit pay dirt. Realpolitik catches up with fiction. Industry just happens to manufacture the device we imagined—Telstar, Waldos, the Bracone collapsible oil barge. . . .

Technology turns a corner around which we have peeked.

You can wake up, as did Cleve Cartmill in 1944, to find yourself answering the questions of suspicious minions from the FBI. "Yes, Mr. Cartmill, but you speak in this story of an atomic bomb. Where did you get that idea? And why did you set your story at Manhattan Beach?"

Cartmill had pretty well laid out the developmental process for an atom bomb, which was then the private domain of the top-secret Manhattan Project. It was a good story and John Campbell published it.

But who could believe such coincidence?

And who can convince a security-conscious minion of the government that there is no way to keep these things secret when knowledge about the steps leading up to such developments permeates an entire layer of world society. There is no way. Despite Descartes, mental and material do not separate.

But nobody seems to believe that a mere science fiction writer can think up such things out of his own head. The question has a definite accent to it: "Where'd you get that idea (pause), out of your head?"

The head of a science fiction author is not supposed to produce the stuff of real crises. We're supposed to entertain, to amuse, to provide interesting food for thought and, occasionally, to bring people up short with a gasp or two.

Vide *1984*.

Vide *Brave New World*.

When you think about it, you realize these two works have influenced our world. Neither *Brave New World* nor *1984* will prevent our becoming a planet under Big Brother's thumb, but they make it a bit less likely. We've been sensitized to the possibility, to the way such a dystopia could evolve.

If we're to understand the relationship between such fiction and a world of real crises, it pays us occasionally to look out at Mount Olympus and append some footnotes.

With the exception of the fancy eugenics, *BNW* presents us with a society that might've been planned by a committee of behavioral psychologists. In many ways, it resembles nothing more than a worldwide *Walden Two*. The universal infant conditioning, the College of Emotional Engineering, and the system of World Controllers ruling by scientific behavioral modification would appear to meet with the approval of *W-Two* author, B. F. Skinner, who, you may recall, has been described as the world's foremost social engineer.

Both Orwell and Huxley were concerned with the ability of our democratic institutions to survive the onslaughts of overpopulation and rising industrialism—mass business, mass government, mass automation, etc. They were concerned with their own understanding of that concept which we call "freedom."

Pause now and consider certain practices by the United States federal government, by state and local authorities here and elsewhere in our world. Consider wiretapping, mandatory lie-detector tests, the keeping of extensive files on citizens alleged to be dissenters, refined electronic surveillance, manipulation of the media, the deliberate distortion of meanings in language. All of this foreshadows *1984*.

Make special note of the ways that have been developed to create demands for goods: the manufacture of goods so shoddy they break down at a predictable rate; a constant stream of "new" models which are not really new; advertising propaganda to maintain demand for goods that have little relationship to human survival (the appeal to sexual and status longings, etc.), and recall Huxley's words:

"As political and economic freedom diminishes, sexual freedom tends compensatingly to increase."

Does that sound familiar?

When people such as Theodore Roszak in *The Making of a Counter Culture* take up these themes, then science fiction leaves the realm of fiction and enters a shadowland between myth and reality. Roszak comments on the repressive desublimation factor in *"Playboy* sexuality" which has taken over American society: " . . . casual, frolicsome and vastly promiscuous. It is the anonymous sex of the harem. It creates no binding loyalties, no personal attachments, no distractions from one's primary responsibilities—which are to the company, to one's career and social position, and to the system generally."

Whether you begin from science fiction or from educational commentators such as Roszak, you can smell a crisis coming.

The promiscuity which Puritans thought would undermine the foundations of society has been co-opted by technocracy and channeled in a way that makes it serve the establishment —maintaining a state of non-freedom, of economic servitude, as well as stability for a social system that allows the technocracy to go its own way.

Our society tolerates drugs such as tobacco, alcohol, barbiturates, and tranquilizers because they serve a useful social purpose. They enable people to endure an otherwise intolerable existence, to remain on the production/consumption treadmill.

Perhaps *1984* isn't all that far away and we may already be living in a *Brave New World*.

In a society of Spocked babies and spooked adults, it gets easier to understand why marijuana, acid, and other drugs are tolerated to help keep the populace under control, especially when you add the mind-numbing properties of TV (audio-visual soma). Whoever said that the realities of twentieth century industrial mass society cannot be endured without outside help may not be far from wrong and the phenomenon of the black-bearded fellow asking a science fiction author for "the answer" becomes more acceptable.

According to Huxley, the greatest triumphs of propaganda have been accomplished not by doing something, but by refraining from doing something. *Silence is greater than truth.* "We'll appoint a committee to study this problem." The assumption by most of today's social engineering types is that independence is not the natural state of man.

Vide *BNW*.

Misfits are removed to their island—"all the people who, for one reason or another, have got too self-consciously individual to fit into community life. All the people who aren't satisfied with orthodoxy, who've got independent ideas of their own."

When they begin feeling out of sorts, the people of *BNW* get a jolt from hypnopaedic memory telling them to take a gram of soma, to enter the "warm, richly colored, infinitely friendly world of soma holiday."

It's clear that both in science fiction and the crisis-beset "real" world, drugs (like magic) need to be taken seriously and considered significant socially as well as individually. Can't you visualize the sincere announcer on TV telling you:

"Drugs can be of significant value when used in a conscientiously applied program of personal hygiene and regular professional care."

In the foreword to *BNW*, Aldous Huxley begins his prescription for the revolution to bring about the world of his book by telling you that, first, the government requires a greatly improved technique of suggestion to make everyone susceptible to the propaganda of the new society. He includes infant conditioning and the use of certain drugs and a greatly transformed "norm" of sexual behavior from that which our fathers openly accepted. Where *BNW* pointed the way, Masters and Johnson or Katchadourian and Lunde follow to fill in the gaps.

You've read all of this in science fiction, of course, and made many of the comparisons yourself, and it's nice to think you're sitting there with the *avant-garde*, first to know what tomorrow's world will be. Let me recommend, therefore, that you study the records of history a bit more carefully. The sexual morality of *BNW* was the norm in the nineteenth century Oneida colony of upstate New York. The Arab culture pioneered in the use of drugs to control the populace a thousand years ago.

If history teaches us that we learn nothing from history, then there may be little point in rehashing these observations on human behavior. Perhaps it'd be better to save this material for fiction, that world of perfection, which is where things operate the way I want. In the "real" world it has all happened before. There's no such thing as a new crisis, just instant replays on the old ones.

It's fun to play the game, though, and to hope that your newest window dressing on the old patterns will tell us something really new. After all, science fiction in its dealings with crises for the sake of story, does indicate other avenues open to us.

We can, for example, assume that behind any accepted morality, fictional or otherwise, is the function of maintaining social stability. When emotions brought out by repression become socially disruptive, dangerous to social harmony, then the repression may be eliminated by the society itself. Our "new morality" so shocking to Middle America could be an evolutionary force to eliminate potentially disastrous social conditions. It could be the social organism's way of dealing with the need for sexual expression without the dangers inherent in producing too many new humans.

As you can see by the foregoing, the science fiction mind is always ready with alternative possibilities—which is part of the game of human change.

Much of our lives we're breaking camp from one set of known surroundings and heading off into an unknown *Other Place* which we hope will become just as familiar as today's surroundings. That's the stuff of science fiction and it is, as well, the stuff of world crises. The hierarchical levels of a future society may very well be sharply defined by categorical birth into different intelligence classes, a birth prearranged from conception. Science of the pragmatic world may give us the aristocracy of the IQ which previous aristocracies attempted to create by mating only with their "own kind." We may look back on *1984* and *BNW* as relatively mild and amusing examples of fictional exploration in social engineering.

Much depends upon the way we integrate the myth world of our wishes into the physical experiences that define who we are as an animal society. This is the crux of all attempts to diagnose current conditions and form some articulated whole that expresses the nature of world crises. If we say, on the one hand, that our world suffers from a certain kind of disease that brings on these recurrent crises, then under present conditions of dependence upon words, the disease we "have" becomes more important than who we are as a people. This could be why we, as a society, suspect the large social diagnoses of the engineers and psychiatrists. We know with a sure and ancient instinct that to be treated and "cured" of such a disease could take from us both the why and the who of our identity.

Certain pitfalls exist in our tendency toward overdependence upon the professional expert, the specialist. When we turn toward such counsel, we begin by admitting that we are helpless and require their *superior* guidance. At the very moment we seek such help, we have created a particular kind of non-symmetrical relationship: the professional, all-powerful and knowledgeable on one hand, and the dependent, abject one on the other hand. One side assumes all of the healthy viewpoint and the other side takes on all of the sickness. With a kind of suicidal totality, we turn matters over to the professional, saying: "Heal me."

This is the situation upon which the politician capitalizes and which psychiatry/psychology have been unable to resolve. Instead, the so-called mental sciences have been seeking political power for many years. This was to be expected as a natural outcome of their power posture. They assumed the position of *all-health* dealing with *all-sickness*. Such non-symmetrical relationships inevitably produce shattering crises.

Remember the old Chinese curse: "May you live in interesting times."

The Chinese of those days valued a serene existence. Their utopian ideal was based on a sophisticated appreciation of the world, on the guiding of the senses into heightened awareness. It's not surprising that Zen found wide acceptance in such a culture. The inner world obviously was where one dealt with consciousness. Thus, external crises were to be avoided. Ignorance, poverty, starvation, and disease were the evils. War was a class monopoly and was to be kept in its own place. Famous generals could not hope for the status of famous teachers. Fear was a tool of statecraft and was to be used to keep down the size of government. Apotheosis (transubstantiation to an immortal state with one's ancestors) was a necessary part of culture.

In such a setting, interesting times were times that changed dramatically, rolled on the wheel of crisis. Those old Chinese could have made common cause with Middle America. Both look to the ideal society as one of social unity, of togetherness as the ultimate social achievement. The distinguishing of one individual from another has to be held within tight limits. To be different is to be dangerous.

God bless the child who has his own. That's the catch phrase, but don't sing it too loudly except on Saturday nights.

This is both a pure and abstract notion. It is the seeking for solace against the physical isolation of the individual identity. It is a barrier against mortality akin to ancestor worship. It is also the stuff of paradox because it brings with it dreams of gods, of nations, and professional experts as the all-powerful arbiters of our lives. This necessarily creates the conditions of crisis because it fails to deal with change. It does not square with a changing universe.

Thus, we get the stuff of crises and of science fiction.

On this relatively small planet well out into the edge of a minor spiral galaxy, we have been simultaneously breeding ourselves an abundance of humans while creating an abundance of material things for a small proportion of that burgeoning life. Against a backdrop of false absolutes, we reduce the variables that we permit in our societies, in our individuals, and in our possessions. By our acts, we demonstrate that we want mass production of a standard human who employs standardized consumer goods. We execute this mass production of sameness in a largely unexamined, unconscious manner.

But *nature* constantly evolves, trying out its new arrangements, its new kinds of life, its differences, its interesting times, its crises. Against such movement, we attempt our balancing acts, our small sallies at equilibrium. In the dynamic interrelationships of the universe around us, we look for models upon which to pattern our lives. But that universe greets us with complexities everywhere we turn. To talk about just one element, carbon, for example, we are forced to deal with combinations whose complexities we have not yet exhausted.

You've read about such things in science fiction; you see the conditions around you which touch your own life. Still, you seek *the* answer.

Our land of plenty was supposed to lead the way to a world of plenty for humankind. Instead, we followed a more ancient pattern, becoming like the worst in those we opposed. We lead the world today in the potential for mass violence. The material doldrums of the 1950s trended gradually into this era, and instead of plenty we find ourselves in a world where, if we shared the world's food supply equally with every living human being, all of us would starve.

Malthus pointed the way. Science fiction has been filling in the possibilities of a Malthusian world ever since. If we experience massive human die-back in such areas as the island of Java by 1980, Malthus and science fiction will have been proven correct.

But at what a cost!

We approach this next level of crises as though we lived constantly in the presence of devils. If no devils appear, we manufacture them. *Give us this day our daily devil.* To counter the unconscious (and conscious) tensions aroused by such a process, we seek seclusion, individual privacy—all the while breeding ourselves out of that vanishing commodity.

Creativity of any kind has become the modern devil.

And the oddball is dangerous.

We want to end all conflicts. They not only kill us, they never seem to produce the glorious and victorious end conditions which we verbally attach to them. But now that the Vietnam war has been brought near a close, we awaken to the realization that we still live in a world threatened by imminent, totally destructive, mass conflict. We cure the disease and find we still suffer from it.

Paradox, paradox: the stuff of crises and of science fiction.

We walk across the ground of our fears and our movement stores up static electricity which shocks us every time we touch the *real* world. Somehow, we are not grounded to the universe. But we go doggedly about those tasks we consider necessary, emulating the muddle-through quality of the ideal nineteenth-century British public servant. And all the time, we fight to repress the sinking feeling that everything we do is useless, that the next crisis will leave us destitute.

Why can't the world be more like me?

Middle America *über alles!*

On the wall of a small hotel in Kabul, Afghanistan, there is a notice, which reads as follows:

MENU

Acid $1
Opium .... 30 Afghanis
Heroin .... 70 Afghanis

Ask Abdul

The hotel, populated in season by large numbers of expatriate American youths, represents a full retreat from crises—retreat from crises into crisis.

You may find it strange that I read this and other signs as heralding hard times ahead for science fiction as we have known it. This is how I read it:

The current utopian ideal being touted by people as politically diverse (on the surface, but not underneath) as President Richard M. Nixon and Senator Edward M. Kennedy goes as follows—no deeds of passion allowed, no geniuses, no criminals, no imaginative creators of the new. Satisfaction may be gained only in carefully limited social interactions, in living off the great works of the past. There must be limits to any excitement. Drug yourself into a placid "norm." Moderation is the key word. And how the old Chinese would have loved that!

In a word, you can be a Bozo, but little else.

Rolling Stone in the fall of 1972 described this world of bozoness:

"Bozos are the huge, fat middle waist in the land. They clone. Everybody tends to drift toward bozoness. It has Oz in it. They mean well. They like their comforts. The Bozos have learned to enjoy their free time, which is all the time."

Among the secondhand, limited excitements permitted in the Bozo world would be reading science fiction, but its creators are in for harsh treatment unless they hew strictly to the well-worn concepts already treated by the field, unless they eschew anything truly new or pertinent.

No more *1984*s. No untimely accuracy. You must stick to such things as *Walden Two*, which is really Edward Bellamy brought up to date. You must look backward, only backward.

Creativity, however, requires wide open alternatives. It fits with the random chaos of the unknown universe and with those limited (and limiting) laws which we learn to apply for our temporary benefit. Science fiction has functioned well against such a backdrop. The more diverse our work, the more profoundly creative, the more luxurious the literature.

The luxury of unbridled investigation carries its own ongoing sense of excitement, one of the attractions of the best science fiction. What will I find around the next corner? This is one of the marvelous lures of pure science, as well. And pure science already is finding itself in the public doghouse. The levelers ask: "Why'd you bastards discover atomic weapons and lasers and bacteriological weapons and all that crazy stuff?"

One of the answers goes this way: "I was driving down this road, see, and there it was."

"But how'd you find the right road?"

"Well, I took that turn back there a ways and, you see, there it was."

The best science fiction and pure science assume an infinite universe where we can look up at the blue sky. That's our playing field. Eton is too confining. That sense of infinity (anything can happen) gives us the proper elbow room. But an infinite universe is a place where crimes of passion can occur, where any dream can be dreamed *and* realized. The reward of investigating such a universe in fiction or in fact is not so much reducing the unknown but increasing it, opening the way to new dangers, new crises. This implies disorder when what we suppose we're seeking is order. The story plot and the scientific law represent order, but chaos lurks at their edges.

Order equals law, a key word for humans.

Law indicates the form by which we attempt to understand order. It enables us to predict and otherwise deal with order. And we don't like the mathematician suggesting to us that we occupy a universe of multiple order*s*, plural, and thus of multiple laws.

Humans want beginnings and nice anthropomorphic motives and happy endings. But motives (intent) are not required against an infinite field of laws. The assumption of infinity opens quite a contrary view. Infinity does not require beginnings or endings. Intent does require them. The essence of infinity is no-beginning, no-ending. Without beginning there is no intent, no motive, mysterious or otherwise. Without ends, there can be no ultimate (absolute) goals, no judgments, and the whole concept of sin and guilt (products of intent) falls apart. Such concepts as sin-guilt-judgment require beginnings which are cut out of an infinitive system, boxed-in, articulated and defined for human motives. They occur as segments of a *linear* system whose infinite surroundings must be represented as nonlinear. Such concepts are ways of dealing with finite, human-created and human-interpreted laws, and are only incidentally (in the fullest meaning of that word) related to infinity.

To project a god, a government, or a professional expert against such a backdrop, we set limits.

Law and order represent a system of dealing with interesting times such that we set our preordained limits upon crises. Law and order is a breeder of crises because it cannot predict everything that will happen.

To accept a universe where anything can happen, however, is to accept a hellish insecurity which is, in itself, an ongoing crisis. We don't know how to understand such a universe. The essence of something we don't understand is that it appears chaotic; it lacks recognizable order. There's a devil in anything we don't understand. It is menacing. It is an outer darkness in which we not only lose a recognizable ground upon which to stand, but we also lose all sense of identity. It is a vision of hell. We must defeat such a devil at all cost.

And we forget that we created this devil.

We say, instead: "This is who I am. This is my absolute god. These are my absolute laws. Get thee behind me, Sathanus!"

Thus, we strive for the illusion of all-knowing in an infinite universe where anything can happen. We seek the basic law to explain a never-ending All which stands as a seething backdrop, as the Vedantic void, that ultimate chaos from which any form of law or order must derive.

In *The God Makers*, I have a religious leader say it this way:

"We have a very ancient saying: the more god, the more devil; the more flesh, the more worms; the more property, the more anxiety; the more control, the more that needs control."

The lost existence of our Eden-Paradise gets further and further from a dichotomized, man-limited world, less attainable every instant. We must turn to science fiction for the temporary illusion, for the *prediction* that once again we will enter into the blissful universe of godlike order. You would be astonished at how often science fiction editors get the Adam and Eve story as the first effort of the aspiring writer. It has become the cliché of clichés in our field. We attempt to deny Eden's ultimate, unchanging conservatism, its essential boredom for the questing intelligence. The very language in which these concepts are couched provides a retreat to match the menu on the Kabul hotel's wall.

Santaroga Barrier puts it thus:

"We sift reality through screens composed of ideas. (And such ideas have their roots in older ideas.) Such idea systems are necessarily limited by language, by the ways we can describe them. That is to say: language cuts the grooves in which our thoughts move. If we seek new validity forms (other laws and other orders) we must step outside language."

We must stand silently and point at the new thing.

This represents an essential Zen concept.

Santaroga portrays an extreme reaction against many of the problems challenging human survival in the 1970s. Technology worship, endless economic growth, human alienation, the limitless powers implied by scientific investigation—all products of today's American-style society—are rejected by Santaroga's counterculture. Santaroga attempts to control change and thus to scale down both the physical and social pace of human life. Isolated, but with a purpose to their hibernation, Santarogans try to make better people for a static world which is necessarily depicted as a valley, a place of high walls, both natural and man-made.

It is the mind, not the artifacts of human ingenuity, on which Santarogans concentrate. However admirable their intentions, the result of their behavioral control is not totally positive. Santaroga is dangerously stable, poised always on the edge of destructive crisis. Its people seem happy but without individual vitality. They are not enslaved by technological innovation, but neither are they much concerned about creativity and personal development. Life for the Santarogan revolves around an archaic super-loyalty to the community which is deliberately akin to nation-state patriotism.

Santarogans indulge in their own form of the step-by-step behavioral engineering you see in *Walden Two*. They also remain self-suspended in time. They have chosen a rather static "good life" to escape the dilemma that Alvin Toffler's *Future Shock* details. The closed society creates its own Berlin Wall to keep out visitors, tourism, the threats inherent in things and people which are different.

Santaroga turns out to be Middle America and Old China brought up to date. As in *Walden Two,* Santarogans extol the merits of their society and permit selective immigration. Essentially, both Santaroga and *Walden Two* ask whether human happiness can be achieved through positive reinforcement techniques and tampering with chemical and psychological characteristics of the species. It is not a question to pass over lightly because every extant culture does these very things, although in a relatively haphazard manner. The difference is that *Walden Two* and *Santaroga Barrier* describe a conscious, "scientific" approach to social conditioning.

Why is it, then, that most people detect something sinister in such a process to produce humans who would behave in a predictable, although "socially beneficial" way? Behavioral control and happiness appear to be inextricably linked in the contemporary social engineering field. Most humans feel, however, that such tampering would not produce happiness, but would force us into new crises.

We have always distrusted Machiavelli.

Is it the coldness? The manipulation of humans by humans? Is it the inevitable separation into the *users* and the *used,* the abject seekers after help and the all-knowing helpers?

The character, Gilbert Dasein, sees the common identity of Santaroga thusly:

"In there behind the facade, Santaroga did something to its people. They lost personal identity and became masks for something that was the same in all of them . . . a one-pointedness . . . such that every Santarogan became an extension of every other Santarogan."

Arthur Clarke, in *Childhood's End,* states it baldly; his entire story represents a comment on differences. He is saying to you that, while men have been able to adapt to wide differences in climate, geography, and threats to survival, they have not always been able to adapt to differences in one another. In the end, the children of Clarke's Earth become what can only be interpreted as a single identity and that identity reflects the myth structure of Western man. Witness the way anthropological studies of acculturation focus on the difficulties a non-Western "underdeveloped" people confront while undergoing cultural assimilation by the West. Almost no studies have been done on the difficult adaptation problem faced by Western men when thrust into a non-Western society.

In fact, Western men tend to refuse such adaptation; we must force others to imitate us. One does not go native!

Why can't the universe be more like me?

Through what is probably a profound unconscious process, the flow of Western scientific/technological development takes on much the same characteristics. Most of science fiction has followed the same channel.

Nature, as a system of systems which we attempt to reduce to some kind of order, has been conceived by much of Western science as flowing from a unified field. Eastern researchers have taken a quite contrary viewpoint, saying that a unified field is inconceivable because even such a mental construct would tend to flow and change. To the Eastern viewpoint, seeking after a fixed, unchanging unified field is the ultimate in conservative thinking. It requires a god (or government, or society of professional experts) who must be worshiped by a mass consciousness that agrees slavishly with everything coming from the god, the government, or the experts.

It is a question of the relationship between human consciousness and the rest of the universe, whether by oneself or through intermediaries. Western culture, selling itself as the last outpost of individualism, has been as quick to stifle this characteristic as the East has been. The West has merely been less aware, and thus less candid, about the consequences of its major decisions. It is also a characteristic of the West that we must believe in absolutes. We demand them. Our language assumes them. We ask: "What *is* it?" And we say: "It either *is* or it *isn't.*"

The verb "to be" betrays us.

Some of the East escaped this pitfall, but shared our tendencies toward the designed state, toward all-inclusive planning. We in the West seduced the East not through guns and massive power, but through engineering and planning. We captured most of the Eastern consciousness through engineered "contingency factors."

An engineer of my acquaintance, servant of a powerful industry, when asked how his industry dealt with unknown contingencies in its long-range plans, said:

"We put a very large item in the budget and label it *contingency.* When the unexpected problem arises, if it's something money won't solve, we borrow facilities from other areas. We patch together a temporary solution until we can fill in the gaps."

He went on to explain that the cost of such solutions was added later to the price which the public pays.

The question of absolutes—absolute solutions, absolute control—remains at the core of our science, our science fiction, and our approach to the solution of crises. It is, without a doubt, a battle of ingrained conservatism against outer chaos. Our utopian dreams of Eden are essentially conservative. We dream of a designed state wherein all the needs of the designers are secure. The main function of paradise is to entertain the needs of its human creators. Everyone must be a Bozo, happily comfortable, and thus limited in severely designed ways. There goes freedom of choice and in come *Santaroga* and *Walden Two.*

And God had better answer our prayers or we'll stop worshiping him. We'll vote for somebody else.

Few seem to have remarked the failure of demanding, ego-centered prayer as an argument for the current revival of satanism, witchcraft, and the like. The morality argument has fallen on hard times recently. Is it significant that both Barry Goldwater and George McGovern, candidates who offered themselves on morality platforms, lost by about the same proportion? There does appear to be an element of moralizing which says: "Why can't you be more like me?"

When the chips were down, the American electorate may have said: "I'll render my own moral judgments, thank you, and you can stuff that preacher pose."

"Judge not lest ye be judged."

In a sense, the struggles of our world, the crises arising from these struggles, and the stuff of our literary creations which reflect on the sensory universe represent a battle over human consciousness and its judgments. It's not so much the minds and hearts of men that are at stake, but their awareness, the ideas they are permitted. The struggle is over what is judged valuable in our universe. Some of the antagonists follow a value system based on what can be measured, counted, or tabulated. They call this attitude "realpolitik." Others base their standards on undefinable terms (undefinable because they change when we touch them) such as freedom, the rights of man, morality, the law of God. . . .

These latter concepts defy programming. They must be continually reinterpreted. Witness the provisions for change in the United States Constitution. Islam provided for *Qazi*, judges who rule on secular matters as they derive from the Koran. *Qazi* must be "adult, free, Muslim and unconvicted of slander."

Even as they are defined, these concepts fall outside current conventions of language which, as a set of symbols, remains finite and forever incomplete as a communications tool. Language opens up the reflection of thought, but by its very nature it also creates boundaries which appear insurmountable when posed against infinity. Language programs us, decides what we see and how we see it—what value judgment we place on anything we see. It is a root of prejudice and a limiter of perceptions as the embodiment of previous experiences which have been judged and catalogued. A new occurrence, pervaded by past perceptions, can be misconstrued. Power—secular and religious—is grounded in language. To assault the barriers of language is to do something dangerous to those who hold power because you open the way to new validity forms, new relationships, new *laws*, new ways of ordering society. Language represents an intervening force when we articulate our dream utopias. It prevents the realization of dreams. It is a sea of paradox, the substance of interesting times, curses and blessings and interesting stories.

Without language there would be no science fiction. What a crisis that would be!

Remember that Thomas More, the author who gave us the word *Utopia* and the dream of uniformity which the Old Chinese and the modern West find so enchanting, conceived his paradise in the form of the army—as does Skinner in *Walden Two*, as the pure-gospel Communists do, as the ancient Essenes did, as they did in the Oneida Colony. . . . The rule appears so very simple:

"From every person according to his ability and to every person according to his needs."

This requires, however, that someone pass judgment on the needs and abilities, setting limits for them. More's *Utopia* provided public kitchens, public clothing repair shops, public laundries, etc., and guidelines for public behavior. I invite you to run your own survey. Ask people who have served in a branch of the military if they judged that a utopian existence. Personally, I recall an unspoken military commandment: "No individual crises allowed!"

Walden One, as seen through Thoreau's prejudices, was a place where the physical universe and the human spirit were to be interwoven harmoniously. Thoreau permitted no machines. Only the simplest things that the earth provided made up his tools. He professed himself perfectly contented in this condition.

Thoreau was not the first on that path. Rousseau drew similar surroundings for his "noble savage." St. Francis of Assisi employed his religious genius in rebellion against life-styles of the thirteenth century. To know God, it was necessary to discard all material possessions and marry nature. He said, in Christ's words, "The foxes have holes, the birds of the air have nests, but the son of man hath not where to lay his head."

And then there were the earlier Pan god prototypes. Pan is still with us.

Religion says: "Love is the answer."

Science says: "There's infinite energy out there just waiting for the right blend of imagination and creativity to bring it into the service of man."

Rebellious youth says: "I'm going back to the farm."

The Black says: "I want it all; share it!"

The American Indian says: "Give it back before you wreck everything."

The social engineer says: "The key to our many problems remains in proper ordering and efficiency."

Listen to the social engineer because he has the inside track. Constant planning is a *Walden Two* obsession. That's familiar, isn't it? There we go again trying to impose our human order on an infinite universe.

However, when we narrow our frame of reference to the earth itself, as Thoreau did, it appears nature is a circle of delicately balanced systems which function efficiently only when man doesn't tamper with them. According to this view, man introduces chaos into what was originally a well-ordered plan, a system of symmetry and balances, and our attempts to establish our own kind of order open us to new complexities and crises.

But the desire for that abstract condition which we call *security* is implicit in our attempts to plan and order our lives. Disorder and chaos, the uncertainties of an infinite universe, threaten our peace of mind if not our physical comfort. Against such a background, behavioral (social) engineers such as Skinner can be heard pleading with us: "Please! Let us plan the world in a way that will set our minds at ease."

Translation: "Why can't everyone be more like me?"

Because the mind at ease is a dead mind.

For civilization to exist as we know it, socializing processes must be strong and pervasively thorough. We are programmed in a multitude of ways, many of them operating unconsciously. By the time we awaken even faintly to the awareness that we have been socially conditioned, we find ourselves so indoctrinated that it's difficult, if not impossible, to break the old patterns. The reinforcements of the system are powerful, many of them rooted in our animal past, and such systems have been taken over entirely by the unconscious socializing programs. Our history also shows us that there has always been a majority in human society which never becomes aware of any need for change.

Survival pressures demanding that we evolve, grow, and change, however, continue to proliferate. We don't want to change, but the floodgates open abruptly and we are overwhelmed.

Crisis!

Western tradition faces such demands with the concept of absolute control. You control the force which seeks to change your world. You build a dam. You organize an army, a navy, an air force, a space service, more efficient police. You control the mob—even that mob in yourself. You control crime or the Mafia or the heroin traffic. Never mind that the control concept is in direct conflict with the American myth of individuality: the thing you fear must be controlled.

How the control concept works with the heroin traffic exemplifies what happens when we apply such pressures to a system without sufficient understanding of the system's internal behavior. Understand first that we have never discovered an upper limit to what the heroin addict will pay for his fix. The *demand impulse* of the system has a wide open upper limit, assumed as infinite. Result: New Yorkers no longer live in Fun City. It's Fear City, made that way by this lack of understanding about the drug traffic. New York at night is effectively in a state of siege reminding one of the Mekong Delta at the height of the Vietnam War. Remember? "The night belongs to Charley." New Yorkers know their addicts will pay any price asked of them—your life, your household goods, anything.

But our dominant approach continues to operate out of that judgmental edict: *Heroin is nasty! Suppress it! Control it!*

Even with our wildest control binge, however, the heroin traffic cannot be completely shut off. Some of it will get through. Remember the industrial engineer's comment on unknown contingencies? You put in a big contingency fund which is passed along to the consumer. Thus, some heroin will enter the United States because the head of a friendly government (or his uncle, or his sister) profits from the traffic; or because a federal agent has been paid off; or because a high United States military officer has become an addict and is forced to use his facilities in the traffic; or, finally, because there are just too many holes through which the stuff can enter the nation.

It may cost a bundle to corrupt a federal official, a general, or a member of the State Department, but what the hell! The consumer will pay.

Ultimately, even if you are not an addict, that consumer-who-pays is you.

Our control efforts do little more than raise the price of the heroin that does get through. There's no upper limit on that price; thus it's a wide open system.

If we really wanted to make a social adjustment to the heroin traffic, our actions would have to be somewhat different. We would have to accept first that our new approach would bring its own problems, that it would not be *the* final and absolute answer. But let's begin by assuming that it's not a good thing to allow a flow of money which can corrupt high officials and whole police departments. Let's assume that we want to stop that flow of corrupting cash. Very well; we take the profit out of the heroin traffic. We make the addict's fix available at a reasonable price—say for about fifty cents and under medical supervision. Then we prepare ourselves to deal with the other socio-medical aspects of the drug problem which would be certain to surface under these new conditions. We could do this by understanding that we would be *dealing with* our mutual problem, not controlling it.

The one-pointed view of the "control it" approach invariably seduces us into making faulty assumptions. A fundamental cause of depressed urban areas has been found to be an excess of low-cost housing, rather than the housing shortages which we assumed to be the problem. City tax bases and legal structures gave incentives for not tearing down old buildings. But aging industrial buildings bring a decline in employment. Residential structures, as they age, attract lower income groups who are forced to use them at a higher population density. Jobs decline while population rises. Then, we come in with our development schemes and add *more* low-cost housing. This attracts more people from the low-income group into the area where jobs are decreasing. Our well-intentioned efforts help to create what Jay W. Forrester of MIT calls "a social trap."

But that wasn't what we wanted at all, was it? My God! We have to control this sort of thing!

Pakistan wanted to control its mosquitoes because the insects are a vector in a runaway malaria problem. However, Pakistan already suffered from the *control disease* which it caught from our Western culture. Having only enough funds and other resources for about a seventy-five percent mosquito control program, Pakistan demonstrated how well it had learned from the West by going ahead with an incomplete program. Result: the surviving mosquitoes are now resistant to former control techniques and malaria is again on a runaway increase.

Attempting to control something "evil," we precipitate a larger crisis. This may be a general human tendency. We feel helpless and alone when faced with large problems. Loneliness influences us to grab for the reassurance of anything offered to us as *the* solution. We want someone to assure us he has the answer and if we'll only follow him. . . . It produces very odd behavior. The more complex a problem appears, the more apathetic we become; the more we turn away, the more strongly we grasp at a proffered solution which is presented with the promise of immediate relief. After all, Pakistan's seventy-five percent mosquito control program *did* ease the malaria problem, temporarily.

We know that a single-pointed attempt to solve a problem is more likely to increase that problem's complexity, make the problem harder to solve and, eventually, confront us with a crisis. The arguments for planetwide planning of human existence are relatively easy to accept, but the danger of massive, single-entry "solutions" remains as long as humans demand "immediate relief."

It is astonishing how many college-level young people writing scenarios for a utopian rebuilding of world society begin their scenarios with a worldwide disaster which kills off ninety percent or more of the human population. The scenarios then have the survivors (including the scenario author, of course) climb back to a planned civilization based on "nonrepressive freedom." The quote is from an actual scenario by a twenty-year-old college junior.

Many of these young writers turn to Herbert Marcuse and Paolo Soleri (strange bedfellows, indeed) for supportive arguments, and they draw heavily from the works of such writers as Robert Heinlein, Ray Bradbury, Arthur Clarke, Ted Sturgeon, Isaac Asimov, Alfred Bester, Jack Williamson, Tony Boucher (W. A. P. White), John Campbell, Lester del Rey, Hugo Gernsback, Henry Kuttner, C. M. Kornbluth, Frederik Pohl, Fritz Leiber, Murray Leinster, Judith Merril, Margaret St. Clair (Idris Seabright), Clifford Simak, Robert Silverberg, William Tenn (Philip Klass), Jack Vance, Poul Anderson, A. E. van Vogt. . . .

This is just a partial list of authors named as sources by students in university classes writing utopian scenarios. The science fiction authors are understandable in this list, but Soleri and Marcuse may need some explanation. Soleri provides them with the concept of arcologies (the single social superstructure, world village) and Marcuse outlines the psycho-mythology of rebellion. It is Marcuse who provides the justification for killing the world's population down to a "manageable" size. Soleri leads the scenario writers to think of mining "the old cities" for materials to construct new super-urban communities linked by high-speed transit. We in science fiction provide social and technological innovations—the frosting on the supercake.

Inevitably, the scenario writers come down to hard judgments, decisions about the limits within which people will be forced to live. Even with London a half hour from New York City and most of the world's surviving population living underground to free the surface for agriculture and other human requirements, the consequent accelerated demand for efficiency produces its own paradox which the scenario writers fail to resolve. They turn to more and more planning, a pervasive planning-octopus which reaches deeper and deeper into the individual life. Current concepts of freedom are abandoned "for the general welfare" and heavy social conditioning is accepted as "inevitable." The demand for more god produces more satan. In come the Skinnerians and another crisis lurks at the end of this road.

Well, the Club of Rome and MIT in their study of the limits to human growth warned us what was happening. They said humans cannot go on increasing their numbers anarchically or exponentially beyond specific limits on this finite planet. They told us that growth must be selective, oriented, governed—that is, *planned*. Equilibrium must be maintained between the human population and its habitat. But this equilibrium cannot be reached if world society remains in a state of imbalance. Social justice and peace have definite ecological impact. But people *en masse* are loath to face up to issues which seem beyond human comprehension and *control*.

World population, which took hundreds of generations to reach present numbers, will double its size in the next thirty years. That means more than seven billion people—all demanding homes, schools, industry, entire cities, highways, harbors, and all the rest of it. No relevant body of opinion has so far faced up to this challenge. There is no *they* out there working on the big answer. Some sort of global planning may be undertaken in this decade, but political pitfalls line the way. The problem may become too big and complicated to be dealt with at all before even the first hesitant steps are taken.

Now *there* is a crisis for you.

Science fiction has explored such fancies and continues to explore them, but the basis for today's world planning concepts remains firmly seated in a commitment to absolute goals—political and physical. The holders of power in this world have not awakened to the realization that there is no single model of a society, a species, or an individual. There are a variety of models to meet a variety of needs. They meet different expectations and have different goals. The aim of that force which impels us to live may be to produce as many different models as possible.

As things now stand, you can be doing something that doesn't need to be done, which in fact is threatening to the survival of the human species, and yet you may be surrounded by a system which says you're doing your job well. The question "Should you be doing this at all?" is seldom asked in a species-wide context. We remain caught in the old "realities" with all of their myth-based self-justifications.

Remember that a way to align your behavior with my desires is to get you to accept my definition of reality. Power rests in getting masses of people to accept your interpretation of events, and this is firmly seated in the structure of language. The words you use, how they are defined as descriptions of events, these carry the weight. Certain definitions are established (Freedom is freedom, dammit!) and these are imposed on our social experiences. The delusional content of the definitions is masked by social pressures. "Historical knowledge" (any past definition) is marshaled to support the way we interpret new experiences. This all occurs within hierarchical structures where the occupants of niches may change but the structures, their myths, and their delusions remain. *There must be an absolute authority which will make everything right . . . eventually.*

What one learns best in this world is how to please those farther up the ladder of authority. Education and social pressures cultivate individuals highly sensitive to the demands coming down to them from above. Most people believe what they are told to believe. The hedge against the unexpected, our social contingency factor, is to continue believing in the possibility of miracles. Of course, if you read the story of Jesus carefully, you'll note that the employment of miracles brought profoundly disruptive crises.

I must take another look at Olympus and recall that it's the source of the most disastrous earthquakes which have struck the northwest corner of the United States. Even a pile of dirt can turn against you.

Perhaps tomorrow I'll call my friend, the industrial engineer, and warn him: "There can be no absolute contingency allowance in an infinite universe."

As long as that's a condition of our existence, the explorations of science and science fiction will continue to turn up exciting discoveries.

But look out for the crises!

Frank Herbert

Frank Herbert has been writing thoughtful and exciting science fiction for more than twenty years; his first novel, *Dragon in the Sea*, is still in print here and abroad, as are many of his other books. In addition, he has published a great many short stories in the science fiction field in such magazines as *Analog, Galaxy,* and *If*.

Probably his best known work to date is *Dune*, published in 1965, and winner of the World Science Fiction Convention Hugo and the Science Fiction Writers of America Nebula awards. *Dune* has attracted international attention both as a novel and as an "environmental awareness handbook."

Mr. Herbert has done research in such diverse fields as undersea geology, psychology, navigation, jungle botany, and anthropology. He has been a professional newspaperman in several West Coast cities— including more than ten years with the San Francisco *Examiner*.

In addition he has been a professional photographer, TV camera-man, radio news commentator, and oyster diver, and has lectured at the University of Washington and other universities around the country.

Mr. Herbert was born in Tacoma, Washington, in 1920, and has recently returned to the Puget Sound area. He now lives in Port Town-send, Washington, with his family.

Dragon in the Sea, 1956 (Doubleday and Avon)
Dune, 1965 (Chilton and Ace)
The Green Brain, 1966 (Ace)
Destination Void, 1966 (Berkley)
The Eyes of Heisenberg, 1966 (Berkley)
The Heaven Makers, 1968 (Avon)
Santaroga Barrier, 1968 (Berkley)
Dune Messiah, 1970 (Putnam-Berkley)
Whipping Star, 1970 (Putnam-Berkley)
New World or No World, 1970 (Ace), editor
Worlds of Frank Herbert, 1970 (Ace)

Soul Catcher, 1971 (Putnam-Berkley)
The God Makers, 1971 (Berkley)
Project 40, 1973 (Bantam)
Book of Frank Herbert, 1973 (DAW)

Theodore Sturgeon

Science Fiction, Morals, and Religion

There is a force operating upon that body of literature called, or miscalled, science fiction, which, quite aside from the substantive content of the field, is moral and religious in nature; and we had better deal with it first.

This force shows itself in critical snobbery, in the "ghettoization" of science fiction, in the wide and erroneous conviction among the general reading (and viewing) public that "Oh, I never read science fiction." What they really mean is that they consciously avoid that which is *called* science fiction, while attending in droves performances of *The Andromeda Strain* or *Lord of the Flies* or any of scores of other science fiction films, novels, and short stories written by "mainstream" writers for the most part—those who have cut their creative teeth elsewhere than in the pages of the science fiction magazines. The assumption is that the magazines themselves, and therefore all of their authors' products, are trash and junk, poorly conceived and poorly written, and concern bolts, nuts, nuclei, zap-guns, and bug-eyed monsters; and anyway, ninety percent of it in concept and execution is trash.

Conceded, but then (and this has come to be known as Sturgeon's Law) ninety percent of *everything* is trash. The best of science fiction is as good as the best of any modern literature —articulate, poetic, philosophical, provocative, searching, courageous, insightful, and virtually anything else you expect of the best. Science fiction alone among the labels is consistently tarred with its own bad examples; the very same reader who knows the difference between *Hopalong Cassidy* and *Shane,* or between Mickey Spillane and Graham Greene, utterly fails to discriminate between the good and the bad in science fiction; utterly fails even to try, and says (in the words of Kingsley Amis), "This is science fiction—it can't be good," or, "This is good—it can't be science fiction"! And with this, we reach the point—the isolation of this genuinely religious force which has created such an injustice to the practitioners of science fiction—and which has committed such arrant robbery upon the reading public. For it has missed many delights, many excitements, and many beneficial explosions of mind.

Our strange species has two prime motivating forces: sex, of course, and worship. We do worship. We will worship. We must. Take the temples away from the people and they will worship a football hero or a movie star; they will go to the shrine, they will touch the hem, they will record the words. This worship, like almost all forms of worship in recorded history, has its pantheon, its sects, its divisiveness, its intolerance, and many, many different objects. The most dominant of all in our age is —science.

And indeed, science meets the specifications for a deity more than any other single thing in the current cultural cosmos. Science has rid us of crippling polio; science (to the lay mind, science and technology are the same) has killed Lake Erie and is murdering the oceans; science walks us on the moon and threatens the pupfish and the revered bald eagle. Science gives us longevity and hints at immortality; poisons the air; creates new sounds, tints, and textures for the creative artist; suggests potency over thunder, earthquake, poverty, ignorance, and the very tides; science, we are told, can sculpt our genes and pro-duce demigods and demons at will, double us into clones, ex-pand our minds, or drive them on pulses of contentment into endless rows of Skinner boxes.

More: science has its acolytes and altar boys, its sextons, vestries, monks, and priests, its roadside chapels ("Seal your social security card in lifetime plastic, 25¢"), and its cathedrals, and within these ("authorized personnel only") its holies. Mary Shelley gave us its devil (Frankenstein) and the Swedish Academy its saints (Nobel Prize winners); it has its scriptures and its credos (though these have been known to change from time to time) and its sacred languages, known only to the elect. *"Doctor, will you explain. . . ?" "Sorry, friend; you haven't the math."*

To put it simply, science is a god-thing: omniscient, omnipotent, omnipresent, master of that terrible trinity of hope, fear, and power. Science-the-god is (to the layman) incomprehensible, unpredictable, and reasonable only in its own mysterious ways. Its graven images are Promethean—sometimes a pillar of fire, sometimes a man in a white coat holding a test tube up to the light, sometimes an untenanted console encrusted with nubs and rounds and faced with a mosaic of gridded screens across which crawl green worms of light, whose body-language may be read only by the ordained. More and more the image becomes a gigantic computer studded with dots of orange radiance and randomly reversing tape reels (while computers themselves, incidentally, become smaller and smaller with fewer and fewer visible features). Science presents all the attributes of an object of worship, and is accordingly respected, feared, sacrificed to, and invoked—that is to say, worshiped.

One of the phenomena of worship is its obverted obeisance —the childishly rebellious act or statement which by its occurrence serves only to acknowledge the authority. When a little boy, indoctrinated and thoroughly warned, yet screws up his courage and says Goddamn, and lightning does *not* strike him dead, he feels roller-coaster scary and a little brave. Such is the swagger of Boccaccio who, in the Age of Faith (which preceded our Age, which in turn precedes the real Age of Reason) told scandalous anecdotes about monks and nuns and probably felt scary and brave, and exactly delineated contemporary Authority. Today nobody bothers to scandalize the cloth; one can get no further than bad taste that way. Instead we have funny stories about insane psychiatrists, mad scientists (more often than not with German accents; the *Übermensch* lie dies hard), and the military, as in *Dr. Strangelove,* and the area of worship is quite as clear as that which Boccaccio inversely incised.

Back now to that mysterious lack of discrimination amongst the reading-viewing public. I know of no other explanation for this strange lack than to submit that there is one target with Science in its title which is as safe to lob bricks at as the home of the only Jew in town: science fiction. Put it down and the lightning does not strike. To sneer at it is perhaps to express a suspicion that perhaps science has become too much the master, that perhaps science will become aware that dissent exists. Science fiction, then, because of its misnomer (it should from the first have been called something else, but it's too late now) is the victim of religious persecution, not from the heretics, but from the devout.

Now to the subject in hand—science fiction, morals, and religion.

Science fiction has been around a long time—at least since Ezekiel saw that flying saucer, and it's not easy to think of anything more religious than an Old Testament prophet. As to morals, it must be said that despite the oft-repeated assertion that science fiction is, or has been until the strictures disappeared in all current literature, a passionless, de- and un-sexed field, with all its gonads on its lurid front-cover art and none inside—science fiction has for a long time explored human relationships—a fair description, I think, of morals in action.

But before citing source, I had better define my terms. *Science fiction:* the fiction of science, a word deriving from the Latin *scientia,* which does *not* mean "system" or "systematic," which does *not* mean "method"—it means *knowledge.* (For the emergence of this true original meaning, see my use of "omniscient" above—"omniscient," knowing all.) *Fiction,* to me, means people; that is to say, the impact of people upon people and of ideas upon people. Fiction, any fiction, primarily about ideas is not fiction at all, but tract. I demand of science fiction that it be good fiction. I demand further that the science—the *scientia*—be so essential to the plot that if it were removed the remainder would be incomprehensible. If a story remains, then it wasn't science fiction; it was the cowboy story on location on Mars. I do not demand of science fiction that it cleave to the so-called Hard Sciences, for as mathematics ascends through pure logic to something approaching philosophy, so does physics advance to areas of uncertainty and intangibility, and above all, mutability. "$E=MC^2$," Albert Einstein once remarked, "may after all be a local phenomenon." Celestial mechanics depends absolutely upon motion, as do chemical reactions; change, passage, transience, evolution, and recidivism of cells and stars—these are the only universal "constants." As to mankind: there is more room in inner space than in outer space, and science fiction, within the wider parameters of true *scientia*, legitimately embraces it all. This is why I claim, for example, William Golding's superb *Lord of the Flies* for science fiction, for it is a study of the sources, in a relatively unindoctrinated group of human beings, of religious and political organization, a fable of cultural structures, with a meaning—a "moral" if you like—far greater than the narrative itself.

Morals: that structure of law and convention within a society which guides the individual in his survival within the group. (Parenthetically, morals are distinguished from *ethics* in that the latter is a structure of thought which is directed toward the survival of the species. Huge families, for example, are at certain times, in certain places, an ethical imperative, and although at first emergence may run counter to contemporary morals, often win out and gradually achieve morality. Limitation of families, on the other hand, may become a survival factor, and the ethical thrust is toward that end, and engenders the same conflict with its society. Ethical thinkers are often decried and persecuted—and in the long run they, or their ideas, are yielded to and their innovations become conventions.) One must be reminded that "moral" and "immoral" should not be confused with "good" and "evil." In a cannibal society it is immoral *not* to eat human flesh.

Religion: For any intelligent discussion, this word and its meaning must be divided into two parts—a concept which I have at times had extraordinary difficulty in expressing. On the one hand it means the religious establishment—the Church and the many Churches, old and new, and all their actual and theoretical divisions and subdivisions. On the other hand it means the force, the pressure, the urge to worship itself, that which underlies the existence of these structures. It is an arduous task indeed to keep these two separate when discussing religion; yet they have been separated sharply—largely by the Church establishment itself.

Recently I saw a photograph of a large youth-rally for Christ, featuring a young man wearing a T-shirt on which was a cross with the legend "1 WAY." Established religions almost invariably proclaim that theirs is the one way, the only way ; it is this which caused the conflict between the Romans and the early Christians. Many Romans were quite intrigued, if not delighted, with Jesus and his works, and were only too willing to include him in their pantheon, with all respect. This the Christians totally, intolerantly refused, an attitude which then cost them savage persecution, which they returned with interest at a later date, directing it even on their own—the Catharists, for example, the Waldenses, and many others.

None of which has anything at all to do with the urge to worship—religion in that sense—and has everything to do with the multiplicity of "one ways." Church establishments, as a matter of record, tend to disdain and even to exterminate any emergence of direct theolepsy—the seizure of an individual personally by a Higher Power—and may be said, in that light, to exist to *prevent* worship!

Both forms of religion—the hierarchal, ritualistic structure, and the infinitely more personal theolepsy, have been a part of science fiction from the beginning. Like religion throughout history, it has had its tides. Lucian of Samosata, who was born around A.D. 125, told in his *Icaromenippus* of voyages, not only to the moon but to heaven, from which he could look down upon all the wickednesses of men and make some biting moral judgments. One of Cyrano's "travels" took him, via rocket, to the Garden of Eden, where he met the prophet Elias, who threw him out. Saint Thomas More in his 1516 *Utopia* takes great pains to describe toleration for divergence in religions, though taking a rock-firm stand against any who might suggest that the soul dies with the body. (The trouble with all utopias, as Sweden's Sam J. Lundwall remarks in his excellent book *Science Fiction: What It's All About*, is that they demand of their citizens: "Think whatever you like, but think *right!*") All through man's literary history, his "moral tales," his fantasies, satires, parables, and allegories have reflected religious influence and are stitched through and through with that metaphorical, fabulous (in the true sense of the word) quality which has now flowered into science fiction.

The novels of C. S. Lewis, most especially his fine trilogy *Perelandra, Out of the Silent Planet,* and *That Hideous Strength,* strongly reflect the religious devotion of their author. Other true giants of science fiction—H. G. Wells and Olaf Stapledon, for example—seem to have largely ignored religion. And it's almost absent, as subject and motivator, in the crude beginnings of science fiction's formative years in the magazines. Not until its sudden explosion of quality, when in the late '30s and early '40s John W. Campbell, Jr., editor of *Astounding Stories,* gathered about him his astonishing coterie—Asimov, Heinlein, del Rey, de Camp, Simak, Russell, Pratt, and so many others—did the field give itself the elbowroom to get into things like religious ideas. Amongst the ever-widening search for variant ideas, it was inevitable that the religious area be touched upon, and finally invaded. One phenomenon of the field was L. Ron Hubbard, who was a slam-bang story machine for *Astounding,* which published the first article on Dianetics. Campbell was an ardent follower of Dianetics for a year or so and then dropped it; Dianetics evolved into Scientology and registered itself as a church, and thrives to this day.

I could not give you an inclusive list of religiously oriented science fiction from Campbell's "golden age" to the present without far overrunning my allotted space here. One cannot discuss religion and science fiction without immediate mention of James Blish's beautifully constructed, provocative novel *A Case of Conscience,* in which a Jesuit unearths the underlying evil in an apparently perfect planetary culture: its ophidian natives have no souls. Equally provocative is Arthur C. Clarke's celebrated short story "The Star," which describes a truly beautiful, powerful, highly cultured alien civilization which is destroyed by its sun's going nova—that nova being the Star of Bethlehem. Here again the central character is a priest, and his view of these fine people and all they have done, versus what has happened here after the ignition at Bethlehem, costs him his faith. Ray Bradbury wrote a shattering story called "The Man," in which the protagonist visits planet after planet, arriving always just after the Messiah has left—and is forced to suspect that his advent is the reason for The Man's departure. Bradbury, by the way, in much of his writing, exhibits that kind of non-Church, absolutely devout religion I tried so hard to describe above. He believes forcefully that the proper worship of man is mankind.

Surely one of the most powerful novelettes ever written is Lester del Rey's For I am a Jealous People, in which the earth is invaded by a reptilian species with an advanced technology. The central character is a small-town minister, who sees his flock decimated and scattered by the invader, which loots and kills and drives him out of his little church. He takes a secret way back in and sees a worship service going on, and on his altar, no less than the Ark of the Covenant. He understands then that God has broken His ancient covenant with humanity and has given it to the aliens; and after some wracking soul-searching, he calls his congregation together and, in a new, potent, Moses-like fury, declares himself against God. "You have in us a worthy opponent. . . ."

In the late '40s a new bright light appeared on the horizon with the founding of The Magazine of Fantasy and Science Fiction, co-edited by J. Francis McComas and Anthony Boucher. Boucher—who was author William A. P. White, who was H. H. Holmes (who reviewed as many as three hundred detective novels a year for the New York Tribune), and who conducted, from one of the finest record collections in the world, a weekly radio program on fine opera, was science fiction/fantasy critic for the New York Times, and one of the best, sharpest, gentlest and most creative editiors who ever lived—was also a devout Roman Catholic. (He was also one of the most relaxed human beings one could meet, and his death in 1968 is a terrible loss.) His was a devotion of wide tolerance and ecumenicism; he would have had a joyful time with Pope John, and if there is high art in heaven he will at this moment be conducting a delightful battle royal with the late Colonel *(Mistakes of Moses)* Robert Ingersoll, and in the Jamaican phraseology, I wud Ghod I were a fly on de wall fe see dat.

A fine writer himself, he wrote a number of stories dealing with religion, probably the most notable being "The Quest for St. Aquin," in which a priest, heavily disguised in an America which had become totally intolerant of all religion, mounts a robot donkey—a "robass"—and follows myths and rumors to a cave in which, it is said, resides a saint. I won't spoil the story for you by telling you what he found; I will say that the dialogue between him and the robass is priceless. In addition, Tony gave a very special kind of house-room to writers with ideas about religion and worship, whether it was whimsical matter, like the endless series of short stories about deals with the devil, or stories of real moment and of towering quality—one thinks especially of Walter M. Miller, Jr.'s, "A Canticle for Leibowitz," which provoked two more novelettes on the same theme—a monastery in a postatomic era which had given itself the duty of preserving knowledge—the three becoming a novel which had even the mainstream critics taking real notice.

Philip José Farmer is one of the most original, one of the most talented, and certainly one of the most fearless writers around. He is deeply preoccupied with (among a good many other things) the profound pressure-to-worship mentioned earlier. "The Alley Man" is a powerful and most unsettling story about a garbage man who is very possibly an immortal Neanderthal and quite possibly a god as well. He is ugly, brutal, sensual, and more than a little divine. Farmer's novel *Flesh* is a marvelous orchestration of commentary on religion, morals, and power politics, in a fast-paced, hard-core science fiction setting. The crew of a starship returns to Earth to find it vastly changed, consisting of a quasi-tribal confederation of states completely under the domination of a savage (in two senses) theology. The captain is taken and processed to be this year's god-in-the-flesh. Part of the processing is to equip him with antlers, which have the effect of turning him daily into a condition of totipotent rut; he is carried naked from town to town and turned loose on the willing female population. He learns that this will continue for some weeks until he dies of it. This wild situation is complicated by his falling in love with a girl he doesn't want to hurt, and of course by her considerably mixed feelings about being in love with him, for all she is a native and understands the ritual. It is this kind of cold-logic-in-the-far-out that is Farmer's hallmark. An underpopulated culture, living a precarious existence in a ruined world in which, however, certain high technologies remain, has several urgencies: to breed as fast as possible; to secure the very best possible for the gene pool; and to give the people a predictable saturnalia during which they can lose their terrors in wild celebration. To accomplish this the government taps every resource of psychology—including that urge to worship, which it adds to the sexual drive, instead of separating them as is done by the Judaeo-Christian and Eastern ascetic philosophies. (Either way serves efficiently to fence a flock during those times when it is not under the direct view of the shepherd.) In *Flesh*, the incarnate dies of his ritual; and even this is used, for the biochemical preparation is ritualized into a surrogate birth process, with the unconscious preparee squeezed out through a narrow opening into public view. The pattern of the deity reborn is a familiar one, and in this context it digs right through the veneer. It can clearly be seen, then, that this narrative is no mere exercise in sensationalism, blasphemy, and porn, but is, underneath, a most astute examination, by comparison, of our own beliefs and convictions, and of the very nature of religion and morality, things which, in the ordinary course, we tend to take for granted, accept as axiomatic. I hold that it is right and necessary to examine these things, for they are vital to humanity. Gregariousness is not a privilege or a play toy. It is essential to our species; and the moral structure, and especially worship—because of its extension from the individual to the group, whereas the thrust of morality is in the other direction—are the peaks of our underlying gregariousness. To celebrate commencement, a faith must pass its finals.

I cannot leave the subject of religion in science fiction without mentioning three writers, who by their reputations within the field are little, middle, and big.

Sam Mines is little only in the sense that his bibliography is so short. He was at one time the editor of *Thrilling Wonder* and *Startling Stories,* and was most notable at the time for the studied gentleness and perception of the magazines' "Letters" columns. He is the author of a story—I call it a "lost" story because I have never seen it in an anthology, and I cannot recall the issue in which it appeared, except that it seems to have been in the early '50s. I am not even certain about the title, but I think it was called "Find the Sculptor."[1] It dealt with a lunar exploration team, a thoughtful and rather ludicrous crewman who happened to be devotedly religious, and another who was agnostic, brash, and the kind of guy who, when he was a boy scout, delighted in pushing the fat kid so he would sit in a puddle. Told too simply, the plot was that the brash one had a joke to play. He had a stone cross with him, and he dropped it on the lunar surface and manipulated matters so that the devout one would find it and pick it up—an artifact!—*a cross!*—on the moon! There would, of course, follow much raucous laughter and 240,000 miles' worth of ribbing. Well, the devout one indeed found the cross, and reentered the ship . . . and he was radiant, he was illuminated. And it came to the meathead to understand that whatever the episode that had lit this flame, regardless of its false and trivial sources, what had happened to his crew mate was *real,* and should not be tampered with. And that was his own illumination. A nice story, and one which reached me personally very deeply.

The levels of this little fable are many, and not the least of them is its recognition of what I have come to call the "infrara-

1. *Wonder Story Annual,* 1952–1953.

tional"—that source of belief, faith, and motive which exists beside and above reason. So conditioned have we been by Aristotle, Kant, and Freud that we tend to believe that any force, object, or problem will yield to rational processes; when they don't, we blame the process and call up yet more logic. The infrarational, however, is a very large component in us, and while reason calls it ignorance and stupidity (viz, trying to talk someone out of a fear of the dark or of snakes), it is neither. It is the infrarational, source of many of our motivations and the tint reservoir of much of our thinking. We will never succeed in reaching our optimum as a species until we learn the nature of the infrarational. We may fail as a species unless we do. The urge to worship—as ubiquitous and commanding as sex—has its origins there.

A "middle" writer is Marion Zimmer Bradley—competent, entertaining, insightful, always worth a reader's time and money. In her new novel *Darkover Landfall*, about a starship, carrying colonists, which strays far off course and crashes on an unknown planet, there is a frightening sequence in which the pollen of a certain flower acts in strange ways on warm-blooded life, indigenous and alien both. Among the people most taken by its madness is a priest (of the Order of Saint Christopher of Centaurus) who, under the influence of the pollen, commits sins which he thought were impossible to him, then murders to eliminate the witnesses, and then begins to suicide—and only at that point recognizes immolation as yet another mortal sin and stops in time. (The details of his sins are in the book. I'm not about to spoil so careful and powerful a piece of writing.) Because human life is so precious in this situation, and because the defense of temporary insanity is so obvious (for everyone was affected during the pollen-drift), Father Valentine is not executed, but is put to burying the dead and setting up a cemetery, working and living alone except for the momentary contact of someone's bringing food. A woman with a problem asks to take him food one day, and this interesting exchange takes place:

"Father, I need your help. I don't suppose you'd hear my confession?"

He shook his head slowly. "I'm not a priest any more. . . . How in the name of anything holy can I have the insolence to pass judgment in the name of God on someone else's sins? . . . How can I honestly teach or preach the Gospel of Christ on a world where He never set foot? If God wants to save this world he'll have to send someone to save it . . . whatever that means. . . ."

"Then you're just leaving us without pastoral help of any sort, Father?"

"I don't think I ever did much in that line," Father Valentine said. "I wonder if any priest ever did? It goes without saying that anything I can do for anyone as a friend, I'll do—it's the least I can do; if I spent my life at it, it wouldn't begin to balance out what I did, but it's better than sitting around in sackcloth and ashes mouthing penitential prayers."

The woman said, "I can understand that, I suppose. But do you really mean there's no room for faith, or religion, Father?"

He made a dismissing gesture. "I wish you wouldn't call me 'Father.' Brother, if you want to. We've all got to be brothers and sisters in misfortune here. No, I didn't say that. . . . Every human being needs belief in the goodness of some power that created him, no matter what he calls it, and some religious or ethical structure. But I don't think we need sacraments or priesthoods from a world that's only a memory, and won't even be that to our children and our children's children. Ethics, yes. Art, yes. Music, crafts, knowledge, humanity—yes. But not rituals which will quickly dwindle down into superstitions. And certainly not a social code or a set of purely arbitrary behavioral attitudes which have nothing to do with the society we're in now."

"Yet you would have worked in the church structure at the Coronis colony?" [Their original destination.]

"I suppose so. I belong to the Order of St. Christopher of Centaurus, which was organized to carry the Reformed Catholic Church to the stars, and I simply accepted it as a worthy cause. I never really thought about it. Not serious, hard, deep thought. But out here on the rock pile . . . Judith, forgive me. You came to me to ask my help, you asked me to hear your confession, and you've ended up listening to mine."

She said very gently, "If you're right, we'll all have to be priests to each other, at least as far as listening to each other and giving what help we can."

Of the many aspects of that multifaceted monolith Robert Heinlein, one of the most fascinating is the development in his work, through the years, of the religious element. One of the boldest thinkers around, he often seems harnessed to conventionality. But has his thinking in this area evolved—or has he been revealing more of what was always there? It's difficult to say.

In one of his earliest stories, "The Year of the Jackpot," which describes the result when all life-affecting cycles—lunar, solar, geological, psychological, meteorological, etc.—happen to peak at the same time: everybody goes crazy. The hero, like so many Heinlein heroes, is a fast-thinking, strong, engineering type, who rescues a girl out of the madness and brings her to a hiding place back in the hills, where they wait it out. They fall very much in love, and what to do? *They're not married!* This is a difficult issue for them; but what seemed even at the time (1952) merely quaint, suddenly became poignant when he and she knelt while he devoutly called upon God as his witness that these two were well and truly married. (In the same story, incidentally, is a most touching passage, in which the girl asks this slide-rule, chrome-plated character if he believes in life after death. "There must be," he says without hesitation. "If there weren't—it would be . . . bad art." I cannot express to you how much I like that.) In *Sixth Column* the United States has been so thoroughly conquered that there are only six patriots left free to fight; they win back the country with a dazzling series of super-, pseudo-, and just plain scientific gadgetry, encasing the whole in a spectacular God-is-on-our-side false front which heartened the natives and demoralized the invader. And to this day I have not been able to decide whether this was cynical commentary on the force of religion or a kind of naïveté. For a long period Heinlein, like a great many of his contemporaries, ignored this aspect—at least, to the best of my recollection; there are, certainly, a great many other things to write about.

Then along came the extraordinary *Stranger in a Strange Land,* a book which infuriates almost everyone who reads it— and with each reader, for a different reason! Aside from the fury, however, most people who read it love it. Heinlein's fusion of the optimum-human concept with religion becomes clear in this book, together with an opening up, not of love (there is always much more of love in Heinlein's works than the casual skimmer can find) but of ways of love. The parallel in *Stranger* between the careers of Michael Valentine Smith and Jesus of Nazareth is purposeful and clear, and, it seems to me, a lot more life-oriented in the former. The gaity in that transubstantiation scene at the end is something that has infuriated some of the infuriated readers; yet it is much closer to the *agape,* the love-feast, of apostolic Christianity than the rather more austere ceremony into which it evolved.

To sum up, then: religion and science fiction are no strangers to one another, and the willingness of science fiction writers to delve into it, to invent and extrapolate and regroup ideas and concepts in this as in all other areas of human growth and change, delights me and is the source of my true love for the mad breed.

As to morality, there is little more I can say about this than I have said above: morals are rules by which the individual survives within the group. More often than not they are out-dated ethical concepts; more often than not they are tools for the established order to keep the order established. They have little contact with necessity; they tend to immobilize rather than to emancipate; they yield readily to straight hard questions, like:

Why must three-year-old girls wear bikini tops?

Why must little boys wear bathing suits at all?

Are the garments worn to worship services by today's females more or less modest than those worn on the beaches in the memory of the oldest parishioners?

Clothing, especially beach wear, is an easy target, a simple test for viability and usefulness in a moral idea. Some are more ponderous and worth pondering:

If all children were slapped every time they used the four-letter word "frog," frogs would achieve more size and more voltage than any frog has ever dreamed of.

Well, you take it from there. Live, and grow, and in the name of a real God, don't let morals stop you.

Theodore Sturgeon

Theodore Sturgeon was born on Staten Island, New York, in 1918. He started writing during the three years he spent at sea after attending Penn State Nautical School; he sold his first sf story, "The Ether Breathers," to John W. Campbell's *Astounding* in 1939, and by that time he had already published forty or more stories in different fields as well as some poetry. Once launched in sf, he produced a long string of memorable short stories, and is celebrated (with Heinlein, del Rey, Asimov, and others) as one of the creators of science fiction as it is today. His stories appeared in all the leading sf magazines, and in 1947 one of them, "Bianca's Hands" won a $1,000 prize from the English *Argosy* (Graham Greene taking the second prize).

Sturgeon's first collection, *Without Sorcery*, appeared in 1948. Then, when *Galaxy* was founded, he began writing for it the psychologically oriented stories which culminated in his novel *More Than Human*, winner of the International Fantasy Award. Since then, he has been accorded innumerable other honors, including both the Hugo and Nebula Awards for "Slow Sculpture," a *Galaxy* story. He has written TV scripts for *Star Trek* and other shows, is preparing a new sf television series, and is married to TV personality Wina Sturgeon. He continues to produce his incomparable novels and short stories. A master of characterization and style, he has been called (by Damon Knight) "the most accomplished technician the field has produced, bar none." His dominant theme is love, which he has examined in all its imaginable possibilities and permutations.

Besides all this, he is a singularly acute and perceptive critic, with the rare ability to illuminate that which he discusses, and has reviewed books for *National Review, The New York Times*, and *Galaxy*.

Without Sorcery, 1948 (Prime Press) with introduction by Ray Bradbury

E Pluribus Unicorn, 1953 (Abelard Press)

More Than Human, 1953 (Farrar, Strauss & Young)

A Way Home, 1955, selected and with introduction by Groff Conklin (Funk & Wagnalls)

Caviar, 1955 (Ballantine)
I, Libertine, 1956 (Ballantine); under pseudonym Frederick R. Ewing
A Touch of Strange, 1958 (Doubleday)
The Cosmic Rape, 1958 (Dell)
Aliens 4, 1959 (Avon)
Beyond, 1960 (Avon)
Venus Plus X, 1960 (Pyramid)
Voyage to the Bottom of the Sea, 1961 (Pyramid)
Some of Your Blood, 1961 (Ballantine)
Sturgeon is Alive and Well, 1971 (Putnam)
The Worlds of Theodore Sturgeon, 1972 (Ace)
Sturgeon's West, 1973 (Doubleday)

Alan E. Nourse

Science Fiction and Man's Adaptation to Change

More than at any other time in history we are living today in an age of furious and bewildering change. Awareness of this fact, with all its disorganizing implications, is thrust upon us daily from all sides. Change permeates every aspect of our lives. In less than a single century we have moved from horse-and-buggy travel to supersonic transports and interplanetary vehicles. Simple bullets and limited battlefields have given way to hydrogen bombs and genocidal warfare. Our insular and agrarian society is rapidly vanishing, swept away by a burgeoning technology that spans oceans and continents. Our political institutions are in turmoil, our social values are shifting radically, and our ethical standards are under continuing attack. The environment of our planet is changing so rapidly that our very existence is threatened. Serious men are seriously questioning our ability as a race to survive at all for very long; others question whether we deserve to survive, or even want to, considering the fearsome nature of the future world we may have to endure. Still others, more optimistic (or more stubborn), search diligently for ways to surmount the problems of change which seem increasingly insurmountable with every passing year.

We know that much of this relentlessly accelerating change is rooted in the vast scientific and technological revolution that began three centuries ago and is still expanding today in exponential progression. We also know that different peoples have suffered differing impacts. In the underdeveloped nations today, change is suddenly uprooting whole societies and hurling millions of people overnight into an alien world they cannot begin to comprehend, much less adapt to. In such areas it has become the function of governments, for better or for worse, to force adaptation upon whole populations, and if the results have often been grisly, the need has been desperate. In our Western world the impact has been less catastrophic. For decades and centuries the winds of change have been accelerating slowly enough that orderly adaptation has been possible—up to a point. But now even here our capacity to adapt is being outpaced. We no longer have time for a slow, evolutionary assimilation of change into our daily lives. Multitudes of people are scrambling ever more frantically to find some kind of foothold, some place to stand, as they try to deal with a changing world which they can neither control nor comprehend. The popular term "future shock" is singularly appropriate: we are staggering beneath a rain of blows, both physical and emotional, as the juggernaut of technology grinds forward ever faster.

There are two ways that man can respond to the change that is thrust upon him: he can resist it, or he can try to adapt to it. Throughout history there have always been some who have found change to be challenging and exhilarating. These people, stimulated by the challenge and regarding change as beneficial, or at the very least inevitable, have searched for ways to adapt to it—that is, to alter their lives in such a way as to accommodate or even utilize the changes that have occurred. The vast majority of people, however, have always found change to be frightening, bewildering, or demoralizing. These people, typifying the forces of reaction or conservatism within the society, have sought to ignore, prevent, or control the forces of change in order to maintain a status quo. In times when change was occurring in a slow and orderly or evolutionary fashion, these opposing forces of adaptation and resistance were more or less evenly balanced, and adaptation was comparatively easy. People had time to assimilate the changes, time to adjust themselves, time to work the implications of change into their lives, and then gently alter the way they were living to conform to the demands of change. Often the same individuals met change with both adaptation and resistance: they would adapt to change a step at a time, resisting further change until earlier change had been fully assimilated and then moving a small step further to assimilate the next change.

We can see this type of successful adaptation to change exemplified in the manner in which the automobile, with its internal combustion engine, edged out the horse and carriage as a primary means of transportation from place to place—an evolutionary process that took place with comparatively little dislocation over a period of decades in the advanced industrial societies, and which is still proceeding today in less developed areas. But as the pace of change has accelerated with bewildering swiftness in recent decades, such orderly adaptation has become progressively more difficult. More and more people regard change as threatening and catastrophic. Without sufficient time to assimilate change in an orderly fashion, even the more adaptive individuals have drawn back into a shell of conservatism, consciously or unconsciously fighting change tooth and nail, seeking desperately to maintain the status quo, however precarious it might be, and responding to the changing world with a vast conservative inertia.

Today we can see manifestations of this inertia on all sides of us. We see it, for example, in the continuing growth of huge and sprawling urban centers, spreading out unchecked into the suburban areas, while the city centers are increasingly beset with poverty, crime, and decay. We know, of course, that the cities have been vital to man's development throughout most of his history, but the city of today is unlike anything ever before witnessed. There is ample reason to suspect that the sprawling metropolis containing tens of millions of people is no longer a serviceable or even a viable social entity, but rather that such cities today are in fact anti-survival and largely unnecessary considering the current state of our technology. Yet with enormous conservative inertia our society not only struggles to maintain existing megalopoli but allows them to enlarge further and seeks even to create new ones. In a related area, the forces of environmental destruction march on virtually unchecked by the token measures we have raised so far to block them, and any truly radical or imaginative approach to stemming or reversing these forces is met with a massive resistance. At the same time our society adheres doggedly to antediluvian values, complacently tolerating corrupt political institutions and ineffective or hypocritical ethical standards which cry out for reevaluation and true reform if the society that is founded on these principles is to survive.

There was a time when conservative inertia and resistance to change were successful in maintaining a status quo; such change as there was came slowly, was bargained with, and was assimilated a bit at a time. But unfortunately the forces of change in our society today can no longer be negotiated. Change is occurring in an ever-accelerating cycle. There is no longer time to bargain, no *quid pro quo* possible. Change is going to continue no matter how man reacts to it, and it is going to *change lives* ever more swiftly and massively, whether men want their lives changed or not. It is no longer even appropriate for us to ask whether change can be prevented, minimized, or controlled; the appropriate question is how change can be dealt with in such a way that individuals and society can survive and prosper in the midst of it. Thus it is hardly surprising that in this past half century of accelerating change a singular popular literature has emerged which deals specifically with change and its impact on human lives.

This popular literature, which we now know as science fiction, is by no means virgin to the twentieth century. Scholars can demonstrate that a literature of romantic fantasy has occupied its own special niche over the centuries. With its curious and rather special outlook on man's relationship to nature and the world, it has always stirred the imagination and evoked a sense of wonder in the face of phenomena that were not clearly understood. But it was only in the first quarter of the twentieth century that science fiction began to distinguish itself by its recognition of science and technology as key factors molding our society. It was at the same time that science fiction became acutely concerned with rational speculation about the impact of science and technology on mankind, as opposed to the supernatural or mystical dream worlds previously explored in romantic fantasy. And just as modern science fiction has evolved side by side with the twentieth century's scientific and technological revolution, it has begun to serve as an increasingly important and singularly effective device for adaptation to changes brought about by that revolution. Science fiction today is an excellent means for pinpointing and identifying the potential hazards that may face us in the future because of accelerating change; in addition, it is also an excellent means for testing or exploring possible future solutions. And it is in this area that science fiction has a surprising potential for preparing its readers to adapt to the swiftly accelerating speed of change, to survive the future shock that this change is bringing about and to modify the untoward effects of change.

Science fiction today is still essentially a popular escape literature, unsophisticated and amusement-oriented. What, then, makes it so useful as a device to ease and abet man's adaptation to change? First, as opposed to mystery novels, western novels, popular love novels, sports stories, or other forms of popular fiction, science fiction is primarily a *literature of ideas*. Quite aside from its entertainment value, science fiction stimulates the speculative imagination. The reader of a science fiction story is invited to suspend his disbelief and embark upon an adventure dealing with events and propositions that have not yet happened but which might very conceivably occur at some time in the future, be it tomorrow or a thousand years hence. Typically a science fiction story begins with a premise which may be untrue but is at least plausible. One story, for example, might contend that the earth has been invaded by invisible aliens who can only be detected with the aid of a galvanometer. Another story might predicate that certain otherwise normal individuals can and do exercise completely unconscious disruptive mental influences over the law of averages. Yet another story might assume a manned space flight to the planet Jupiter, and take as its premise the proposition that one of Jupiter's larger moons has engendered a life form totally different from our own yet equally intelligent. In each case the science fiction story then proceeds from its initial premise to explore what such a premise might mean, what might be expected to happen in such circumstances, how people might respond to such a turn of events, and how it might influence their lives. Once the reader has been induced to suspend his disbelief it is the *idea* in the science fiction story that becomes paramount, and "what would happen if—" becomes the main thrust of the science fictional entertainment.

Second, science fiction stories deliberately and specifically look to the future. This is not, as many believe, an attempt at prophecy or specific prediction; rather, it is an attempt at rational speculation about the various patterns the future might assume, given what we know about the present. Writers and readers of science fiction accept as an unspoken premise that what might happen tomorrow is directly related by cause-and-effect to what is happening today. The invisible aliens are discovered among us only because our scientific and technological advancement has provided us with an instrument—the galvanometer—by which we can detect them. Perhaps these invisible aliens have been among us for centuries without our having any awareness of their presence before this momentous discovery is made. Conceivably this unsuspected presence could explain multitudes of phenomena which hitherto were recognized but totally unexplained. But the story's concern is what the discovery may mean in human terms *tomorrow* and what human beings *tomorrow* are going to do about it. Similarly, in the story of the man whose mind unconsciously influences the law of averages, the story is concerned not so much with the phenomenon itself as with implications, speculating as to what influence such an individual might have on the world at large. It is assumed that the hero's extraordinary mental powers have evolved from certain characteristics or qualities already known to be present in humans, or else to have appeared according to the rules of genetic variation and mutation; there is nothing magical or supernatural about it. And granted this cause-and-effect premise, the story then concerns itself primarily with what this suddenly appearing mental power might mean to its possessor or to other human beings around him, what changes it would necessitate in society, and *how man might adapt* to the appearance of such a phenomenon if it were to occur.

Thus science fiction is predominantly a *speculative literature* in which the reader is invited to ponder in some detail the effect that a given advance, change, discovery, or technological breakthrough might have upon society as we know it and upon human beings as we know them. While engaging in such speculation, however, science fiction clearly recognizes the importance of future variables in the lives of men. In particular it takes into account the appearance of *unpredictable variables,* such as might arise as a result of rapidly accelerating and unexpected change, and then seeks to predict where such unpredictable variables might reasonably lead. For example, it is not at all implausible that a virulent mutated virus might appear as an unpredictable variable in our own immediate future, and could lead to massive changes in the lives and health practices of whole societies. Science fiction can imagine such an unpredictable variable and then, given the premise that such a mutated virus had appeared, can ask what our society would and should do about it, how we should deal with it, and how we might work to resist it or to adapt to it. Similarly, the unexpected discovery of physical principles that could make faster-than-light travel possible by one means or another might very plausibly appear as an unpredictable variable in the world we know today. Such a variable would have a profound effect upon man's ability to explore and possibly better understand the universe. Science fiction has long been speculatively concerned with precisely such exploration, even when its concepts of what such an exploration might mean and the conclusions it might arrive at may be extremely provincial and naive.

But how can a popular literature which is often regarded as "crazy" or "fantastic" by those least acquainted with it actually equip its readers to adapt to social, cultural, or technological change? First and foremost, science fiction prepares the minds of its readers with certain concepts or attitudes toward change that are not always widely shared by others. For example, the science fiction reader is powerfully acclimatized to the underlying idea that *change is going to come about, come what may.* There is no nonsense in his head about resisting, thwarting, or evading change. The science fiction stories he reads dwell upon future societies that *have* changed from the present. In these stories change is regarded as inevitable; indeed, science fiction frequently predicates rapid, radical, or abrupt change as probable in the pattern of the future. From his experience with the simple process of extrapolation—taking current trends and patterns and tracing them to their possible logical future implications—the science fiction reader *knows* that the changes proceeding about him today, however sweeping they may be, are as nothing compared to the changes that may be expected in the near and distant future.

Second, the science fiction reader is encouraged by his reading not to fear or dread change, but rather to accept it as a fresh and exciting challenge. After all, science fiction seems to say, the winds of change—however violent they may seem—are of man's making in the first place, and it should be within man's power to temper them. This is not to say that the science fiction reader necessarily *likes* the idea of change, or welcomes it, or even approves of it. He may well react quite negatively. He may elect to move heaven and earth in an effort to modify its impact, but total rejection is unlikely to enter his head. Rather, his thinking will be directed to identifying *what might be wrong* with a specific direction of change, which kinds of change to resist and which to applaud, what deleterious influences might come about as a result of change, and how those undesirable effects might be prevented from happening. Indeed, there are a number of prominent science fiction writers, and multitudes of their readers, who quite actively detest the process of technological change and the direction in which technology seems to be drawing mankind. But even the most adamantly pessimistic of these "anti-science" writers nevertheless recognize the inevitability of change and seek in their writings to modify its impact rather than to attempt to turn the clock back. And even at that, these writers and their readers are the exception rather than the rule. Most science fiction writers and readers approach the idea of change not with the negative mental set of "what can we do to halt it or minimize it?" but rather with the more optimistic mental set of "how can we use it, adapt to it, make our lives with it, around it, or in spite of it? How can we deal with it most effectively?"

Third, science fiction readers in general are equipped by their reading to accept scientific and technological discovery and advancement as a major and potentially beneficial instrument forcing change. Rather than ask, "Why do we need this advancement?" they are asking, "Why haven't we had this advancement sooner? Why aren't we applying it more widely? Why didn't we recognize its potential twenty years ago, and why aren't we using these changes to better advantage?" There are very few "back to nature and the simple life" thinkers among science fiction readers, very few hand-wringers, very few indeed who are concentrating on past faults, failings, and frailties of mankind. Thus, for better or for worse, science fiction readers are probably more realistically oriented to the inevitable forces of change than most other people. At the same time, science fiction readers are prepared by their reading to cope with the natural ambivalence that scientific and technological change generates in people's minds. These readers clearly recognize that all scientific and technological progress is not necessarily good, and that for every benefit of science there are likely to be hazards or disadvantages. Thus they are able to direct their thinking toward neutralizing or counteracting these hazards or disadvantages while at the same time nurturing and developing the benefits. And if worst comes to worst, science fiction readers are prepared *to accept the worst and deal with it*. They are long familiar with the ironic concept of Finagle's First Law as scientists and engineers apply it to any scientific experiment in the laboratory: *If something can go wrong, it will*. But the science fiction reader is also aware that this perverse principle applies just as universally to life situations as it does to scientific or engineering experiments in the laboratory.

In short, science fiction prepares its readers for successful adaptation to change first by accepting the fact of change, whether desirable or not, as inevitable; second, by seeking to adjust to the change wherever possible; and third by modifying the change when possible or necessary in order to reduce its negative impact on our lives. On the other hand, much adaptive failure arises, first, from refusing to accept change as an inescapable factor; second, fighting against *all* change, the good as well as the bad; and seeking to resist or negate changes in attempting to return to or to restore past circumstances that are more familiar and comfortable. The non-adaptive individual is frightened by the unfamiliar and seeks unsuccessfully to resist it. The science fiction reader is dealing constantly with the unfamiliar and is equally constantly, and successfully, seeking familiar patterns or trends in it.

Thus we can say that science fiction engenders a *positive adaptive attitude* in the minds of its readers. What is more, it furthers adaptation toward change by developing in its readers the elasticity of mind—the sheer imaginative grasp—to enable them to grapple with change constructively. The typical science fiction reader is capable of conceiving many possible futures, each different from the other, and is comfortable dealing with change one step at a time in approaching these possible futures. Critical to constructive adaptive thinking is the sort of elasticity of mind typified by the concept of fairy chess—a modification of the classic game in which an already complex game operating within a rigid framework of rules is made even more mind-stretching by the simple expedient of arbitrarily modifying certain of the rules at the beginning of each game. Thus in fairy chess the players might agree that for the purposes of the game they are about to play the knight will always have the option of moving either two spaces forward and one to the side or three spaces forward and one to the side, thus significantly altering and extending the ordinary power of the chessboard knight. All other rules of the game remain unchanged from the classical pattern. In another game the players might agree that the pawns can move only on the diagonal and capture only straight ahead, directly the opposite of the classical rule. Each such minor modification presents the players with an unfamiliar context that still bears familiar patterns or trends. It also forces the players to stretch their minds beyond the limits of the normal chess game and to cope effectively with the unfamiliar. On a somewhat similar level, the introduction of wild cards into a poker game is a clear extension of the fairy chess concept, and players in such a game are forced with each declaration of a wild card to adjust their thinking with regard to the odds and the values of cards and hands. The adaptive player grapples with such unfamiliarity, learns to calculate the shifting odds, and wins; the non-adaptive player cannot cope with the change, gets his toenails trimmed, and returns to the more familiar classical pattern of the game as quickly as the deal comes his way.

Science fiction readers are constantly playing fairy chess with their reading. The rules are ever-changing. The notion that "nothing is certain" or that "nothing is quite what it seems" becomes familiar and acceptable; the stretching of the mind is challenging and exhilarating, not frightening or demoralizing. Indeed, it is this very mind-stretching quality of science fiction that draws the great majority of its readers to this literature.

Consider for a moment how the rules for adaptation that we have been discussing might apply specifically to a broad and emotionally loaded area of change facing us as individuals in the future: the part that computerization is destined to play in the area of health care. To a non-adaptive the notion of introducing a machine, however complex, into the human equation of health care is anathema—a repugnant and threatening concept. It does not matter to the non-adaptive that the pattern for this change is already set, and that computerization of many areas of medical care is inevitable if universal, expert, and inexpensive health care services of high quality are to be made widely available. In spite of all this the non-adaptive fights doggedly to resist the change. He seeks to retain or to restore the ancient and comfortable concept of human ministration and laying-on-of-hands by the personal, concerned physician, even when it can be demonstrated that today's physician equipped with today's medical knowledge cannot possibly do as good a job using only the classical techniques of medical art and science as he could do by availing himself of modern computerized services. The adaptive individual, on the other hand, sees clearly that computerization offers certain very major advantages and opens the door to immensely more competent, comprehensive, and scientifically thorough health-care services, *together with certain built-in losses and disadvantages as well.* He recognizes clearly that the human physician working in close partnership with the computer can practice a far superior quality of medicine than the physician working alone, but that certain human touches in the doctor-patient relationship, a certain element of human concern on the part of the physician for his individual patient will very probably be lost. The adaptive then says, "How can we avail ourselves of all the advantages while taking the rough edges off the disadvantages?"

For a simple example, consider the matter of medical history-taking. A patient's medical history—a summation of all past illnesses, a discussion of apparent symptoms of the present illness, if any, an accounting of family and social history and a careful review of symptoms relating to the various organ systems—has always been the solid core, the *sine qua non* of accurate diagnosis. This is the patient's opportunity to tell the doctor what is wrong with him, and the doctor knows that somewhere in this mass of data he will find the diagnostic clue he is seeking. Yet the physician approaching a difficult diagnostic problem knows that it is unlikely that he will be able to elicit a *complete* medical history no matter how painstaking and thorough he may be. Such a medical history would require hours of penetrating interview with a patient, hours that no physician has available to spend and that no patient can afford to pay for. Thus at best the physician can take only an abbreviated medical history, and although he may be carefully trained and widely experienced in eliciting useful data quickly, vital bits of information may elude him. The computer, on the other hand, can be programmed to take an utterly exhaustive medical history and, through the utilization of time-sharing principles, can in fact take medical histories from dozens or hundreds of patients simultaneously while each individual patient has the illusion that the computer is devoting its full and entire "attention" to him. What is more, the computer can easily be programmed to flag for the doctor's attention *precisely those items of medical history data that are most likely to help him reach an accurate diagnosis.* In truth, the doctor-computer team can achieve a level of competence and efficiency in diagnosis that no doctor can hope to achieve any other way.

Obviously, then, it can be a very real advantage to the patient to have computerized history-taking facilities available. Despite these advantages, however, the non-adaptive individual objects to the coldness, the impersonality, of the machine-taken history. He does not like the idea of a machine asking personal questions; he does not trust the utilization of the information given to the machine. Early attempts to computerize medical history-taking ran aground on precisely such objections as these; the results were anything but satisfactory and the prospect seemed discouraging. Fortunately a form of science fictional thinking suggested a solution to the dilemma—a solution which is currently under intensive development and appears likely today to guarantee that computerized medical histories will soon completely replace the human physician's history-taking. The solution was simply to make the computer seem "more human" to the patient—that is, to program into it an element of superhuman courtesy, superhuman patience, expressions of consideration and concern—in short, to create an illusion that the computer was very much like a person with a very human concern for the individual patient, even as the patient knew quite rationally in a corner of his mind that the machine really did not and could not have such a concern.

We are not speaking now of some crude punch-card system, or a list of multiple-choice questions for the patient to answer. Rather, we are considering now a highly sophisticated computer carefully programmed for medical interviewing. Such computers are being developed and tested for everyday use even today—computers that have all the time in the world to spend with a given patient, and to which a patient can pour out his heart as the computer listens and listens and listens. Computers of this sort have been programmed to be so warm, so understanding and "human" that patients in test programs have actually preferred them to the living physician. Such a computer encourages the patient to talk about himself; it gently prods his memory; it sympathizes with his discomfiture; it offers him a cup of coffee; it urges him not to feel rushed; if the patient seems tired, the computer suggests a five-minute break and plays pleasant music for the patient while he's resting; it is polite, solicitous, concerned. Indeed, the computer can be programmed in such a way that when a patient has finished giving the computer his medical history the patient knows in his heart that that computer *really cares* about him and his health, and *really wants to help him.*

Of course we know rationally that the machine cannot really care about anything. It is merely doing what it is told to do— but if it is told to act uncannily like a concerned human being, that is precisely what the machine will do. And if, by utilizing such a "humanized" machine to elicit medical histories, we can promise a vastly larger number of sick people a vastly more careful and accurate diagnostic work-up than can conceivably be possible in the traditional doctor's office, with vastly less likelihood of human error, misdiagnosis, or omission, then surely this is a change which offers far more advantages than disadvantages. Indeed, under such considerations, the disadvantages that the non-adaptives fear and rail against may actually seem quite superficial. Once again the reader of science fiction is encouraged, through his reading, to look beneath the superficialities of impending change, to look deeper and to imagine in greater detail the more profound implications which cursory attention or superficial consideration might miss. In short, the reader is encouraged not to fear change simply because it is change, but rather to think more lingeringly on its implications for good as well as for ill.

We can find many examples of science fiction-inspired adaptation to change both in the past and in the present. For example, very few science fiction readers indeed were startled at the launching of the first Sputnik in October of 1957. They may have been frustrated and disappointed that the first such earth-orbiting satellite should have been launched under the auspices of Soviet technology and not our own, but to these readers the accomplishment itself, in all its implications, had been taken for granted as an inevitable eventuality for decades. Science fiction readers, indeed, had gone from the first German buzz bombs of World War II to the orbiting-earth satellite in a single leap. These readers assumed and accepted this eventuality as a matter of time and nothing more; by the time it had occurred they knew and understood the physics and technology behind it; they were fully acquainted with the logistic requirements of such a shot; they had already explored—and largely discounted —the military implications of such an accomplishment (a widespread but superficial and shortsighted concern) and instead were quite accurately recognizing the Sputnik as a first solid step in man's eventual exploration of the solar system beyond the earth. What is more, throughout the subsequent fifteen years that ultimately led to the first moon landing, science fiction readers were continuously far in advance of others in their thinking and acceptance of the implications of the space program. By the time the first exploring party finally did set foot on the moon, science fiction readers had long since been working out the logistics of permanent moon colonies, debating specific techniques for interplanetary exploration elsewhere in the solar system, and were chafing at the apparent physical limitations which seemed to make travel to other star systems something less than practical as a short-term goal.

By the same token, few science fiction readers were seriously startled at the emergence of the uranium fission bomb on the scene in 1945, or at the subsequent staggering technological developments that made fission and fusion weapons such an unparalleled influence on the course of human affairs in the twentieth century. At the time the first fission bomb was released, science fiction readers were already fully aware of the unthinkable quantities of energy trapped in the atomic nucleus. Indeed, in their speculative explorations they had already moved on to consider not only the enormously horrifying military aspects of these power sources, but also the enormously beneficial aspects as well. They had been prepared by their reading to assimilate the concept of nuclear weaponry, on the one hand, and to adapt to the idea of nuclear power as an immensely important energy source of the future on the other hand.

Finally, in a society which to date is still very much shaken and disturbed by the sudden emergence of the computer as a frighteningly competent partner to human endeavor, science fiction readers have moved further than anyone else in their acceptance and adaptation to the idea of a massively computer-oriented society of the future. Here again we are speaking of a change the pattern of which is already set. Perhaps the most revolutionary and far-reaching of all technological changes destined to take place in our society in the next quarter century will be the introduction of modern and sophisticated computer terminals into the individual home, operating on a time-sharing basis with existing telephone lines and television cables for input and output communications. To vast multitudes of people today the computer is still a mysterious and threatening device that seems tolerable at all only at a vast distance from everyday experience. Yet science fiction readers have long since looked beyond the superficialities to recognize the home computer terminal as a vital partner to human endeavor with profoundly beneficial potentials, a device that is destined to become as important and as necessary to the average household as the telephone, the television set, or the electric refrigerator. Already aware of the vast potentials of such a device and experienced through his reading in exploring adaptations of its use to his everyday life, the science fiction reader has already adapted. He may not understand precisely how the computer will function, nor by any means everything that it may be able to do or enable him to do, but he does see it as an inevitable adjunct to his everyday life in the future. And by the time this is reality he will be prepared for its use and able to modify it splendidly to his needs.

As a potent device for enabling man to adapt to change, science fiction today deserves far more serious attention than it has yet received. Yet for all its potential, and for all its growth in popularity, science fiction suffers from one grievous limitation which severely restricts its successful application. This limitation lies in the imaginative fertility, the inventiveness, the emotional and literary maturity, and the insight of its writers. For all its inventive and imaginative *potential*, science fiction has actually proven discouragingly mundane in many areas. Only a few of its writers have begun, most tentatively, to grapple with human beings as human beings rather than as caricatures or stereotypes. Far too much modern science fiction is more empathetic to scientific advance and technological progress than it is to human beings dealing with human problems. Too often science fiction's insights into human psychology are embarrassingly naive, and its grasp of sociological implications are distressingly provincial. And although multitudes of imaginative problems may be explored in science fiction, the solutions all too often fail to stand up to mature scrutiny. Thus, for all its speculation about future societies and future problems, as far as I can recall science fiction has failed to come up with a single new concept for a plausible alternative political or social organization since the utopian novels of the 1920s.

Fortunately, a few writers of science fiction are beginning to grasp this limitation and are seeking to do something about it. But far more writers must join in this effort if science fiction in the future is to have the beneficial impact which it ought to have. If science fiction is to realize its potential as a powerful force for adaptation to change, its writers must vastly expand their horizons and their imaginative and inventive capacities. At the same time, the readers of science fiction must immensely expand the demands that they place upon the science fiction medium. In its present state of evolution modern science fiction is a sleeping giant, a medium of immense but largely unrealized potential. Whether the writers and readers of the future will surmount these limitations and bring about appropriate changes in the medium is a matter for grave speculation today.

Alan E. Nourse, M.D.

Alan E. Nourse was born in Des Moines, Iowa, in 1928, and spent his childhood in Iowa, New York, and New Jersey. After graduating from high school, he started his pre-medical studies at Rutgers in 1945, but these were interrupted by two years in the Navy's hospital corps. In 1948, he returned to Rutgers, where he received his B.S. in 1951, and was admitted to the University of Pennsylvania School of Medicine. After getting his M.D. in 1955, he interned in Seattle, and then devoted two years to freelance writing before entering general practice at North Bend, Washington, in 1958. In 1963, he returned to full-time writing.

His first national publication was a short story, "High Threshold," published in *Astounding* in 1951, and this was followed by some sixty sf stories and novelettes which appeared in virtually all the magazines of the time. In addition, he published a short novel, *A Man Obsessed* (Ace Books, 1954) and wrote *The Invaders Are Coming* (also for Ace) in collaboration. His writing, at the time, helped to pay for his medical education, and of course still reflects a strong medical orientation.

Nourse has published fiction and nonfiction in a great many magazines: *Saturday Evening Post, Playboy, Argosy, Ellery Queen's Mystery Magazine, Better Homes and Gardens, Boy's Life,* and so forth. At present, his work in progress includes (in addition to fiction) two medical guides: *The Ladies' Home Journal Family Medical Guide* and *The Outdoorsman's Medical Guide* (both for Harper & Row) and *The Backyard Astronomer* (for Franklin Watts).

He lives in North Bend with his wife and four children, and also maintains a writing retreat in eastern Washington, where much of his work is done. His hobbies include reading, fishing, hunting, and backpack hiking in the mountains.

NONFICTION

Nine Planets: Astronomy for the Space Age, 1960 and 1970 (Harper & Row) and 1962 (Pyramid Books)
The Management of a Medical Practice, 1962 (Lippincott); with Geoffrey Marks

So You Want To Be a Doctor, 1964 (Harper & Row); one of a series all for the same publisher, including *So You Want To Be a Lawyer; a Scientist; a Nurse; an Engineer; a Physicist; a Chemist; a Surgeon; an Architect,* several of which were collaborations, (various dates)

Universe, Earth and Atom: The Story of Physics, 1969 (Harper & Row)

Venus and Mercury: A First Book, 1972 (Franklin Watts)

SCIENCE FICTION AND JUVENILE FICTION

Trouble on Titan, 1954 (Holt, Rinehart & Winston), 1964 (Lancer Books)

A Man Obsessed, 1954 (Ace Books)

Junior Intern, 1955 (Harper & Row)

Rocket to Limbo, 1958 (Ace Books) and 1957 (McKay)

Scavengers in Space, 1958 (McKay) and 1960 (Ace)

The Invaders Are Coming, 1959 (Ace) with J. A. Meyer

Star Surgeon, 1960 (McKay)

Raiders From the Rings, 1963 (McKay)

The Universe Between, 1965 (McKay)

PSI High and Others, 1967 (McKay)

The Mercy Men, 1968 (McKay)

SHORT STORY COLLECTIONS

Tiger by the Tail and Other Science Fiction Stories: 1960 (McKay)

The Counterfeit Man: More Science Fiction Stories: 1965 (McKay)

Rx for Tomorrow: Tales of Science Fiction, Fantasy and Medicine; 1971 (McKay)

Thomas N. Scortia

Science Fiction as the Imaginary Experiment

"The thing I like most about science fiction," a physicist friend of mine once remarked, "is that all of the experiments work." His rather plaintive remark was prompted by the frustrations of a lifetime of experimental science. It was generated by the anguish of seeing a year's work disappear in pages of meaningless measurements while the elusive quantity he was studying vanished in the complexity and noise level of his instruments. Such frustration was further compounded by those too frequent instances in which someone in Paris would report an observation, using a new technique, and he and his colleagues would labor for months in vain in an attempt to duplicate the observation.

The whole basis for experimental science, of course, is the unquestioned faith that the experiment that works in Paris will work in New York or San Francisco. It is not uncommon, however, that the data gathered in San Francisco is not quite the data gathered in Rome. Indeed, it seems sometimes as if the laws of physical science aren't quite the same in San Francisco and in Rome. This is a problem rather pointedly ignored in technological science fiction. The purely human factor is ignored blithely except in those instances where the author is postulating some psi influence on the experiment. In most stories the experiments, even when they don't work as planned, always yield the same data at any spot in the universe.

Behind all of this concern for the repeatable experiment are two tacit assumptions, almost articles of faith: that the number of factors influencing an experiment are finite and predictable, and that the laws of nature are the same throughout the universe. If this were not so, there would be little point in developing an experimental science. Why bother to codify laws of nature that vary, depending on the location of the experiment or the nature of the experimenter? Yet, there always remains the nagging suspicion that some quality of the experimenter may influence the nature of the data derived from the experiment. If this were so, a natural consequence of this phenomenon would be the realization that the laws of the universe are not truly ordered and subject to rational interpretation. This is the ultimate blasphemy in the hierarchy of faith we call modern experimental science.

Yet, modern physics is aware that there is a quality in nature called randomness, that on an atomic level mechanistic determinism doesn't quite seem to work. The laws of nature that we formulate on the macro-level are in the final analysis statistical laws. The assumption that mathematics may be used to describe the interaction of moieties in the real universe ignores the fact that mathematical formulations of natural laws are, at most, what mathematicians call "curve fitting." A simple formulation such as the Universal Gas Law, for instance, is an approximation that becomes less and less exact as the molecules of the gas become more compacted to the point where their separation is of the same order as the real dimensions of the molecule.

Such a problem rarely arises in science fiction. Here the laws are all idealized and the experiment, when it works, follows rather precise mathematical definitions. Such fictional experiments are always unambiguous, even when they yield results that the scientist-hero did not expect. Implicit in such stories is the humanistic assumption that the laws of nature are amenable to the interpretation of human logic and, more than this, amenable to logical extrapolation. It is this tacit assumption that nature will yield her secrets by the application of logic and extrapolation that underlies all of science fiction, even that science fiction which at first glance appears to be anything but hard-core technological fiction.

There is a tradition in modern physics known as the *"gedankenexperiment,"* a term coined by Heisenberg. The term means literally "thought experiment" and describes a mental experiment in which the physicist imagines a precise set of experimental conditions or sets up a well-defined series of assumptions and tries to infer logically the results of the experiment. That such an exercise in logic has become important to modern physics is understandable when one considers that modern physicists concern themselves with the very stuff of space, time, and energy on such minute or on such grand scales that meaningful experimentation is often beyond the capabilities of mere human experimenters.

The science fiction writer is in the truest sense a professional fabricator of *gedankenexperimenten,* whether he is exploring the narrow consequences of a new scientific or technological development or whether he is considering the broader consequences of a social trend. If he has done his groundwork well in setting up the story, he has presented the reader with the necessary premises on which the story is based. He conscientiously avoids the *deus ex machina* in the same way that the mystery writer avoids introducing the murderer in the last five pages of the whodunit.

The rules of the game are as simple as that. The writer may assume that time travel works in such-and-such a fashion or that antigravity with certain characteristics has been invented or that a given social trend will continue. Once he has established those constraints, he must honorably be bound by the state of human knowledge as it now exists. There are, of course, rare writers who can throw such rules aside and still produce a viable and exciting story. Probably the most notable exception to the rule is A. E. van Vogt, who not uncommonly will suddenly introduce "a little known [and fictitious] physical law" that conveniently allows him to rescue his hero from an untenable situation. (He does this in *The World of Ā* by postulating a Law of

Three-point Similarity so that his hero may simply disappear from the spot where he is about to be killed and reappear in another less perilous place.)

Most writers are reluctant to pull such rabbits out of the hat, however. While a technical *deus ex machina* may be used to solve a plot problem, the reader is either prepared for the appearance of the device by an early plant in the story or the writer takes great pains in developing a sophistic structure that seems technically to justify the device. In my own *Artery of Fire* (Doubleday, 1972), a so-called "black-field effect" is postulated to rid a plasmoid stream, traveling a quarter of the speed of light, of an inconvenient amount of kinetic energy so that the metallic U-235 of the plasmoids may be plated out on the moon.

Such a justification is not always considered necessary when the device has become through frequent use a convention of the genre. Thus, few writers feel it necessary to explain the workings of a time machine as did H. G. Wells in his pioneering novel *The Time Machine,* nor does a writer feel compelled to explain what he means by a "space warp." It suffices that the story may not move without the assumption that faster-than-light travel is possible, and the convention "space warp" solves the problem without slowing the story for a long-winded explanation.

The conventions of science fiction, however, often violate fundamental logic. Time-paradox stories are a case in point. The ultimate exercises in such paradoxes are Robert Heinlein's story "All You Zombies," in which the hero is his own father and mother, and David Gerrold's Random House novel, *The Man Who Folded Himself.* In this latter *tour de force* the hero repeatedly travels through time, altering the future and establishing alternate time lines, in the process having a love affair with his female counterpart and participating in a beach-side homosexual orgy with himself.

However, even in the use of conventions the writer will often wish to define more precisely the conditions of his device, especially when his basic story line proceeds from some peculiar restriction which he places upon himself. As an example, the recent search for the tachyon, a hypothetical faster-than-light particle not excluded by relativistic theories, has resulted in a spate of faster-than-light drives based on this particle as a reaction mass. It has served as a special explanation of time travel. Other writers have faced the contradictions inherent in the postulation of a space warp and have restricted their ships to less-than-light speeds while relying on the relativistic time-dilation effect to allow their astronauts to survive voyages of centuries.

Many of the conventions of science fiction betray basic errors of science. While one may argue that the assumptions in such conventions as faster-than-light travel and time travel are in an area not clearly explored by modern science, other science fiction conventions are clearly violations of known physical laws. Such a violation is found in the often used convention of giant ants or other living creatures expanded beyond their usual size. Here the writer encounters the problems of the square-cube law. Doubling the linear dimensions of the beast will quadruple the cross-sectional area of legs and the absorptive area of lungs and gut while multiplying the mass of the creature by eight times. It becomes obvious that after several such expansions, the beast's legs will not support it while the lungs will not be able to absorb enough oxygen or the gut enough food to sustain the mass of the creature. (This relationship can be illustrated by comparing the simple lungs and digestive tracts of insects with the complex branching lungs and convoluted alimentary canals of humans.)

The closely reasoned technological story has come to be known as a "hard-core science fiction story." Robert Heinlein and Dr. Isaac Asimov have long been the leading adepts of this difficult subspecies. More recently, Larry Niven in *Ringworld* and Frank Herbert in *Dragon in the Sea* and the monumental *Dune* have shown themselves masters of the difficult art of constructing a story line that adheres to an internally consistent technical or social structure. Hal Clement too has been particularly facile in building completely consistent technical structures in such novels as *Mission of Gravity.*

Because the fabrication of such stories is so demanding, it is not surprising that hard-core science fiction is relatively rare.

Few of the newer writers have been rigorously schooled in the sciences, and a great many of them rely on the large body of science fiction conventions for the underpinning of their stories. The writer, however, who fails to account for a basic physical law or who commits a gross error of logic in his scientific extrapolation may still expect cries of outrage in book reviews and in the readers' pages of the magazines.

Technical slips in logic and extrapolation do appear in the best of the hard-core science fiction stories. A surprising example of such a technical *faux pas,* considering the background of the author, is *The Curve of the Snowflake* by W. Grey Walter,[1] the British physiologist. In this rather peculiar novel the author has postulated a weightless vehicle constructed like a three-dimensional version of the snowflake curve. The snowflake curve series is a progression of closed figures with an increasing number of projections. The first in the series is an equilateral triangle whose sides are trisected and a new equilateral triangle constructed in the middle third. This process may continue indefinitely, yield more and more complex figures with subtriangles increasing without limit. Grey's argument for the weightlessness of his vehicle is that it rests on an infinite number of points and, since each of the infinitely small points bears an infinitesimal portion of the weight, the total weight born by the points is itself infinitesimal. Anyone familiar with theory of limits or with the calculus will spot this error immediately since the progression of a function by a summation of infinitesimal increments to a finite limit is the whole basis of the calculus.

Some years ago physicist Dr. Sidney A. Coleman, in a talk before the Northwestern University Science Fiction Society, pointed out an amusing contradiction in the famous Grey Lensman series by Dr. E. E. Smith. The faster-than-light spaceships of the Lensman series are powered by an "inertialess drive," a device that cancels the inertia of a mass and allows instant acceleration or deceleration. (The semantics of the discussion breaks down somewhat at this point since those two words imply the presence of inertia.) Dr. Coleman pointed out that a

1. W. W. Norton and Company, 1956.

truly inertialess starship would be at the mercy of every collision with even a hydrogen molecule, forever bounding from gaseous molecule to gaseous molecule. However, he had a ready solution for navigation, reasoning that the starship captain might reach his destination by applying well-known statistical calculations to predict the mean free path of the starship.

As might be expected science fiction has often shown a remarkable ability to foresee technological developments in its *gedankenexperimenten* even though it has been somewhat less successful in anticipating social and political changes. Science fiction's function as a framework for the imaginary experiment has surprisingly been formalized in such government-supported "think tanks" as the Institute for Defense Analysis and Dr. Herman Kahn's Hudson Institute. This latter institute has for years been engaged in writing scenarios projecting a series of alternate futures, depending on possible developments in the social and political forces now at work. This, of course, is the purist exercise in the science fiction *gedankenexperimenten.*

In the area of space travel, science fiction writers wrote knowledgeably years before about rocket ships and staging principles, space satellites, atomic power, and a host of other present realities. Arthur Clarke predicted the usefulness of communication satellites long before they were a reality. A classic example of technological prediction is Cleve Cartmill's famous story "Deadline" in the March 1944 issue of *Astounding Science Fiction.* Cartmill's description of a fusing technique for a fission bomb which was then under consideration by the Manhattan Project (but later discarded) was based on data from the open literature but nevertheless brought a quick visit by Intelligence to the offices of editor John W. Campbell. (Campbell finally convinced his visitor that there had been no leak and persuaded him to allow publication of other stories on atomic energy by the argument that their sudden disappearance from his pages, where such stories had appeared regularly, might be even more compromising.)

Frank Herbert in *Dragon in the Sea* described a limp plastic balloon that functions as an undersea crude oil barge to be towed by a submarine, raiding foreign offshore oil deposits.

Soon after the appearance of the novel, such a device was perfected and patented in England. Herbert also described a "vampire gauge" that gave instantaneous readings of blood carbon dioxide content. Such a device now exists.

H. G. Wells's 1908 novel *The War in the Air* describes a frighteningly realistic air raid on Manhattan; the villains of the piece are the Germans and the Japanese. (The Japanese pilots fly heavier-than-aircraft in full uniform with samurai swords at their belts.) The most striking part of the novel is Wells's conclusion that the fundamental weakness of air power in war is that, while aircraft may interdict territory to the enemy, they cannot hold ground to become the decisive force in a war. Indeed, Wells's enemy forces retire to strongholds from which they make periodic sorties against the surrounding countryside without effectively curtailing the social vigor of their antagonists. This is a remarkable insight for one writing in 1908, an insight that has not yet been granted to our leading military minds in the Department of Defense.

The list of successful technological predictions is impressive. The list of failures on the other hand is overwhelming. One might suggest that the explanation for the successful predictions is simply that, if one makes enough wildly varying predictions, some of them must invariably come to pass. While this is a tenable hypothesis, particularly since the professional writer must continually generate a variety of extrapolations simply to keep food on the table, the writers with good technological educations score in an improbably high percentage of their stories. The success of these writers in anticipating technological trends is the success of the gifted experimenter contrasted with those with less insight and less·thorough preparation.

The science fiction writer, as we remarked before, is somewhat less successful in his extrapolations of social and political trends. Here he is dealing with alternate futures and must restrict the premises of his extrapolation to a relatively few factors or to even one. The historical process is compounded of many forces with no reliable technique other than intuition for identifying the dominant ones or the significant interactions. Morever, completely unsuspected factors may develop in the future to alter the whole historical or social process.

The science fiction writer then finds himself very much in the same position as the physicist setting up a *gedankenexperiment;* where he is concerned with the social sciences, he is first cousin to the think-tank scientist at the Hudson Institute extrapolating the historical process in a *gedankenexperiment* in a scenario. The physical scientist, the social scientist, the science fiction writer . . . all are concerned with answering the question "what if ?" Each by his own techniques defines an imaginary experiment and through logical extrapolation or interpolation attempts to find one of the possible answers to the question. It is well to note that none of these workers truly believes that he can arrive at a unique and unqualified solution to the question.

The science fiction writer, as are his colleagues, is engaged in a kind of knowledgeable speculation whether it be in describing the results of a simple imaginary experiment or at a higher level of extrapolation describing the consequences of his basic story assumption. It is worth noting that his speculation may be an extrapolation toward an unknown future or an extrapolation directed to the unknown past or may be in the truest sense an interpolation. In the later instance the writer is concerned with alternate explanations for the world as we see it now.

This continued emphasis on the word *speculation* in discussions of science fiction has prompted Robert A. Heinlein to suggest "speculative fiction" as a more meaningful term than science fiction. Unfortunately, such a term would by definition have to include a great deal that is only marginal science fiction such as *Fail-Safe* or *Marooned* and much that is clearly not acceptable under present definitions of science fiction. The single criterion that seems to satisfy the intuitive definition that everyone has of science fiction is the use of the literary *gedankenexperiment.* Extrapolation of any form, particularly linear extrapolation, is a process with well-known pitfalls. The classic examples are amusing to remember: the 1890 projection of U. S. buggy whip manufacture to fantastic levels in 1930; Simon Newcomb's calculations that show quite clearly that no energy source is sufficiently compact to carry a manned vessel to the moon; the list is endless. The buggy whip extrapolation failed because no one predicted the advent of the automobile. Simon Newcomb, who used nitroglycerine in his calculations (nitroglycerine is, coincidently, a major component of the Poseidon missile propellant), failed completely to consider the mass ratio advantages of staging.

Since it is impossible to anticipate all of the factors that will influence an extrapolation, science fiction stories are not intended as exercises in prediction even though, as we have noted, successful predictions have occurred. In many instances they follow the pattern that engineers know as "exploring the boundary conditions of the function." Very often in such an exercise the writer's purpose is intended as social warning or as satire and he clearly shows in his speculation that he does not believe that the situation he describes will necessarily come to pass.

Many of the present-day ecological stories are of this nature. The chief intent of the writer is to develop a logical extrapolation of what will happen if a present trend remains unchecked. It is (to borrow a Heinlein title) an exercise in "if this goes on." In such an exercise the writer follows the fictional situation through its ultimate expansion to the boundary condition of the function.

Two writers who have proven particularly adept at this kind of extrapolation and who have used their extrapolations for social and political satire are Pohl and Kornbluth. In the novels *The Space Merchants* and *Gladiator At Law* they envisioned two situations, one in which advertising had assumed a dominant social position in a world with shrinking sources of raw materials, and one in which urban sprawl brought on by an unregulated building industry had led to a complete deterioration of interpersonal social relations. Both of these novels represent science fiction social *gedankenexperimenten* used as vehicles of social comment. In reading the novels, the audience can identify in distorted form the factors in their own world that have led to the nonviable worlds that the authors postulate.

Since the death of Kornbluth, Frederik Pohl has carried this technique a daring step further into the dangerous realm of the *reductio ad absurdum*. This classical exercise in logic has been used to show the invalidity of an extrapolation by demonstrating that its boundary conditions are patently illogical and absurd. Pohl has developed such extrapolations in, for instance, "The Man Who Ate the World." In seeking to comment on the insanity of the American way of conspicuous consumption, he has envisoned a world in which a citizen is penalized for not consuming and the penalty is a demand for even greater consumption. It is quite obvious that Pohl does not believe his story line. Rather he is concerned with showing the insanity of such thinking carried to extremes. That the story is rich with a manic humor only serves to heighten the satiric qualities of his comment.

Mainstream science fiction has been traditionally a literature of ideas and the science fiction critic has rightly spent a great deal of his time examining the internal logic of the extrapolations in a story. There has been, in the last decade, however, a decline in this attitude that insists that the scientific extrapolations be as logical as possible. Indeed, one writer has advanced the thesis that the sole requirement of the modern science fiction story is that the science "feel right." He proposes that completely sophistic structures are perfectly acceptable, recognizing that to manufacture such "science" requires an endless number of *dei ex machina.*

This trend may well have had its beginning in the writings of van Vogt, whose use of manufactured physical laws has been mentioned. It certainly gained stature and general literary acceptance in the works of Ray Bradbury who cares little about scientific extrapolation in his poetic stories. In the words of critic Damon Knight[2] ". . . he does not even take the trouble to make his scientific double-talk convincing; . . . worst crime of all, he fears and distrusts science."

In recent years the growth of the self-styled "New Wave" has carried this trend still further. The New Wave authors are frequently unschooled in the physical or social sciences and—more —are heirs of the new distrust of the sciences growing in our culture. In science fiction they form the core of an attitude that

2. *In Search Of Wonder,* Advent Publishers: Chicago, 1956.

reflects the general national mood that has embraced astrology, witchcraft, and mysticism.

This is not to say that excellent extrapolative stories may not be written in which such mysticism plays a valid part. Heinlein demonstrated this repeatedly in the forties, particularly in his novella *Waldo*, in which a Pennsylvania hex doctor quite logically solves the breakdown of a universal transportation system. Under John Campbell of *Analog Magazine*, writers developed a bewildering range of speculations about the hidden powers of the mind, and the "psi story" is now firmly entrenched as a part of science fiction.

The writers of the so-called New Wave are not interested in developing closely reasoned extrapolative stories, however. The concept of science fiction as a *gedankenexperiment* is not so much rejected as ignored. The science fiction of this movement is based on the manipulation of the literary conventions we have discussed and concentrates its interest on other story values. The result of this change in emphasis has been, interestingly enough, to develop a body of fiction concerned with strong social and satiric comment. It appears now that there is a merging of these two creative streams to yield still a "newer wave" of writers who can construct valid scientific extrapolations while concentrating on the humanistic and social values explored by the New Wave. Two impressive examples of such novels are David Gerrold's recent *When Harlie Was One* (Ballantine, 1972) and Joseph Green's *The Mind Behind the Eye* (DAW Books, 1972).

The function of the science fiction story as a vehicle for the imaginary experiment has gained new importance with the advent of space flight, atomic power, and a host of other once impossible developments. The remarkable progress in molecular biology since the elaboration of the genetic code has resulted in a number of stories dealing knowledgeably with speculations on the role of DNA and RNA in genetics, and in the biological storage of information. New observations on quasars and other astronomical arcana are quick to find their way into stories and novels. The whole spectrum of ecological endangerment has been the source of some frightening works.

With the rapid growth of technology, rapid changes in the social order are inevitable. Toffler's *Future Shock* (Random House, 1970) has become a source book for many science fiction writers. We are worried about where we are going and the science fiction writer, working within his structured imaginary worlds, offers a variety of scenarios . . . predicting, warning, satirizing. Much of the hard-core science fiction presently written is strongly pessimistic, an indication of the dread with which we face the future.

Yet, face the future we must. It would be foolish to ignore the menace of the future and equally foolish to turn our backs on its promise. Science fiction, quite apart from its entertainment value, has served an honorable function in showing us the alternates and identifying the critical decision points in the historical process. Where science fiction has served as a literary *gedankenexperiment*, it has fulfilled that function well. It has at the least served as a potent catalyst in teaching us the complex techniques for thinking about what will come, and has offered us, with all of its doomsday warnings, a chance to consider alternate courses for our inexorable voyage into the future.

Thomas N. Scortia

Thomas N. Scortia was born in Alton, Illinois, on August 29, 1926, of German and Rumanian parents. He entered the Army at seventeen, served in the infantry in the Pacific Theater in World War II, and went on to a year's occupation duty in Japan. He took his A.B. in chemistry at Washington University in St. Louis and did graduate work in biochemistry at the same school. Returning for a second period of two years' service with the Army (Chemical Corps) from 1951 to 1953, he commanded the last operational Heavy Chemical Mortar Company and later was the assistant commandant of the 3rd Army CBR School as well as being for a short time chief chemical officer of the XVIII Airborne Corps. After discharge he sold pharmaceuticals for a while before returning to a research position in industry. He was assistant manager of the Special Products Division of Union Starch and Refining before leaving to join the newly formed Propellex Chemical Corp. as Director of Research and Development. He left Propellex and he and his wife, Irene, moved to Ashville, North Carolina, when he joined Celenese's Amcel. A year later he accepted a position with United Technology Center, Division of United Aircraft, in Sunnyvale, California, where for nine years he headed the Advanced Propellants Branch.

His first story, "The Prodigy," appeared in *Fantastic Adventures* in February 1954, and he wrote sporadically for some years, publishing a short novel, *The Shores of Night*, in the Bleiler-Dikty *Best Science Fiction Stories of 1956* and a mainstream novel, *What Mad Oracle?*, for Regency in 1960. During this period he published in all but one of the existing science fiction magazines, and left the aerospace industry in 1970 to become a full-time freelance writer, an ambition of many years. Since then, he has sold extensively to both genre and men's magazines as well as to a large number of anthologists. A novel, *Artery of Fire*, was published by Doubleday in 1972, and an anthology which he edited, *Strange Bedfellows*, came out in 1973. Upcoming is an anthology co-edited with C. Quinn Yarbro from Ballantine Books; *Two Views of Wonder*, and a novel, *Endangered Species*, for Fawcett and Random House. He is currently collaborating with Frank M. Robinson on a novel, *The Glass Inferno,* which is due from Doubleday in the spring of 1974. *The Glass Inferno* was recently purchased by Twentieth Century-Fox, Inc., for Irwin Allen (of *Poseidon Adventure* fame) for $400,000 and five percent of the adjusted gross. Movie rights for *Endangered Species* are presently under negotiation with two major companies.

Reginald Bretnor

Science Fiction in the Age of Space

Now that we have (at least tentatively) entered the Age of Space, the future of science fiction, which heralded and defined that age, like our own future, seems full of strange uncertainties and highly arbitrary *ifs*—and therefore doubly interesting because announcing and examining such futures is what so much of science fiction is all about.

However, before attempting to discuss it, I had better define just what *I* mean when I say science fiction, for the meaning of the term has been confused by a plethora of definitions and by the tendency, in recent years especially, to derationalize the field and give it a non-scientific and even anti-scientific orientation. The definition I prefer, and to which I will adhere in this chapter, is a simple one which satisfies me:

> *Science fiction:* fiction based on rational speculation regarding the human experience of science and its resultant technologies.

This is the central fact of science fiction, and if we accept it we can apply it also to *science fantasy* as part of the whole, distinguished from science fiction proper simply by being permitted greater freedom in choosing its bases for extrapolation. (Therefore *sf* is an especially useful term, for it can embrace both without explanation.)

Except for this central fact, then, sf is governed by precisely the same literary and dramatic requirements as any other form of literature. Nor is there any need to quibble about what the word *rational* means; the dictionary definition is quite adequate for our present purposes. While characters in science fiction can think and speak and act as irrationally as story necessities demand, the writer himself cannot afford to lapse into irrationality—for once he indulges in its easy luxuries, he probably will no longer be writing science fiction.

The main point I am making here is that science fiction *cannot and must not* be divorced from science—from an awareness of what the scientific method is and means. One of the stock arguments of those people whom C. P. Snow calls the "literary intellectuals," and who may perhaps better be described as *non-scientific* intellectuals, has always been that cold, inhuman science is somehow at war with everything warm and good and beautiful in man's nature, and that consequently science fiction, preoccupied with cold things and colder forces, cannot touch the human emotions, which must therefore remain the province of the non-scientifically, or anti-scientifically, oriented "serious" writer. This argument is based on a profound misunderstanding, for science is as human as man himself. On this earth at least, man alone has conceived, defined, and employed the scientific method; and the fact that in so many cases he has failed to use its products sanely, or misused them for insanely destructive purposes, cannot be blamed on *science* as an abstraction, or used to justify abandoning it for less rational approaches. It simply dramatizes one of the main dilemmas of modern man: that, individually and collectively, he has not yet come to terms with himself—that he still is fighting the artificial war of "the emotions" against "the intellect," still stating his most urgent problems in inaccurate, confusing, and emotionally abrasive terms, still letting himself be manipulated by unsane individuals for unsane purposes. Were it not for the weapons science and technology have given him to use against himself, the powers provided him to use against other living creatures and the earth, his situation would not be so critical.

As matters stand, divided man cowers in terror, creates new terrors to cower from, and then takes refuge in an irrationality that can do nothing to diminish these terrors or the tensions born of them. He would do better to seek a clearer understanding of the scientific method, of the new areas—parapsychology, for instance—to which, with the aid of new devices and techniques, it is now being successfully applied, and to wait for answers and discoveries which can give him a better understanding of himself and a better map of cause and effect in his affairs.

Here lie the main challenges and perils for science fiction in the immediate future, and here too lie our greatest opportunities. How we meet them, and what we make of them, will depend partly on ourselves, but also very largely on the intellectual environment within which we will have to work. Therefore let us examine that environment as it is now.

The Age of Alienation

The alienation of man is the dominant characteristic of society today, and particularly of Western society, with which here I naturally am most concerned: the alienation of men from other individual men, of citizens from government, of trades, professions, and special interest groups from the community, of cultural and linguistic segments, of races (real or imaginary), and—most terribly—of the young, not just from one another, but from their ambient reality. (Of this last I shall have much more to say.)

Why has it occurred? I would like, very briefly, to propose a theory: that the process started with the application of the scientific method to the problems of the material world, and the resulting—and dramatically profitable—development of those technologies which brought about first the Industrial Revolution, then the wholesale destruction of established aristocracies, and finally, in our own century, the virtual dissolution of any *self-determined* intellectual middle class—in other words, the elimination of any effective counterbalance to political and commercial short-range pragmatism. It did not take long for physical scientists and technologists to acquire great prestige, and to begin threatening the previously unchallenged security of non-scientific intellectuals. The reaction was in part subconscious: Rousseau's idea of the "noble savage," for example, followed by the Romantic Movement early in the nineteenth century, then by the pseudo-Medieval pre-Raphaelites, and finally by that curious intellectual renunciation of the intellect which has, during the past sixty or so years, given us such aberrations as poetry, prose, drama, and painting devoid of definable form or content, and "intelligible" only to an elite of self-sanctified *illuminati*. On a conscious level, the reaction took a rather different form. The non-scientific intellectual hurried, neither to become a scientist nor to acquire a more or less scientific general orientation, but to ape the outward forms of the scientific process and, of course, all of its prestige symbols. Where the physical scientist, of necessity, invented new languages to describe newly discovered and demonstrated processes accurately, the non-scientific intellectual could (and did, and indeed still does) concoct his private languages almost at random, and then proclaim his discovery of new "sciences" as prestigious and momentous as anything out of the laboratory. In its essence, the process closely resembles the attempts of a child or a savage to copy a sophisticated mechanism—an alarm clock, for example. The hands are there; the numerals may even be in the correct order; the sign reads "Master Clockmaker": the only trouble is that it won't work. And here we have the essential flaw in those semi-sciences and pseudo-sciences which we now support so generously not only in our universities but in so many other areas of our lives: they lack the two essential elements of any *applicable* science—reproducible performance and predictability.

A beautiful example of this sort of pseudo-scientific proclamation is the Marxist teleology, which purports to explain man's history, his behavior in the present, and his future all in the ultrasimplistic terms of an early nineteenth century economic theorist. Another is the equally simplistic Freudian formulation.

153 | Science Fiction in the Age of Space

Here, indeed, we have the origins of the conflict between Snow's "Two Cultures," and if we consider one other factor in connection with it, we can begin to understand the reasons for our alienation. The *social* impulse behind scientific discovery has always been an unbalanced one—the desire for profit, monetary or political—on the part of those who, in whatever socio-economic system, have controlled the necessary resources. Hence, scientific research and its technological exploitation have usually been directed into money-profitable or power-profitable (and to a lesser extent into prestige-profitable) channels. The best example, and probably the most important, is that of the mass media, which without science and technology could never have come into being.

Scientific discovery and technological development progress exponentially. (A dramatically simple example is the frightening curve showing the history of artillery: a slow, almost imperceptible climb over several centuries, then a sharply steepening one for several decades, then in the space of a single generation the leap from guns with a maximum range of, say, thirty or forty miles to projectiles capable not just of spanning continents but of bridging the gap between the worlds.) Similarly, social waves stirred up through the increasing application of science-generated techniques and devices must also proceed exponentially, first perhaps as ripples, then as heavier seas, and suddenly —sometimes before we know it—as tsunami.

It took a long time for non-scientific intellectuals, in their eagerness to make their own astonishing discoveries, to demolish the old ideal of a good general Classical education and to substitute for it a narrow and often premature specialization which, they argued, was more "practical" and more "relevant." It took even longer for them to establish their new semi-sciences and pseudo-sciences on the same prestige level as that enjoyed by the physical sciences and traditional disciplines, and to begin that general dilution of the educational process, in the name of progress, which not infrequently produces high school graduates who are quite literally illiterate, and men with higher degrees who have no picture of history, almost no idea of the geography of the world they live in, and no concept whatever of their culture's artistic and literary heritage. Not content with this, they managed to undermine parental authority and prestige without offering any effective substitute.

In this process, that once self-determined intellectual middle class to which I have referred (which included innumerable skilled craftsmen, farmers, and the like in addition to business and professional men) began to find its self-assurance undermined. These were people who, by and large, had always known how to conduct their lives, how to rear their children, how to choose the books they read and the things they needed. They knew that they were part of the community, and were reasonably sure of their status in it. Though they were, like all men, influenced by fashion and by the propaganda of the times, their response to pressures of this sort was not yet Pavlovian. In short, a very high percentage of them were capable of making up their own minds.

Perhaps the best evidence of this is the fact that for about fifty years in the United States, until the late 1920s, they—as a class, if not invariably as individuals—managed to support more than twenty major general magazines which dealt with all those subjects which are of interest to educated, cultured men: *Scribner's*, the old *American Mercury*, the *Bookman, Current History*, the *Dial*, and at one time or another many more. These were magazines designed for the reader, not for the advertiser or "consumer." They published speculative and discursive articles and essays, purchased largely on the open market and therefore representing a wide and spontaneous cross section of American thought. What is left of these magazines today? *Harper's* and the *Atlantic*—and even these have the smell of Madison Avenue manufacture about them. Nothing has emerged to take their place. The academic quarterlies, with minuscule circulations, are read by almost no one but academics.

The disappearance of the serious general magazines and subsequently of the better general slicks—the *Saturday Evening Post, Collier's*, and the *American*, for instance—is of course only one symptom of the massive de-intellectualization and vulgarization of the intellectual middle class by diluted education and by the mass news-entertainment media. The process became readily noticeable in the 1930s and '40s, but its culmination did not come until TV became universal in the early '50s, for television was able to accomplish something no other communications medium could ever do—provide a world of total unreality, a world which demanded *nothing* of the viewer, not even an effort of imagination, and which, *regardless of its quality or content,* inevitably alienated its addicts from the actual world.

This statement may appear extreme, but consider the statistics of TV viewing today. The *average* for every child in the country is more than three hours a day. The average set is on for five and a half hours; these are hours when there can be no meaningful communion between children and their parents, between men and women. In the alienation process, this has been—and still is—the true *tsunami.* Without it, the rupture could never have been so complete—and the counter-culture could never have been born.

This is of critical importance if we are to assay the part science fiction is going to play in the immediate future, for the counter-culture has proven to be eminently salable, and the temptation to go along with its sometimes suicidal irrationalities will be—and indeed already is—extremely strong.

Science Fiction and the Counter-Culture

The voices of the counter-culture have been so strident, its militants and propagandists have employed shock and abrasion to such good effect, and its middlemen—academic, religious, and commercial—have decked it out in so much pseudo-moralistic and pseudo-scientific claptrap, that its real nature has been pretty much obscured.

Stripped of all the McLuhanesque verbiage, there is nothing new about it. Until a few years ago, it was an under-the-counter culture, varying in detail, varying in legality, but essentially the same animal. For centuries, it has thrived in every major slum from Marseilles to Marrakech, from Port Said to Bombay. It is a culture of fear, and of fear-born irrationalities and excesses. It offers us no new discoveries: the age-old flight into "mind-blowing" drugs, the age-old flight into unrestrained and immature sex, the child's resentment of all rules (those governing personal cleanliness, for instance,) his blind faith in his immediate impulse rather than measured judgment, his temper tantrums when he can't have his way, and—in every area of activity— that antithesis of the scientific spirit, the uncontrolled experiment.

Why have so many young people drifted into this? I myself believe that, in their alienation, they are searching not so much for a better and brighter future as for a past they have been denied by adults whom they have really scarcely met. The generations with which we are now concerned—and there are as many generations as there are days in the year—have had the TV unreality from birth, not as entertainment in the traditional sense, *but as a major life activity.* In schools where pupils outnumber teachers by fifty or a hundred to one, they have grown up in what is essentially a children's society, and this has continued in their colleges and universities, where dormitory living is now increasingly the rule, and where too many professors, playing their "publish or perish" pecking order game, leave the greater part of the teacher-pupil relationship to often immature teaching assistants. For many kids, the experiences and associations which used to lead to adulthood are no longer available. Practical lessons in civilized survival, civilized competition, civilized restraints, adult resiliency and adaptability— children seldom can learn these from other children, and young adults cannot mature fully unless they do learn them, unless the survival skills and the necessary graces of their culture are communicated to them in their earliest years by adults.

And they know it. The counter-culture is retrogressive. It copies not just the pre-adult behavior of the child and the savage, but even the superficial trappings of past generations and preliterate cultures. It has created no new styles, not even in its clothing. Some it has taken from nineteenth-century Europe, others from Edwardian England, others still from the scrap heap of the 1920s. This is true also of its poses and transient beliefs. In Berkeley, at the main entrance to the University of California, all a boy needs is a beaded headband and a peyote button to be an instant medicine man. Give him a grubby loincloth and he's an instant *guru*. By wearing clodhopper boots and a Dogpatch hat, he can become a hardy mountaineer; and a Boer War tunic, a string of trade beads or an *ankh*, a ponytail and a pair of Viking braids can transmute him into something adequately archaic but never previously assembled in pop art. Even his music is unoriginal—fake folk, pseudo-African, or just plain noise.

The best way to judge the counter-culture is in the measurable statistics of how men and women treat each other. These people claim that they are "liberated," that they have shaken off the repressions of a cruel society and an evil past; they claim that they are animated by love of all men and veneration of the earth. If that is so, why is it that among them unwanted pregnancies, cases of VD, hepatitis, and the dirt-borne diseases, drug freak-outs and psychoses, suicides, and crimes of violence are far more common than ever before, and are still increasing? Why are they not rising instead among the repressed Mormons or the unliberated Amish?

Because behavior is a better standard by which to judge people than any number of pronouncements, I frankly cannot see how the counter-culture can help science fiction, for it is nothing more than the unscientific alienation of human beings carried to an unsane extreme. It can provide us with no ideas we could not get elsewhere. (It has not even managed to come up with any coherent scenarios for the new world it is proposing.) It can almost certainly produce no science fiction writers of any stature—not if the field is to retain any of the rationality of the scientific method or any of the discipline of literature and the arts. Its one service to us can be to provide material for extrapolation and for satire—for stories like Fred Pohl's "If All the World Were Like Berkeley," and Clancy O'Brien's "Generation Gaps," (*Analog*, September 1972).

And there is always the question of what it may turn into:

It's a new cult—the abandonment of civilization, poverty and nature, peace and beauty, beggars for the love of God. . . .

A reference to the hippie segment of the counter-culture? No, a description of the *wandervögel,* those alienated youngsters who, after World War I, roamed the German countryside —destined to form a nucleus of Hitler's storm troops. Philip Gibbs, who wrote it in the early 1920s, in a story prescient with anxiety, put those words into the mouth of a Berlin waiter.[1]

The counter-culture appears to be moving in a similar direction, for the search of alienated youth is not only for a past denied to them but for a lost or never-known authority. The counter-culture's uglier involvements—with slum underworlds, with demoniac cults, with sadistic and rapacious street and motorcycle gangs, with far-out terrorists and deftly organized and managed "urban guerillas"—all point in this direction. So do the increasing adulation of "the thoughts of Mao Tse-tung" and the continuing influence of Mr. Marcuse.

These are matters with which science fiction writers should be deeply and rationally—never hysterically—concerned, for science fiction cannot thrive in any atmosphere of fear or repression, whether it be imposed by revolutionists or by an established society trying to prevent revolution.

I have, of course, been dealing in great generalizations. What are the parameters of the counter-culture? Where does it begin and end? In treating it as a coherent whole, are we not, perhaps, being unjust to innumerable individuals half in, half out of it? I think not. The Egyptian army, in 1967, probably included many men as brave as lions, eager to give their lives for Nasser and whatever else they thought they were fighting for. If so, they failed to stem the panic-stricken flight of the majority— and it is with majorities that we most frequently must deal, not with the odd exceptions to the rule. The fact that science fiction has many readers—and indeed many intelligent and inquiring readers—within the counter-culture does not and cannot outweigh that culture's general influence, which is essentially anti-

1. Philip Gibbs, *Little Novels of Nowadays.* New York, 1924.

scientific and anti-rational, and which can only deepen the false split between the "intellect" and the "emotions" dividing modern man against himself.

Even without the counter-culture and its irrationalities, the world is going to be a complicated enough place for science fiction writers during the next decade, for we are going to have to cope with—among other things—the new and curious fact of academic recognition. Twenty years ago, when I edited the symposium *Modern Science Fiction, Its Meaning and Its Future* more than a hundred reviews of the book came to my attention; of these, the few that were academic consisted of little more than sneers at science fiction and at the hacks who allegedly were writing it. Now suddenly the academic world, prompted perhaps by the undeniable fact that men have landed on the moon (and possibly by a growing shortage of materials for the Ph.D. mill) has not only discovered our watering place but is splashing around in it with all four feet. Personally, I think that this will prove to be a somewhat mixed blessing.

The Academic Involvement

Were the academic involvement confined to those dedicated teachers who delight in practicing what is one of the most creative of professions, and whose critical publications, if any, are of secondary importance to them, it would indeed be a blessing. However, it will not be so confined, for at the other end of the academic spectrum, the minority of critical mandarins have already, with considerable *éclat*, defined the role which they intend to play.

Like so much nonscientific and pseudo-scientific "research," academic literary criticism has become very largely a word game, a game of inconstant perspectives and uncertain, shifting values. Often, because many careers depend on it, it is a spiteful, cutthroat game. Even more often, when its play becomes a substitute for teaching and its ploys a substitute for learning, it is a foolish and wasteful one.[2] The dramatic experience, whether on stage or on the printed page, must be *whole* for the audience or the reader. To succeed fully, it must touch and involve the *whole* man, "intellectually" *and* "emotionally." Where it does indubitably succeed—in the Greek tragedians, in Shakespeare and Molière, in Tolstoi and Ibsen and Thomas Mann—it does precisely that. A cultural matrix may be needed for it to have its full effect, but even this is minimal. It is universal. Shakespeare, for example, translates and has been translated into splendid Japanese. Because we are all similarly conceived and born of woman, we all have something of Oedipus and Electra in our souls. If we are at all intelligent and sensitive, we also are, in some small part, Hamlet and hunchbacked Richard and Anna Karenina and the brothers Karamazov, Don Juan and Don Quixote and the Ancient Mariner. We really need no tortuous explication either to feel the impact of what the authors have conveyed or, on the "whole man" level, to understand it. The reader of Jane Austen or the Brontës can derive no benefit from a study, no matter how cleverly footnoted, of (say) their putative toilet-training. Nor can he really profit from a psychological exploration of the subconscious drives of Her-

---

2. In his wise and challenging work *The American University, How It Runs, Where It Is Going* (Harper & Row: New York, 1968), Jacques Barzun very pertinently says:

> Reconsider research, and benefits to the university will include: less general anxiety, less preoccupation with money, fewer arrangements— to interrupt teaching and go away, to get research assistance, to get printed, etc.; and further: smaller subsidies to university presses for useless books serving only the author's claim to more salary; libraries and journals relieved from the pressure of having to cope with what comes out of the foundry under forced draft: we are perishing from publishing and must keep down that which is premature and that which is artificial.
>
> "But if a man doesn't produce, how do we know he's a scholar?" Answer: "How do you know now from reading titles?" In the end, you take the fact on faith from close observers who know the man. They could just as easily tell you even if he never published a line. Teachers in college and university should be scholars. But scholarship and publication are not identical. Of the two, higher education should prefer scholarship. It is not as visible as jaundice, but it is often far more visible in one man's lecture than in another man's book. The teaching scholar should be able to say what Loup de Ferrieres wrote to Charles the Bald: "I desire to teach what I have learned and am daily learning."

man Melville or Edgar Allan Poe. It would be more to his enrichment if his general education made him familiar with the courtesies and cruelties of early Nineteenth-Century England, of how the sea and sweat smelled in the forecastle of a New Bedford whaler, or even simply how it felt, dying, to write by candlelight in the raw cold of a New York winter.

The psychoanalytical illusion of penetrating and exhibiting the soul of man is strong meat for those egos who would magnify themselves by doing so. Put into practice by "qualified" professionals—isn't the going rate now fifty dollars for the fifty-minute hour?—it can claim virtually no predictability and can guarantee no result.[3] In other words, in great measure it is a put-on—a very prestigious and profitable put-on, but a put-on nonetheless.

What are we to think, then, of its employment by people who are, at best, sketchily trained in its disciplines, and whose understanding has been further muddled by the fashions and rivalries of contemporary formal criticism?

Not many years ago, when the so-called New Wave was first emerging, science fiction was given its initial taste of this sort of thing. Suddenly, with all the awed excitement of a small boy's

3. In a curious and interesting book, *The Mind Game, Witchdoctors and Psychiatrists* (New York, 1972), E. Fuller Torrey of the National Institute of Mental Health, on pp. 108–9, has this to say of:

> . . . therapists in our culture who are thought to employ techniques based on modern science.
> The truth is not even close; it is a quantum jump away. The techniques used by Western psychiatrists are, with few exceptions, on exactly the same scientific plane as the techniques used by witchdoctors. If one is magic then so is the other. If one is prescientific, then so is the other. The only exceptions to this are some of the physical therapies, in particular some drugs and shock therapy, which have been shown in controlled studies to be effective in producing psychiatric change. None of the psychosocial therapies has been so shown. In fact efforts to show this— so called "outcome studies"—have been notoriously negative. . . . Psychiatry is just as scientific—or prescientific—in rural Nigeria or the mountains of Mexico as it is in New York or San Francisco.

To do Dr. Torrey justice, he is not saying this in criticism of his profession, but as part of his argument that "indigenous therapists"—shamans, witchdoctors, *curanderos,* and the like—should be accredited and admitted to psychiatric practice, at least within their own cultures and subcultures.

discovery of his genitals, critics in the field itself solemnly proclaimed its symbolisms: now every rocket was a penis; the firing of each booster stage an orgasm; and every monster-haunted cave on an alien planet Mommy's womb.

Let us assume, for fun, that they were right.

What of it?

If such mean, infantile comparisons do indeed reveal the wellsprings of our creativity, why—once they are recognized—must we labor them? What is so impressively profound in dredging up, and capering over, our own pre-adult drives? Why not accept them, integrate them into a more mature synthesis of our survival struggle in the world and in the universe, our goals and purposes, our relations with our fellow men—and then, as working artists, let them recede into the background? Any artist, unless we abandon all traditional definitions of what this means, must be like the accomplished fencer, the finished horseman. The fencer must practice and absorb all those exercises of cut, thrust, lunge, and parry which over several centuries have proven their effectiveness. The horseman similarly must understand his aids: reins, legs, weight, and voice. The sculptor and the painter must first master the chisel and the brush, must learn the texture of hard stone and the way colors combine on the palette. But once any of them have attained these masteries, then their preoccupation must be with what they have in hand: the bout with sabre or *épée*, the steeplechase or polo game, the statue or the portrait. Any underlying reasonings, any underlying drives, must be subordinated into the act of skill, the act of art, the act of love. In all this, the role of the doer's intellect must be an *editorial* one, monitoring the act the whole man is performing while itself remaining, not uninvolved, but—as far as possible—unswayed and undisturbed.

Nothing is so destructive of the arts as self-consciousness in the artist—which cripples both intuition and spontaneity—and there is no better way to render him self-conscious than to over-emphasize the importance and value of hidden drives and occult meanings, real or imaginary. (In science fiction, the miserable result—now unhappily too common—is the sort of story that makes the sophisticated reader close the book with the comment, "Sorry, chum, your Psych. 1-A is showing.") Yet these meanings and motivations are the critic's stock in trade. He is compelled to seek them out and find them, and indeed often to invent them. They, and his supposed ability to sniff them out, put him above the commonalty; and when the commonalty accepts his own appraisal of himself, as it does now, he acquires power and status, and becomes another middleman—or perhaps, on the academic level, we might say middle-mandarin.

The rise of middlemen to positions of power over the arts began with the Industrial Revolution, when a culturally insecure newly rich started to displace a more self-assured aristocracy and upper middle class as art buyers. These people needed guarantees of quality and worth, which dealers and "authorities" were only too ready to provide. This started the alienation of the working artist from the community, and gave rise to the now common fancy that artists are incapable of accurate self-evaluation, and need appropriately anointed "experts" to judge them and even to manage their affairs.[4] The pretty notion of the artist working and starving in his garret as a necessary part of the creative process not only served the middleman's purposes, but was also "romantic" enough to obscure the injustice and ugliness of the reality.

The middle-mandarin may protest that, unlike the more commercial middleman, he doesn't get a direct rake-off from the artist's earnings. Nevertheless, his need to minimize the importance of the working artist—at least until that artist is sufficiently well known to be profitably exploitable—is just as great. As matters stand in the United States today, it is quite commonly accepted that only *great* or *famous* writers deserve a decent living, and that "hack" writers merit no support at all;

4. An anecdote from my own experience illustrates this very nicely. In the early '50s, I sold a story to the quarterly of a large and very rich Texan university. It wasn't too bad a story; at least it made Martha Foley's "Distinguished" list. I was paid the princely sum of twenty dollars—half a cent a word. A year or so later, I requested what I thought would be a routine reversion of reprint rights, and was informed that, if I would tell them who was publishing the anthology, and who was editing it, and give them some idea of its contents, they would if they saw fit release the necessary rights because—I quote verbatim and the italics are my own—they *considered themselves trustees for the author!*

I have heard this voiced by hack professors, hack lawyers, and (God save us!) even a hack proctologist.

The attitude is reflected very clearly in the academic involvement with mainstream literature. For years, the mandarins have cried their deep concern for poetry in the Philistine society, for the short story as an art form, for the "serious" writer and especially the serious *young* writer; and there always seems to be money available for new university reviews, usually expensively produced, in which to publish cries and criticisms.

But all these reviews together—and we have a regiment of them—*in any year spend less than one professor's salary to purchase the work of poets and short story writers.* Most of them either pay nothing whatsoever or pay in a few free copies. A very high percentage appropriate all rights. A bare half dozen offer poor pulp rates. This is indeed a magpie charity.

What has happened to American poetry since these people made it so much their personal province? To a great extent, it has become formless, unreadable, and unintelligible; and a nation which, when it was much smaller and poorer, always supported at least some poets now can support none at all—except for an odd tame specimen or two kept as showpieces on campuses.

What has happened to the "serious" short story since this involvement? First, on one aesthetic pretext or another, it was devitalized into the non-story: deliberately over-sensitive slices out of the meaningless lives of utterly uninteresting people, invariably larded with the toothsome obscurities so dear to the interpretive middleman.

And what is going to happen to science fiction now? Certainly, *as a group,* the academic mandarins can contribute little or nothing to the field. However, what they can *do* to it, and especially to our younger writers, is quite another matter. One can only hope that among them there will be enough men with the prudence and good taste to walk carefully and considerately over ground they have not tilled and crops they have not cultivated.

Dedicated teachers, and genuinely creative writers on college faculties, are of course something else again. Certainly, no one can do anything but welcome their enthusiastic interest and participation, for from now on much of the responsibility for maintaining the artistic and intellectual integrity of science fiction in the Age of Space, the Age of Alienation, the Age of Crisis will rest upon their shoulders.

Science Fiction and the Working Writer

Professional science fiction writers—and by this I mean those who either write full time or sincerely wish they could—face a strange situation as we enter this new age. For years, they have been prophets without honor. Now, in the dazzle of new recogniton, they still run the risk of receiving honors without profit.

As the Science Fiction Writers of America managed to convince a number of publishers a few years ago, the field depends very heavily on the professional for its steady flow of printable material. Without him, it never could maintain its quality or more than a fraction of its present volume. Yet today, despite a growing readership, he still confronts a world where the average working writer is grossly underpaid, and where in order to make a bare living he frequently has to work sweatshop hours. Let us consider the economics of writing science fiction, and then estimate the effect the market has on the producer and the product.

The would-be professional writer enters a world where, as far as he is concerned, the tail wags the dog. The topless-bottomless dancer in a Barbary Coast night spot makes her few hundred a week by entertaining a few hundred drunks for a few hours; the dentist and the attorney and the plumber do not have to work on masses of humanity to gain a livelihood. But—with very few exceptions—the writer must be a mass producer and mass entertainer before he can hope to be financially successful; he must become a product that can be packaged and peddled to the millions. My first short story, "Maybe Just a Little One" —it was sf, by the way—I sold to *Harper's*. It was reprinted in *Fantasy and Science Fiction*, translated into French and Spanish, and anthologized in *Best From F. & S.F.*, which also went into a Science Fiction Book Club edition. At a very conservative estimate, it has certainly been read by half a million people, and as I have never met anyone who didn't enjoy it, I think I can fairly assume that it has given the world at least a hundred thousand individual hours of fun, and possibly a good deal more. My earnings from it total just under $360—about as much as an anesthesiologist makes using other men's techniques to put one or two patients to sleep for an afternoon.

I cite this story simply to illustrate the fact that not only pulp writing is underpaid, and that literary level has no bearing on this economic law—a law which, by the way, operates much more harshly now than it did in, say, the '20s, when the break-even point in sales for the hard-cover publisher was much lower than it is today and the number of magazines buying freelance fiction much, much higher.

The effect on the professional and would-be professional is that, generally speaking, only the mass-producer can survive (which tends to militate against careful craftsmanship and to discourage the less prolific writer, regardless of his ability). As a consequence, great numbers of young people, who should at least get a fighting chance to write for a living, never get to first base—for the more the market becomes a mass-market, the more important becomes the middleman, and the harder it is for the new writer to break in. Television, which has pulled most of the rungs from the new short story writer's ladder, has not become an open freelance market; its producers will almost never even read material unless submitted through an agent. This is true also of the motion pictures. And, of the surviving magazines, an increasing number are following the practice, though fortunately it has not yet spread to the sf and mystery fields.

Actually, the writer's best break today is given him by the standard hard-cover publisher. Royalty rates are usually at least fair; contracts can be negotiated, and the distribution system is by no means as stupidly wasteful as the paperback publisher's. As a real money-maker for writers, the "paperback renaissance" is very much a myth. The average paperback original (at, say, fifty thousand words) makes its author roughly twelve hundred dollars. This means that, limited to this market, a man who writes no faster than Thomas Mann would, if he sold every line, come out with about four thousand dollars for his year's labor. Of course, there are exceptions. There are paperback houses that do much better for their authors—but there are others who do worse. And there are paperback editions that sell and sell and sell, and keep on selling. But again, it is not the exceptions that make the rule.

Conservative estimates, made after careful surveys of the subject, indicate that today more than three hundred college-level courses in sf are being taught in the United States. Other studies show in colleges and high schools together the courses now number about a thousand. Granting all this, and averaging out differences in pay and in the number of courses in instructors' schedules, in the colleges alone we now have probably the equivalent of at least one hundred full-time professors' salaries spent on teaching science fiction, at roughly $12,500 a year.

There aren't fifty science fiction *writers* in the country averaging $12,500 a year.

It should not be necessary for writers of real competence either to turn out a million words annually or to teach or to dig ditches on the side to keep going—any more than it is necessary for teachers or electricians or cocktail waitresses or accountants to dig ditches; and it should be a prime concern of the academic friends of writing and the writer to do everything in their power to remedy the situation. One way would be to revive the market for short stories by finding buying funds for academic magazines. If existing university and college reviews could each secure between five and ten thousand dollars a year for the purchase of short stories, and then pay approximately what the *Atlantic* pays now, the old freelance market for short stories would very largely be restored—and if that market's unprejudiced impersonality were restored with it, then the new writer's most important ladder would have a lot of its rungs back again.

How much would such a program cost a year? Less than any foolish Federal project to "rehabilitate" a big-city street gang. Less than McGraw-Hill paid Mr. Irving as an advance on his fraudulent biography of Howard Hughes. Infinitely less than it costs to keep up the pretense of educating the semi-literate in one of those unfortunate colleges now required by law to accept and keep *any* high school graduate for a year or even two.

Ways must be kept open for new writers to become professionals, and for professionals to maintain themselves, for the challenges and problems and opportunities presented by science fiction in the Age of Space will, more than ever, demand the maturity and expertise of the professional. Contrary to present popular belief, genius cannot be manufactured by technicians or institutions; its appearance, in any field and at any period, is very much a function of available patronage and of the number of individuals of seemingly average talent given the opportunity to work freely and independently. In science fiction especially, these men and women will require, not just a market, but one paying enough so that, instead of having to become high-pressure word machines, they can have leisure to read and think and talk, to build their individual backgrounds for interpretation and synthesis. They will have to come from many different fields, because of the natural complexity of science and technology, because of the lack of a new synthesis to replace our almost vanished general educations—and because this diversity of knowledge and experience has always been a major factor in the enrichment of a literature. They will have to be as various as the world they live in.

The Challenge to the Writer in the Age of Space

When the first Sputnik went into orbit, and when the first astronauts landed on the moon, almost every sf writer was, I think, asked the silly question: "Well, they've caught up with you—where do you go now?"

The answer, naturally, was : "We just keep going."

The progress of science and technology—as long as it receives nourishment—is open-ended and exponential, and this applies also to science fiction, which exists by leaping beyond scientific fact and theory. When and if we encounter our first space-faring alien race, science fiction writers will lose nothing—except perhaps a temporary divergence of reader interest—and will gain immeasurably. Regardless of whatever discoveries may be made, this will continue to be the case. The only danger to progress in the field lies in the intrusion of the semi- and pseudo-sciences—in the Leninization of science fiction, for example.

Our greatest opportunities now lie, not in the overemotional rehashing of themes already long-established, but in reexploring, reevaluating, and stating them anew, as well as in devoting more attention to those we have generally ignored. Consider the recurring theme of *war*, on this earth and in space. Where war on earth has been concerned, by far the greatest emphasis has been on the "what ifs" of utter horror. Stories of this sort have, only too frequently, been utterly realistic—and utterly neurotic. But how many writers, comparatively, have even attempted to explore science fictional alternatives, detours away from Armageddon? A few only, mostly in hard-core sf; certainly not enough. Nor have we had enough explorations of the inevitable side effects of super-weapon development, where it is mathematically demonstrable that these weapons not only will continue to increase in power and effectiveness, but must also inevitably become simpler to produce, cheaper, and more generally available. Within the past two generations, we have seen more than one madman ruling a great nation. What of the innumerable "sovereign nations" now surrounding us, many of them just "emerging" out of savagery into military dictatorship? What of independent terrorists and criminal groups? "Disarmament" isn't going to solve that problem, because you *can't* disarm a technological society, or individuals in a technological society, *even if they want to be disarmed.* We have a fertile field for science fiction here.

War in space, still very much with us, is quite another matter. Future all-out war on earth has generally overwhelmed the minds of writers with its weaponry, but in writing of space-war, the tendency has been to underestimate, not the development of cataclysmic weapons, but their effect on warfare itself. The weapons are developed and described, but they are almost never *realized* in the writer's mind, and so are automatically absorbed into the military behavior patterns with which he is familiar. Therefore we still find World War I aerial dogfights being reintroduced as individual combats between pilots of spaceships armed with planet-busters and moving at speeds only computers can cope with. We also keep encountering the persistent nitwittery of sword-armed space-farers—as though any race measuring its energies in star-travel terms would keep on lugging around weapons almost as primitive as stone hatchets—and of sword-and-spear-armed natives successfully repelling invaders from the stars. This sort of thing is plausible only when the board, the pieces, and the rules are artificially and logically set up and adhered to, as in Jerry Pournelle's recent *A Spaceship for the King* and Poul Anderson's delightful *The High Crusade*. But when it comes to hordes of mounted barbarians charging triumphantly against spacemen armed with laser weapons and the like—uh-uh. Anyone doubting it would do well to read a 1964 study on weapon lethality prepared for the United States Army.[5] The values it gives are illuminating:

Weapons	Lethality Index
Sword, pike, etc.	20
World War I machine gun	12,730
French 75-mm gun	340,000
World War II medium tank	2,203,000
One-megaton nuclear airburst	661,500,000

We can go on from there.

Actually, there is one aspect of war in space which has not received too much thoughtful treatment in sf, and that is whether races who have not learned to control their own destructive drives can even make it into space, let alone found empires and fight wars, either against themselves or against extraterrestrials. Project the curve suggested in the study, consider it in the light of what the world is today, and it becomes

5. Historical Evaluation and Research Organization, "Historical Trends Related to Weapon Lethality," 1964.

obvious that unless solutions are found to some of our domestic problems, and that right speedily, the Age of Space for man may die before it can be properly born.

Another possibility to be considered is that martial races which have not, as we have, been disunited may already have made it into space, but here again we come up against the same rule on a different plane—can rival warring races, considering the energies at their disposal when they attain interstellar capability, survive even in space against each other?

In any case, the argument would appear to be undeniable that it is to man's interest to unite, to make common cause against any and all apostles of disunion, Left against Right, race against race, religion against religion, or whatever. We almost certainly will not make it into space warring and divided, and if by some miracle we make it anyhow we'd better be united to meet whatever may await us there. Here we have one of the most important sf themes today—a theme great enough to challenge any writer, and any number of writers: *how can man survive against himself?*

And this, in turn—because our problem is so much a problem of our own confusions—leads directly into another area we have inadequately treated: that of the communications failure, the understanding failure, the world-view failure, that of semantics, of what we mean when we make noises or put marks on paper.

Science Fiction and the Problems of Meaning

Forty years ago, Count Alfred Korzybski published *Science and Sanity, An Introduction to Non-Aristotelian Systems and General Semantics,* a profound, revolutionary, and seminal work which has had considerable influence, not only on scientists but on science fiction writers—Robert Heinlein and John W. Campbell, for example. (S. I. Hayakawa's *Language in Thought and Action,* a useful introductory simplification of Korzybski's formulation, is more widely known and available, but is not an adequate substitute for the original text.)

The essence of Korzybski's system is that the languages we use in daily intercourse are essentially primitive in structure, that they perpetuate false-to-fact concepts, and that they literally dictate contra-survival behavior. An analogy may be made to a world map—let's say Ptolemy's—that has been added to, altered, subtracted from, but never fundamentally revised. Were we to rely on such a map, we'd have one hell of a time trying to find our way from Patagonia to Peoria—it would be as difficult as it is now to find our way from hatred and suspicion to love and trust, from destructive anarchy to creative order. Korzybski pointed out that, for this reason, the developing sciences had been *forced* to invent entirely new maps—new languages (including the mathematics) designed to describe phenomena accurately. He emphasized the fact that, while all languages abstract only *certain* data from the reality with which they purport to deal, unconsciously their users confer on them an *allness* which is not only delusive, but psychologically crippling. He devised and described techniques by which individuals could train themselves to become conscious of abstracting and to avoid confusing orders of abstraction.

A very simple example will suffice. The word *spider* refers to any individual specimen of an entire order of creatures, the *arachnida*, the majority of which are harmless, some of which are useful, and only a few of which (at least in the West) are in any way dangerous to man. Yet to many individuals it is a word of fear, triggering instant and usually nonfunctional reactions. We don't have to look far for other, even sadder samples: words like *nigger, Fascist, imperialist, wop, pig, Jew*—the list is endless.

The result of a study of Korzybskian techniques is to de-fuse many of these words, and to expose the falseness of the intellectual-emotional meanings they convey—and of those terrible psychological push buttons manipulators of men have used throughout man's history. It is, I think, no exaggeration to say that anyone who has really worked at these techniques can scarcely read a political speech again without translating most of it into *blab-blab-blab-blab-blab*. Or listen to the hard-sell advertising of the mass news-entertainment media. Or take the glossolalia of the pseudo- and semi-sciences very seriously.

Naturally, the Korzybskian formulation was greeted with considerable antagonism by many non-scientific intellectuals, and particularly by those whose careers had been built on what he would have considered the unsane use of language—for few men are big enough to acknowledge even the possibility of error when their prestige is founded on it. Korzybski's influence, in the academic community and among intellectuals generally, while by no means negligible, was never able to realize its initial promise. However, at this juncture in human affairs, science fiction writers especially would do well to become familiar with it, for it is the only formulation, at least to my knowledge, offering us any really sane, *uninvolved* approach to those problems of meaning which are letting us tear ourselves apart—and which could follow us into space if we succeed in getting there.

Of course, they have already done so in our fictional adventures and encounters among the stars, limiting our imaginations where alien beings and civilizations are concerned just as they limit our imaginations with regard to man's affairs. They will not be easy for any of us to cope with, either in the personal dramas we present or the social frameworks which must contain them. But if more of us at least make the effort, our scope will be extended vastly—and so, perhaps, will be our contribution to mankind.

In his chapter for this symposium, Alan Nourse takes science fiction to task for its failure, in recent years, to invent new and alternative societies; and it is true that generally writers simply transpose old orders and old anarchies into new settings, usually not even endowing them with new insanities. It is as though our self-confinement in the stockade of our languages has made it almost impossible for us to imagine societies other than those evolved around their unconscious structural matrices; for almost always, where any truly alien society or truly new society is concerned, we take refuge in the explanation that its way of thinking or of doing things is simply unexplainable in human, or in contemporary human, terms.

Years ago, I made a very simple attempt at a departure from

this pattern in a short story, "High Man, Low Man," published in *Beyond* (May 1954). It concerned a society of intelligent beings evolved, not from tree-climbing ancestors, but from earth-digging creatures similar to badgers. Their whole survival drive had been *downward*, for at bedrock they were safer from their enemies than anywhere. Consequently, their social value-system was the reverse of ours. In their history, slaves had been the highest social class; their Emperor had always been addressed as *Your Abysmal Lowness.* They plumbed the bottomless depths of science, philosophy, and ethics. They fell to success, and rose from grace. If they admired one of their fellows, they said that they looked down on him, and called him the lowest of the low. Their stockbrokers, confronted by a market crash, didn't jump out of their office-building windows; they slammed their elevators up into the roof.

A light and rather inconsequential story, it proved disquieting to an ed. or or two—probably those who had worked hard to rise in the world. One of them (not a science fiction editor) returned it with an agitated note which she addressed to *Dear Miss So-and-so*—her own name.

I mention it here only as an example and a possibility. How would the world look to beings dwelling in their own carapaces on the ocean floor, seeking refuge in caves and crevices? What social value-gradients might they not adopt? For that matter, how do porpoises express such concepts as "superior" and "inferior," both of which derive from the basic physical fact that the chap higher in the tree could often brain his enemy without being hurt, or catch his dinner without it seeing him?

These are simplicities. The science fiction exploration of variant meanings and symbologies will, in many areas, go far beyond them. The first issue of *Vertex* contains an article by Larry Niven, a highly original and beautifully reasoned article, "The Theory and Practice of Time Travel," in which the semantics of time travel are considered:

> The English language can't handle time travel. We conclude that the ancestors who made our language didn't have minds equipped to handle time travel. Naturally we don't either; for

our thinking is too dependent on our language.

As far as I know, *no* language has tenses equipped to handle time travel. No language on Earth. Yet.

But then, no language was ever equipped to handle lasers, television, or spaceflight until lasers, television, and spaceflight were developed. Then the words followed.

If time travel were thrust upon us, would we develop a language to handle it?

We'd need a basic past tense, an altered past tense, a potential past tense (might have been), an altered future tense, an excised future tense (for a future that can no longer happen), a home base present tense, a present-of-the-moment tense, an enclosed present tense (for use while the vehicle is moving through time), a future past tense ("I'll meet you at the bombing of Pearl Harbor in half an hour."), a past future tense ("Just a souvenir I picked up ten million years from now"), and many more. We'd need at least two directions of time flow: sequential personal time, and universal time, with a complete set of tenses for each.

We'd need pronouns to distinguish (you of the past) from (you of the future) and (you of the present). After all, the three of you might all be sitting around the same table someday.

Those creative minds who can conceive of such perspectives can also face the challenge of the meaning-gap in human affairs, and—perhaps simply by dramatizing the precision and beauty of the scientific method, perhaps by contrasting it with the destructive misuse of technology by non-scientific men, perhaps even by exploring new ways of seeing—can at least help to prepare the way to a new understanding and a new synthesis. This may not be easy, for it is much harder to make such subjects interesting in fiction than simply to fall back on the well-known tricks of shock, excitation, and abrasion.

From its beginnings, the best of science fiction has at least *tried* to provide entertainment for the *whole* man—lover and hater, son and father, worker and adventurer, *and enquirer and problem solver*—and perhaps today its most important function may be to help men realize their wholeness, that each man should indeed, to some degree at least, play all these roles, and thereby to repair some of the damage done by premature individual specialization, by the divisive forces in society, and by the sub-intellectual pressures of manipulators and the mass news-entertainment media.

Because every writer is a propagandist whether he wants to be or not, this means that, in the Age of Space, the science fiction writer must do his best to achieve, at least in his perspectives, the Renaissance ideal of the universal man. He must try to swallow the world whole. We have been told that this is no longer possible, for the facile reason that "in Leonardo's day one man could learn everything there was to know; today, there is so much to learn that all anybody can do is specialize."

This is very much like saying that, because no man can possibly know every town and hamlet, coastline and stream and mountain range in the wide world, a clear and accurate world map which he can understand cannot be drawn. It is not necessary to *be* a scientist to understand the uses and implications of the scientific method. It is not necessary to *be* an engineer to comprehend the workings of technology, or a mathematician to see that the mathematices are languages, supplementary to the tongues we speak.

These are areas in which our general educations are hideously deficient—and this deficiency today is much more critical even than the failure to transmit our "cultural" heritage, for it prevents us from coping successfully either with ourselves or with the world. Actually, in order to revive the ideal of a general education and of individual universality, the first step should be to introduce epistemology as a grade-school subject and to continue emphasizing it until the formal education is completed.

For this, science fiction can be at least a partial substitute— but only if its writers, new and old, are given the essential freedom and the necessary resources to penetrate and develop themes that still lie on the frontiers of our knowledge.

Writers must have the freedom to think, to discuss, to write and publish. (I wonder how much good *science* fiction has not been written, even in our own relatively open society, simply because of "security" regulations?)

Writers also need freedom of time, which can be translated bluntly as *enough money.* To cite expert testimony in support of this contention, I shall again quote Dr. Torrey. (Though of course he is referring to shamans, witch doctors, medicine men, and other highly qualified personages, perhaps we can apply his words to writers also.):

> It is the dignity which brings the real payoff. If we accredit indigenous therapists but relegate their pay and status to that of a janitor, then we must expect to get janitor-level performance.[6]

The doctor has a real point there—for the responsibility of the serious science fiction writer in the Age of Space is, if not more important, certainly wider in its scope than the therapist's, indigenous or otherwise.

It is to do his utmost, while entertaining his readers, to make sure that there will *be* an Age of Space, and that the old Norse prophesy—

> Wind time, wolf time—
> There will come a year
> When no man on earth
> His brother shall spare.

—shall not be fulfilled.

6. E. Fuller Torrey, *The Mind Game, Witchdoctors and Psychiatrists,* p. 108.

Reginald Bretnor

Reginald Bretnor was born in 1911 in Vladivostok, Siberia, where his father was a banker. His family moved to Japan in 1915, and he lived there until brought to the U.S. in January 1920.

He received a haphazard education in a number of private and public schools and in one or two colleges, and has no degrees. During the War, he wrote propaganda to Japan and the Far East for the Office of War Information, and afterward continued with the Department of State's OIICA until he resigned in February 1947. Since then he has been freelancing, and is now living with his wife, Rosalie, in Oregon.

His fiction, much of it humor, has appeared in a wide variety of magazines: *Harper's, Esquire, Today's Woman,* a few academic quarterlies, the major sf magazines, *Ellery Queen's Mystery Magazine,* and so forth. Many of his stories have been anthologized.

His articles, on public affairs and military theory, have been published in such periodicals as the *Michigan Quarterly Review, Modern Age,* and the *Military Review;* and he is the author of *Decisive Warfare, a Study in Military Theory,* 1969 (Stackpole Books).

As editor, he published *Modern Science Fiction: Its Meaning and Its Future,* 1953 (Coward-McCann), a now-standard critical symposium, for which he wrote the final chapter on "The Future of Science Fiction." He is also the author of the article on sf in the last two editions of the Encyclopedia Britannica.

His interests include Japanese swords and related areas of Japanese art; antique and modern weapons (he is the inventor of an automatic mortar on which a U.S. patent has been issued); military and naval history and theory; parapsychology; people and their stories; the world at large; and the great adventure of the Age of Space. He is a member of several organizations which reflect these interests.

The Art and Science
of Science Fiction

James Gunn

Science Fiction and the Mainstream

Science fiction is a relatively recent invention.

So is the mainstream.

We can uncover predecessors and cite precedents but they only obscure the fact that the first successful science fiction writer—in the sense that science fiction made him immensely popular and a sizable fortune—was Jules Verne, whose first science fiction novel, *Journey to the Center of the Earth,* was published in 1864, not much more than a century ago.

The word *mainstream,* on the other hand, is not listed in any metaphorical sense in that ultimate authority on word origins, *The Oxford English Dictionary; Merriam-Webster's International* does not list it until its 1961 edition; *Random House,* in 1968; and none of them mention its literary meaning.

Clearly the use of the term goes back half a century if not twice that far, but it should also be clear that the state of mind described by *mainstream* is contemporary. In fact, *science fiction* and *the mainstream* may have been created by the same conditions: the tendency toward specialization which produced, among many other aspects of our society, the all-fiction magazines beginning with *Argosy* in 1896 and the category magazines beginning in 1906 with the *Railroad Man's Magazine,* continuing with *The Ocean* in 1907, *Detective Story Monthly* in 1915, *Western Story Magazine* in 1919, and culminating, for science fiction readers anyway, with *Amazing Stories* in 1926.

In the nineteenth century all kinds of fiction might be given different names—Jules Verne's novels were called *voyages extraordinaires* and H. G. Wells's science fiction novels were called "scientific romances"—but almost all (if we omit such publications as "penny dreadfuls" and "dime novels") were part of general fiction. Most nineteenth-century writers—including Verne and Wells and Kipling and Twain, as well as Poe and Hawthorne and Balzac and Haggard and Doyle, among many —wrote a variety of fiction dealing with contemporary life, history, adventure, and so forth, and did not feel that they were writing something markedly different when they wrote science fiction.

The readers of Conan Doyle's Sherlock Holmes stories were likely to read his historical novels and *The Lost World* as well, John Brunner has pointed out; and those who read H. Rider Haggard's *King Solomon's Mines* and his Egyptian historical novels probably also read *She* and *Ayesha.*

The nineteenth century was the period when the impact of science and technology on the Western world became obvious to everyone—steam and its impact upon transportation led the list but it was followed quickly by electricity, submarines, balloons and other aircraft, telegraphy and the telephone, explosives, canals, weapons, medical advances such as anesthesia and Pasteur's work with bacteria, mesmerism, improved metal processes, the chemical industry, plastics, commercial oil wells, recording, photography, the internal combustion engine and the automobile, motion pictures, the incandescent lamp, and X rays.

More important, perhaps, than any of these was a theory: Darwin's theory of the *Origin of Species* which presented a different concept of man, not as a special creation but as a natural and evolving creature; and Darwin's speculations about natural selection and the survival of the fittest soon were translated into social, economic, and even political action.

And fiction: naturalism took much of its inspiration from Darwin, and H. G. Wells found inspiration for his first scientific romances from Darwin through Wells's inspirational biology teacher, Darwin's foremost champion, Thomas H. Huxley. With Wells science fiction began to take form and direction; it became more a medium of ideas than a variety of adventure, and the ideas that Wells incorporated in his stories and novels created whole new thematic lineages down to the present, from time travel through alien invasion, forced evolution, invisibility, overspecialization, urban development, and so on and on.

And still there was no mainstream. When relatively few people can read and relatively few books are published nice distinctions between kinds of fiction are unnecessary. General literacy was another product, in the English-speaking countries at least, of the last third of the nineteenth century. Until then the reading of fiction, at least, was almost exclusively restricted to a small upper class. The great majority of the people were illiterate or, at best, literate enough only to read their Bibles.

Compulsory primary schooling was a product of the post-Civil War era, when enthusiasm for the power of education swept all parts and levels of the nation. By the mid-1890s thirty-one state legislatures had made elementary school attendance compulsory.

With more young people completing elementary school, attendance in high school shot upward. In 1870 only sixteen thousand boys and girls were graduated from high school; in the next thirty years the number of high schools jumped from about five hundred to six thousand and the number of high-school graduates to nearly ninety-five thousand a year. Americans were being educated for upward social and economic mobility and as citizens and workers in an increasingly technical and urbanized society; as a side benefit, they were being taught to read fiction.

In England a similar process was launched by the Education Act of 1871 which organized the British and national schools into a state system and supplemented them with board schools and a system of degrees by examination which created the correspondence colleges. By the last decade of the century, H.

G. Wells noted in his autobiography, "The habit of reading was spreading to new classes with distinctive needs and curiosities. . . . New books were being demanded and fresh authors were in request."

This was the period, also, when the mass magazines originated, beginning with George Newnes's *Tit-Bits* in 1881 and *The Strand* ten years later, imitated in the United States in 1893 beginning with *McClure's Magazine*. The development of mass magazines was made possible by the inventions of the rotary printing press in 1846, the linotype and wood-pulp paper in 1884, and the half-tone engraving in 1886.

The processes which were creating a greatly expanded reading public with new and untutored reading tastes, and the popular magazines to publish the material that public wished to read not only were creating popular fiction, including science fiction, to fill these magazines, but also the critical necessity to distinguish between mere "popular" entertainment and "serious" fiction.

Of course, even the short story and the novel themselves are relatively young. "The only new pleasures invented since Greek times have been smoking and the reading of novels," a French critic once commented. Although man always has invented narratives to amuse his fellows or to transmit cultural information, and we can trace the development of story through Greek and Roman episodes and incidents, Medieval fables, epics, and romances, and English and Italian tales, the novel as we know it did not develop into a formal kind of storytelling until the eighteenth century, and the short story, which became a peculiarly American specialty, was not consciously formulated into an art form until the nineteenth century, with writers like Hawthorne and Poe, Mérimée and Balzac, and E. T. A. Hoffmann. The reading of fiction was closely associated with the emergence of the middle class as the dominant element in European and American society.

The impulses that finally produced science fiction when the conditions were right go back to times as early as the development of narrative itself: the desires to entertain and to be entertained, to instruct, to explain, to illuminate, to invent, to imagine things that are not. Homer's *Iliad* gave the Greeks a common heritage, but his *Odyssey* naturalized their Mediterranean universe. Not until the facts of change created by man through his growing control over nature and the possibility of controlling change became apparent to perceptive men and then to most men, however, did science fiction become possible: that is, somewhat after the Industrial Revolution, generally dated about 1750. Considering the cultural inertia of the eighteenth century, that it took another hundred years to produce the first true science fiction writer is not surprising.

Some sixty years after the publication of *Journey to the Center of the Earth*, Hugo Gernsback founded *Amazing Stories* and the first science fiction magazine was born. Between Verne and *Amazing Stories* science fiction had existed in individual books and in the pulp fiction magazines—*Argosy, All-Story, Popular, People's Cavalier, Blue Book, Black Cat, New Story*, and others —where science fiction stories, mostly adventure in remote places, were found adjacent to adventure stories, western stories, sea stories, war stories, romantic stories, and other kinds of popular fiction.

In 1914, Edgar Rice Burroughs's *Tarzan of the Apes*, when it appeared in book form, still could be reviewed, even by such newspapers as *The New York Times*. Thirty years later Burroughs's books were excluded from most public libraries, along with those of the other famous storytellers of the first two decades: Garrett P. Serviss, George Allen England, and A. Merritt. In fact, during the thirties and forties virtually no hardcover science fiction was being published; only after the end of World War II, first with the fan presses and then with publishers such as Simon and Schuster, Doubleday, Frederick Fell, Random House, and Pellegrini and Cudahy, did science fiction return to book form. Even then it received no critical attention. A bit later, when most science fiction novels appeared as paperback originals, they shared the critical fate of all paperbacks: oblivion.

One faculty member told me in 1950, "Science fiction is at best subliterary."

What had happened to the genre since H. G. Wells's novels

were welcomed by such literary figures as Henry James, who was filled with "wonder and admiration" by Wells's early work and spoke of reading the *First Men in the Moon: "à petites doses* as one sips (I suppose) old Tokay," and of allowing *Twelve Stories and a Dream* "to melt, lollipopwise, upon my imaginative tongue"; and Joseph Conrad, who wrote to Wells how much he liked his work, particularly *The Invisible Man:* "Impressed is *the* word, O Realist of the Fantastic!" and added: "It is masterly —it is ironic—it is very relentless—and it is very true." Both James and Conrad kept after Wells to improve his description, his characterization, his subtlety, but they were not put off by his material.

One thing that happened to science fiction was a change in criticism and the appearance of the mainstream as a concept. More important than both, however was the creation of the science fiction magazine. Today the observer of the science fiction scene can recognize that magazine science fiction was a ghetto, but in the early days of the magazines readers and writers had no such concern. The discovery of *Amazing Stories* was a joyful recognition that now readers could enjoy their favorite kind of reading without having to winnow it out of general magazines or search it out in obscure corners of the public library. Fans, and Gernsback discovered many of them, now could read, collect, and even communicate with one another, first in the letters columns of the magazines, then in clubs and fan magazines.

Science fiction became a refuge and a mission. Science fiction writers were the missionaries: they worked in strange lands, they were underpaid, and they preached salvation and a better world. Gernsback believed that readers would be introduced to science and technology through science fiction and some of them would be inspired to become scientists and through science create a better world; one of the early fan feuds centered around the contents of a fan magazine: should it be devoted to science fiction or science?

At first *Amazing Stories* ran only reprints, mostly from Verne, Wells, and Poe, but gradually new writers were discovered and introduced. The first generation was composed primarily of pulp writers who had to write very fast and in a variety of categories—adventure, sea, detective, war—in order to make a living. They helped give science fiction its subliterary reputation; by necessity their stories were constructed to narrative formulas and they were hastily written by people who did not know much about writing and cared somewhat less. There were no H. G. Wellses among them.

Among that first generation of science fiction writers, however, were men like E. E. Smith, Jack Williamson, and Edmond Hamilton who did not know a great deal about writing but were eaten up with wonder and the desire to create it themselves. They were fascinated by *Amazing Stories* and the creations of Verne and Wells and Merritt, and they were inspired by the cosmic visions of scientists like Einstein and Hubble and Rutherford and Planck and de Broglie and Heisenberg and Jeans and Shapley, who were peering into the atom and staring out at an expanding universe.

The second generation were writers more like Smith and Williamson and Hamilton; they had grown up reading science fiction magazines—not only *Amazing Stories* but its competitors, *Wonder Stories* and *Astounding Stories*—and they had learned something about ideas and science and speculation and a little bit more about writing, mostly learned from other science fiction writers. Many of them read little except science fiction and perhaps some science and philosophy and history, but they could tell a story and they could build on the ideas of other science fiction writers. They were men like Isaac Asimov, Robert Heinlein, Theodore Sturgeon, and A. E. van Vogt, who all came along in 1939, not long after John W. Campbell took over as editor of *Astounding Stories* (shortly to become *Astounding Science Fiction)* in December 1937.

Now science fiction was truly a ghetto, and it began breeding its own traditions, its own myths, its own history, and its own storytellers: the third generation—some, like Ray Bradbury, were in the second—came largely out of fandom. They wanted to be better Asimovs, Heinleins, Sturgeons, and van Vogts. They were largely ignored by the world outside, but greatly admired within the ghetto itself. That seemed enough.

The fourth generation . . . But I will get to that a bit later.
Meanwhile science fiction had begun developing a philosophy and a concept of the future based upon that philosophy—a sort of consensus future history. This vision of man's destiny saw him conquering space, spreading his colonies through the solar system and the nearer stars and finally the galaxy itself (sometimes meeting alien races but most often not), experiencing a breakdown in communications or government which left isolated human communities to develop along divergent paths until a new galaxywide government arose to bring mankind back together, wiser and kinder and stronger than before.

From the vantage point of that future, earth was viewed as an ancestral home, sometimes remembered, sometimes recalled only in myth or legend, or a backwater of human progress, a planet ravaged by radioactives, as Isaac Asimov speculated in *Pebble in the Sky,* or a burial ground for earth's far-flung trillions, as Clifford Simak speculated in *Cemetery World.*

Donald Wollheim, in his personal history of science fiction, *The Universe Makers,* traces the beginnings of that consensus future history to Asimov's *Foundation* stories, which began with "Foundation" in 1942, although there were predecessors like Edmond Hamilton and Doc Smith, and Robert Heinlein contributed significantly with his future history of the next two centuries. In the ghetto, however, as the stories and ideas passed, so to speak, from hand to hand, they were refined and added to like an oral epic until general agreement was reached —no one was bound to it, but through most stories ran the same general assumptions about what was likely to happen.

That future was so significantly like our present that we can say we are today living in a science fiction world.

Behind the assumptions of that future history lay a concept of man which was at the same time arrogant and humble. It was a concept that grew out of the dominant literary and scientific movements of the nineteenth and early twentieth centuries: realism and naturalism on the literary side, Darwinism, sociology, Marxism, and Freudianism on the scientific.

Realism, which helped shape critical standards of what fiction ought to be, sprang up about the middle of the nineteenth century mostly in reaction to romanticism; realism—"the truthful treatment of material," William Dean Howells called it—was the ultimate in middle-class art, focusing its concerns on the immediate, the present, the specific action, and the clear consequence; it was democratic, emphasized character and ethics, that is, issues of conduct, and believed that art should imitate life (*i.e.*, be "mimetic," in the language of criticism), and since life had neither plot nor symmetry, realistic fiction should also eliminate them.

Naturalism, which followed but did not succeed realism, shared with realism its concern for fidelity to detail and reaction to the assumptions of romanticism, but it shared with romanticism a belief that the action was important not so much for itself as for what it revealed about the nature of a greater reality. Naturalism was the application to fiction of the principles of scientific determinism; it drew much of its inspiration from Darwin but also was influenced by Newton's mechanistic determinism, by Marx's view of history as a battleground of great economic and social forces, by Freud's concept of inner and subconscious determinism, and by Comte's view of social and environmental determinism.

Under the influence of naturalism, science fiction adopted a view of man as an animal selected by environmental pressures for intelligence, aggressiveness, possessiveness, and survival; from the scientific optimism of the times, science fiction saw man also as an animal whose passions, aspirations, and understanding had given him a tragic nobility: he might not be divine but in his hubris and his understanding he partook of divinity —he had eaten of the tree of life and of the tree of knowledge of good and evil; he was a creature who could dream of greatness and understand that it was only a dream.

"Man is the only animal that laughs and weeps," Hazlitt wrote, "for he is the only animal that is struck with the difference between what things are, and what they ought to be."

Man exists, science fiction said, and he must continue to exist, for the process that evolved him selected survival characteristics of dominance, intelligence, adaptability, and endurance.

Arthur C. Clarke illustrated that philosophical position with an early story called "Rescue Party." A spaceship manned by members of a race who "had been lords of the Universe since the dawn of history" discovers that earth's sun is to become a nova in seven hours and that earth, examined only four hundred thousand years ago and found to have no intelligent life, has developed a civilization. After searching an abandoned earth, the ship finally discovers in the lonely void far beyond Pluto a vast, precise array of chemically powered spaceships. Alvaron, the old, wise captain of the alien ship, gestures (with a tentacle) toward the Milky Way, "from the Central Planets to the lonely suns of the Rim," and comments:

> "You know, I feel rather afraid of these people. Suppose they don't like our little Federation. . . . Something tells me they'll be a very determined people. We'd better be polite to them. After all, we only outnumber them about a thousand million to one."
>
> Rugon laughed at his captain's little joke.
>
> Twenty years afterwards, the remark didn't seem so funny.

Robert Heinlein, in his juvenile novel *Have Spacesuit—Will Travel,* set up a situation in which a teen-ager faces the responsibility of representing man's right to survive before a Council of Three Galaxies which has accused humanity of being a danger to all other intelligent creatures. The boy finally can endure the unfairness no longer:

> "It's no defense, you don't *want* a defense. All right, take away our star—you will if you can and I guess you can. Go ahead! We'll make a star! Then, someday, we'll come back and hunt you down—all of you!"
>
> Nobody bawled me out. I suddenly felt like a kid who has made a horrible mistake at a party and doesn't know how to cover it up. But I meant it. Oh, I didn't think we could *do* it. Not yet. But we'd die trying. "Die trying" is the proudest human thing.

Pride in humanity has been one of science fiction's most significant attitudes (alternating, of course, with feelings of shame, dismay, and disgust; misanthropy has been a persistent ingredient in the mix; I do not wish to suggest that science fiction writers have been single-minded but that certain attitudes represent the main current)—but pride not so much in the qualities a creature must have to survive, though survival is basic and without it everything else is frivolous, but pride in the qualities a creature that must survive can develop and sustain in spite of unrelenting adversity. Man, says the science fiction main current, must be tough and aggressive, but his glory is that he can temper his toughness and aggressiveness with an appreciation for beauty, with artistic creativity, with self-sacrifice, with a capacity for love. And that paradox is what it means to be truly human.

Naturalism held no such pride in man nor hopes for him; what it seemed to demand was understanding of man's predicament and through understanding an amelioration of the harsh judgments and treatments inflicted upon him. Science fiction moderated its naturalism, its Darwinism, not merely with optimism but with rationalism.

Leo Rosten concluded a recent book with a story about Destiny:

> Destiny came down to an island, centuries ago, and summoned three of the inhabitants before him. "What would you do," asked Destiny, "if I told you that tomorrow this island will be completely inundated by an immense tidal wave?" The first man, who was a cynic, said, "Why I would eat, drink, carouse, and make love all night long!" The second man, who was a mystic, said, "I would go to the sacred groves with my loved ones and make sacrifices to the gods and pray without ceasing." And the third man, who loved reason, thought for a while, confused and troubled, and said, "Why I would assemble our wisest men and begin at once to study how to live under water."[1]

The man who loved reason had the rational approach of a science fiction writer. The spirit he represents finds alien the dismal view of man displayed by the mainstream when its writers venture into the genre, like Aldous Huxley with *Brave New World* or Nevil Shute with *On the Beach;* it is not so much that their view of man is tragic nor even that they perceive him as an emotional rather than a rational being, but that they underestimate him. If threatened by destruction, science fiction says, man will not surrender peacefully; he will struggle to the end, studying how to live under water, on a frozen or a flaming earth, in outer space, on the most hostile worlds. It seems to me that this is the truer picture of man's character. That concept is not unique to science fiction, of course. "I decline to accept the end of man," William Faulkner said in his 1950 Nobel laureate speech; and "I believe that man will not merely endure: he will prevail." And Dylan Thomas wrote:

> Do not go gentle into that good night, / Old age should burn and rave at close of day; / Rage, rage against the dying of the light. . . .

But rationalism—the belief that the mind is the ultimate judge of reality and can be relied upon to provide an answer to any problem—even rationalism modified by experimentalism does not completely describe science fiction's philosophic position. Independently it arrived at a position which approximated existentialism, described by Jean-Paul Sartre in these terms:

> Atheistic existentialism, of which I am a representative, declares with greater consistency that if God does not exist there is at least one being whose existence comes before its essence, a being which exists before it can be defined by any conception of it. That being is man or, as Heidegger had it, the human reality. What do we mean by saying that existence precedes essence? We mean that man first of all exists, encounters himself, surges up in the world—and defines himself after wards. . . .
>
> Man is nothing else but that which he makes of himself. . . . If, however, it is true that existence is prior to essence, man is responsible for what he is. Thus, the first effect of existentialism is that it puts every man in possession of himself as he is, and places the entire responsibility for his existence squarely upon his own shoulders.
>
> And, when we say that man is responsible for himself, we do not mean that he is responsible only for his own individuality, but that he is responsible for all men. . . . When we say that man

chooses himself, we do mean that every one of us must choose himself; but by that we also mean that in choosing for himself he chooses for all men. . . .

Even before Sartre, though not before Kierkegaard (whose influence upon science fiction is doubtful), science fiction said that man was responsible and that each individual was a representative of humanity. Even if he is a conditioned animal, through his passions and his understanding he has free will; he can choose between actions and between fates. Even in a hostile universe deserted by God and meaning, he still must struggle to remain human, to do the human thing. The human thing varies: it may be to survive, to keep evolving, to keep improving, to explore the ultimate potential of the human form, the human mind, the human spirit, or of intelligence itself. In this sense, the arrogance of the science fiction man is a kind of humility before the blind creative processes which produce him, and a determination to assume the responsibilities of choice. Carried to its ultimate form this philosophy results in not only individual but racial sacrifice: if some alien race or intelligence, natural or artificial, proves itself superior, better fitted to think, to understand, to create, to survive, man has a responsibility to step aside and, perhaps wearily, perhaps gratefully, lay down the earthman's burden. Science fiction writers almost always considered this solution even if they did not always choose it; mainstream writers venturing into the genre never consider intellectual superiority or promise.

In a story called "Resurrection" (also, "The Monster"), A. E. van Vogt illustrated science fiction's pride in humanity and its still unrealized potential. An alien spaceship descends upon an earth where life has been wiped out by an unexpected cosmic storm. The aliens recreate men from fragments of bone and destroy them as soon as they suggest a possibility of danger; each resurrected man has greater powers until the fourth understands the situation at the moment of his rebirth, vanishes instantly, and revives the rest of mankind to fulfill man's interrupted destiny.

Other stories demonstrate science fictional man's concern for the survival of his successor if not himself. Nietzsche called man a rope stretched between the animal and the superhuman; Arthur Clarke calls man the organic phase between the inorganic. "It's hard to see," he has said, "how on a lifeless plant an IBM computer could evolve without passing through the organic phase first." The intelligent machine may be man's successor.

Clifford Simak, in a collection of related stories called *City*, imagined that man's successors would be dogs and robots. In John Campbell's story "Twilight," it was too late for dogs: "as man strode toward maturity, he destroyed all forms of life that menaced him" and eventually, because of their interdependence, all other forms of life. Now man was dying because he had lost his curiosity, but the machines still operated perfectly. A visitor to that distant future "brought another machine to life and set it to a task which, in time to come, it will perform. I ordered it to make a machine which would have what man has lost. A curious machine."

On a more immediate level, science fiction tests mankind and the future against the principles of scientific positivism, a philosophy which rejects metaphysics and maintains that knowledge is based only on sense experience and scientific experiment and observation. The basic attitude of serious, main-current science fiction speculation about the future and man's role in it is pragmatism. "It is not what you believe to be true that will determine your or humanity's success," John Campbell's *Analog* insisted, "but what works." A substantial body of science fiction is dedicated to overturning prejudice and prior judgments, romanticism and sentimentality; and some writers have created careers out of asking themselves what mankind and its folk wisdom hold dear and then demonstrating fictionally that the opposite makes more sense.

The ultimate expression of this pragmatism is embodied in Tom Godwin's "The Cold Equations." A girl, hoping to see her brother, who is a member of an advance group on a frontier planet, stows away aboard a one-man emergency delivery ship sent out by an interstellar liner with vital serum for another exploration party on that planet. The amount of fuel necessary to reach the planet has been carefully calculated because the "frontier" demands the strictest economy. Interstellar regulations state that a stowaway must be jettisoned immediately upon discovery; otherwise the ship will crash and kill eight people instead of one. The cold equations say that the girl must leave the ship, that she must die; she does.

"The Cold Equations" looks at humanity from the viewpoint of the universe; the universe is indifferent to the feelings of individuals. It doesn't care whether they live or die, whether mankind itself survives; its cosmic processes involve the titanic birth and death of suns, of galaxies, and of a universe itself slowly running down toward the universal heat death called entropy, and even for these things it does not care. Those who infer purpose or concern in the universe may find comfort, but they also assume risk; and what they hazard is not merely their own lives and the lives of others but the waste of those lives, those human efforts, those human purposes, through sentiment or ignorance.

Viewpoint is a key to the writing of fiction. More than fifty years ago, Percy Lubbock, in his classic study called *The Craft of Fiction*, wrote: "The whole intricate question of method, in the craft of fiction, I take to be governed by the question of the point of view—the question of the relation in which the narrator stands to the story." The kinds of viewpoints that science fiction adopts, however, are more than questions of narration; in a larger sense, irrespective of the point of view from which the story is narrated, the viewpoints of science fiction, whether implied or explicit, have made science fiction what it is; they create the tone and perspective which have distinguished science fiction from other kinds of fiction, and more than anything else, subject or scene, created the effects it has achieved.

These viewpoints detach the reader from his anthropomorphism, from his blind involvement with the human race; for the first time, perhaps, he is able to see man—and hopefully himself —from afar and judge objectively his potential and his accomplishments, his history and his prospects. The most distant, coldest, most objective view is the indifference of the universe. Another, a bit closer and a bit more subjective, is the view of man from space. One reason for getting into space is to attain this perspective, and one of the values of the space program was the photography of earth from space, and the comments of the astronauts. From this group of extroverted pragmatists came such remarks as Neil Armstrong's "I remember on the trip home on Apollo 11 it suddenly struck me that that tiny pea, pretty and blue, was the earth. I put up my thumb and shut one eye, and my thumb blotted out the planet earth. I didn't feel like a giant. I felt very, very small." To Bill Anders the sight of earth from space evoked "feelings about humanity and human needs that I never had before." Rusty Schweickart said, "I completely lost my identity as an American astronaut. I felt a part of everyone and everything sweeping past me below." Or Tom Stafford: "You don't look down at the world as an American but as a human being." Michael Collins: "I knew I was alone in a way that no earthling had ever been before." Or Ed Mitchell: "You develop an instant global consciousness, a people orientation, an intense dissatisfaction with the state of the world and a compulsion to do something about it."

Any of those statements could have come from Reverend McMillen in my 1955 short story, "The Cave of Night," in which the first man to venture into space gets stranded there and radios back:

> "Up here you wonder why we're so different when the land is the same. You think: we're all children of the same mother planet. Who says we're different? . . .
> ". . . I have seen the Earth . . . as no man has ever seen it— turning below me like a fantastic ball, the seas like blue glass in the sun . . . or lashed into gray storm-peaks—and the land green with life . . . the cities of the world in the night, sparkling . . . and the people. . . ."

What the astronauts felt is what science fiction, at its best, can achieve. What other kind of fiction has this capability?

The view from space brings humility. In those photographs from space, where were man's monuments? Where were the signs of his civilization? "Is there life on earth?" I. S. Shklovskii and Carl Sagan ask in their book *Intelligent Life in the Uni-*

verse, and go on to remark, after searching Tiros and Nimbus satellite photographs of the eastern seaboard of the United States and the southern tip of India and the island of Ceylon, "The regions depicted in these photographs are among the most heavily populated and densely vegetated areas of the earth; yet even close inspection shows no signs of life at all. New York appears deserted; India and Ceylon appear barren . . . when the resolution is no better than a few kilometers, there is no sign of life on Earth."

The farther into space one travels the less significant become the passions and agonies of man, and the only matter of importance in the long morning of man's struggle to survive is his survival so that his sons could be seeded among the stars, just as the only importance of the long, terrible efforts of gilled creatures to live upon the land was that they became the ancestors of all air-breathers, including man, and the only importance to the life of a man is what he passes on to his children or the children of his race in the form of a physical, genetic, or intellectual legacy.

In 1969 Ray Bradbury said, "Space travels says you can live forever. Now we are able to transport our seed to other worlds. We can be sure that this miraculous gift of life goes on forever."

Another detached viewpoint of science fiction is the future. Much of science fiction has looked back at man from this vantage place: from there the important function of the present is to make possible the future—or, at least, not to make it impossible. Ted Sturgeon made use of this viewpoint in his 1947 story "Thunder and Roses," in which the United States has been attacked with atomic bombs from both the east and the west; it is doomed, although a few survivors still are searching for the secret trigger that would send off the atomic weapons of the United States in a retaliation which would destroy all life on earth. One woman, a popular singer, tries to get across the message that "we must die—without striking back."

> "Let us die with the knowledge that we have done the one noble thing left to us. The spark of humanity can still live and grow on this planet. It will be blown and drenched, shaken and

all but extinguished, but it will live if that song is a true one. It will live if we are human enough to discount the fact that the spark is in the custody of our temporary enemy. Some—a few —of his children will live to merge with the humanity that will gradually emerge from the jungles and the wilderness. Perhaps there will be ten thousand years of beastliness; perhaps man will be able to rebuild while he still has his ruins. . . ."

He looked down through the darkness at his hands. No planet, no universe, is greater to a man than his own ego, his own observing self. These hands were the hands of all history, and like the hands of all men, they could by their small acts make human history or end it. Whether this power of hands was that of a billion hands or whether it came to a focus in these two —this was suddenly unimportant to the eternities which now enfolded him. . . .

"You'll have your chance," he said into the far future. "And, by Heaven, you'd better make good."

Here is science fiction pointing out the ultimate horror of holocaust—the horror is not that so many will die so horribly and so painfully (all men are doomed to die and few deaths are easy) but that it destroys the future of mankind, all the unachieved potential, all the untested possibilities, all the art and love and courage and glory that might be; it is not just that some idiot kind of total warfare might destroy the present (the present is being destroyed minute by minute as it is pushed inexorably into the future) but that it might destroy eternity. From this viewpoint, from the viewpoint of our distant descendants, no matter what their alien forms, ways, beliefs, the ultimate crime is not murder but stupidity, as pollution, global war, civil strife, and other contemporary carelessnesses that threaten racial survival are stupid. In a metaphorical sense, science fiction might be considered letters from the future, from our children, urging us to be careful of their world.

A final detached viewpoint is that of the alien—sometimes the alien to our society such as the visitor from the future, as in Fredric Brown's "Dark Interlude," or the visitor from a distant planet, as in Robert Sheckley's "Love, Incorporated," or the earthman in an alien society, as in Sheckley's "The Language of Love" or Roger Zelazny's "A Rose for Ecclesiastes," or the man from the present in a future society, as in Edward Bellamy's *Looking Backward,* Wells's *When the Sleeper Wakes,* or Frederik Pohl's *The Age of the Pussyfoot,* sometimes the extraterrestrial beings who visit earth for conquest or exploration or judgment, as in Murray Leinster's "Nobody Saw the Ship," Ross Rocklynne's "Jackdaw," Jack Williamson's *The Trial of Terra,* or Gordon Dickson's "Dolphin's Way," or the alien conquerors of Arthur Clarke's *Childhood's End,* or the ultimate alien—the Creator—of Eric Frank Russell's "Hobbyist." From the alien viewpoint we can see more clearly the relativity of our most cherished beliefs, the ridiculousness of our traditions, our mores, and our concerns, and the temporality of our societies; and we can learn to share the broader vision that encompasses all living creatures, all thinking beings—as in Clifford Simak's *Time Quarry* and other stories—which by extension renders trivial the minor differences between races or individuals.

These viewpoints—there are others and innumerable variations upon them—help determine how a reader is going to react to science fiction; some readers welcome perspective on themselves or on humanity; some find it painful or silly or are unable to make the imaginative leap necessary to dissociate themselves from their unshakably earthbound preconceptions —they are unable to get outside their own skins and their own viewpoints. This may be one reason fewer women have read and written science fiction than men; genetically or through conditioning women seem to be more emotionally committed to their own viewpoints.

Edmund Crispin pointed out in a 1962 *London Times Literary Supplement:*

> All these things being thus, it would be surprising if science fiction were to be popular. Nobody can take altogether kindly to the thesis that neither he personally, nor anyone else whatever, runs much risk of unduly bedazzling the eye of eternity. . . . The best seller lists are scarcely, if one comes to think of it, the place to look for fiction which instructs us, no matter how cheerfully, in how completely trivial we all are. . . . In medieval times Man was commonly visualized as being dwarfed against

a backdrop of stupendous spiritual or supernatural agencies; yet not dwarfed ultimately, since the Christian religion consistently averred him to be a special creation. From the Renaissance onwards that backdrop shrank, or was more and more ignored, with a corresponding gain in stature to the actor in front of it. What science fiction has done, and what makes it egregious, is to dwarf Man all over again (this time without compensation) against a new great backdrop, that of environment. Leopold Bloom has Dublin, and Strether has Edwardian England, and Madame Bovary has provincial France; but the relative nonentities in science fiction have the entire cosmos, with everything that is, or conceivably might be, in it.

The mainstream and the literary criticism that created it emphasize instead the overriding importance of the individual. Crispin writes of science fiction as "origin of species fiction" in which a man is important only in his relationship to humanity; to focus on any individual "is as if a bacteriologist were to become fixated not just on a particular group of bacteria but on one isolated bacterium." Opposed to that is D. H. Lawrence's conviction that "only in living individuals is life there, and individual lives cannot be aggregated or equated or dealt with quantitatively in any way."

F. R. Leavis, the English literary critic, quoted Lawrence's statement in Leavis's 1962 rejoinder to C. P. Snow's "The Two Cultures." A brief summary of that debate may be illuminating here: Snow was describing the scientific culture, but for that we might, without significant distortion, substitute science fiction; and Leavis was defending the literary culture, but for that we can substitute "mainstream," that at its best is the literary culture's mode of expression. Through an examination of the positions taken in the debate we may be able to understand why the mainstream became what it is and why until recently science fiction was excluded from it.

After expressing regret over the fact that most scientists are ignorant of literature and greater regret over the fact that almost all members of the literary culture are ignorant of science, Snow attacked literary intellectuals as "natural Luddities" who "have never tried, wanted, nor been able to understand the industrial revolution, much less accept it. . . . Almost every-where . . . intellectual persons didn't comprehend what was happening. Certainly the writers didn't. Plenty of them shud-dered away, as though the right course for a man of feeling was to contract out; some . . . tried various kinds of fancies which were not in effect more than screams of horror."

Snow saw "those two revolutions, the agricultural and the industrial-scientific" as "the only qualitative changes in social living that men have ever known" and noted that "with singu-lar unanimity, in any country where they had the chance, the poor walked off the land into the factories as fast as the factories could take them." Against this Leavis placed a "vision of our imminent tomorrow in today's America: the energy, the trium-phant technology, the productivity, the high standard of living and the life-impoverishment—the human emptiness: empti-ness and boredom craving alcohol—of one kind or another" and compared it with "a Bushman, an Indian peasant, or a member of those poignantly surviving primitive peoples, with their mar-velous art and skills and vital intelligence."

"If the scientists have the future in their bones," Snow said, "then the traditional culture responds by wishing that the fu-ture did not exist."

Leavis inherited his critical principles from Matthew Arnold who said, "Literature is the criticism of life." Of course Arnold meant "criticism" in the broad sense of judging and evaluation rather than faultfinding, but the standards of literature—and literary comparisons with past successes—have led to more faultfinding than programs for improvement. In 1913 Bertrand Russell pointed out:

> In the study of literature or art our attention is perpetually rivetted upon the past: the men of Greece or of the Renaissance did better than any men do now; the triumphs of former ages, so far from facilitating fresh triumphs in our own age, actually increase the difficulty of fresh triumphs by rendering original-ity harder of attainment; not only is artistic achievement not cumulative, but it seems even to depend upon a certain fresh-ness and *naiveté* of impulse and vision which civilization tends to destroy. Hence come, to those who have been nourished on

the literary and artistic productions of former ages, a certain peevishness and undue fastidiousness towards the present, from which there seems no escape except into the deliberate vandalism which ignores tradition and in the search after originality achieves only the eccentric.

And H. G. Wells noted in 1929:

> We are constantly being told that the human animal is "degenerating," body and mind, through the malign influences of big towns; that a miasma of "vulgarity" and monotony is spreading over a once refined and rich and beautifully varied world, that something exquisite called the human "soul," which was formerly quite all right, is now in a very bad way, and that plainly before us, unless we mend our ways and return to mediaeval dirt and haphazard, the open road, the wind upon the heath, brother, simple piety, an unrestricted birth-rate, spade husbandry, hand-made furniture, honest, homely surgery without anaesthetics, long skirts and hair for women, a ten-hour day for workmen, and more slapping and snubbing for the young, there is nothing before us but nervous wreckage and spiritual darkness.

One source for such accusations might be Ruskin, who noted in the mid-nineteenth century "signs of a slavery in our England a thousand times more bitter and more degrading than that of the scourged African, or helot Greek. Men may be beaten, chained, tormented, yoked like cattle, slaughtered like summer flies, and yet remain in one sense, and the best sense free"; and Ruskin went on to praise the age of nobility and peasantry when "famine, and peril, and sword, and all evil, and all shame, have been borne willingly in the causes of masters and kings."

In this context Leavis wrote that the human faculty above all others to which literature addresses itself is the moral consciousness, which is also the source of all successful creation, the very root of poetic genius, and to maintain that great literature asks deeply important questions about the civilization around it, but "of course, to such questions there can't be, in any ordinary sense of the word, answers." The questions, moreover, will all be of the sort to make society hesitate, slow down, lose confidence in the future, distrust both social planning and technological advance.

In support, the *Spectator* remarked that "philosophy . . . takes the form of that effort to impart moral direction, which is to be found in the best nineteenth-century English writers."

If Snow's scientists have the future in their bones, the literary culture claims moral direction.

Professor Martin Green pointed out in 1962 that "for the last ten or fifteen years the study of literature, and to some extent the general intellectual climate, has been increasingly dominated by a movement very largely antithetical in tendency—a movement which insists on narrow intense knowledge (insights), on the need for personal freedom within the best-planned society, on the dangers of modern science and technology, on the irreducibility of artistic and religious modes."[2]

Webster's New World Dictionary defines *science* as "knowledge as opposed to intuition," and Maxwell Anderson described the work of art as "a hieroglyph, and the artist's endeavor is to set forth his version of the world in a series of picture writings which convey meanings beyond the scope of direct statement."

By what criteria is literature evaluated? Theories of criticism have not so much evolved as alternated: beginning with the classical criticism of Aristotle, Longinus, and Horace criticism moved through the ecclesiasticism of the Middle Ages, the classical revival of the Renaissance, various attempts like that of Sir Philip Sidney's to find a new theory of criticism, the neoclassicism of Alexander Pope, the romanticism of Wordsworth and Coleridge, the impressionism, growing out of romanticism, of Walter Pater, the realism of Matthew Arnold and then of William Dean Howells and Henry James, the naturalism of Émile Zola and Frank Norris, and finally arriving in this century at the new humanism of Irving Babbitt and Paul Elmer More, Marxist pragmatism, and the New Criticism of Robert Penn Warren, Allen Tate, and Cleanth Brooks.

M. H. Abrams in *The Mirror and the Lamp* suggests that criticism can be categorized according to the dominance of one of four elements in "the total situation of a work of art": the work, the artist, the universe, and the audience. If the critic judges the work on how well it imitates the universe, he is using "mimetic theory"; in terms of its effect on an audience, "pragmatic theory"; in terms of the artist, "expressive theory"; in its own terms, "objective theory."

"Mimetic theory"—imitation—was dominant in Aristotle and his successors, "pragmatic theory," from Horace through most of the eighteenth century; "expressive theory" came in with romanticism; "objective theory"—the work itself for its own sake—emerged in the nineteenth century and became dominant in the twentieth.

Modern criticism—and the popular book-review media which, insofar as they contain criticism rather than reviews, are subconsciously influenced by prevalent critical standards and modes—has ignored science fiction for most of its recent history not only because of the crudeness of its craftsmanship, the ephemeral nature of its medium, and its nondiscriminating popular audience but also because its philosophy was optimistic and scientific in a pessimistic, anti-scientific literary climate, because its values were accessible only through mimetic and pragmatic theory in a period dominated by expressive and objective theory, and because modern criticism finds nothing to say about its style and content.

Hilary Corke, British poet and critic, says of Snow's novels, "Their emphasis is on plot, not character," and "A paragraph of a Snow novel yields nothing whatever to deep analysis; his merits lie in the structure and ordering of the whole."

The same comments might be made about a well-constructed science fiction novel.

All of this was true until recently. About half a dozen years ago—a time roughly coincident with the student riots, not only in the United States but in France and Great Britain as well—revolution came to science fiction. Perhaps a revolution was inevitable against the apparent inhumanity of a viewpoint which could equate the Vietnam War with Wat Tyler's Rebellion, Discrimination with serfdom, individual tragedy with the crushing of a cockroach, which could think of mass starvation as a possible long-term good, plague as a genetic boon, humanitarianism as genetic suicide, and war as merely another means of redressing Malthusian imbalances. Although science fiction has been consistently egalitarian, libertarian, and fraternitarian, its penchant for the long view ultimately created a new breed of writers who focused their concerns on the short term, on individuals and their inalienable worth, on men's passions and perplexities rather than their reason.

But it was no coincidence that the revolution in science fiction—Judith Merril called it "the New Wave" in her later *SF: The Year's Best* anthologies—occurred at the same time as the campus disturbances over civil rights and the Vietnam war, which spilled over into university governance and even the structure of the college curriculum. The New Wave was more than a reaction to the scientific positivism that had become the main current of science fiction; it was a response by young writers to the spirit of the times which was rejecting intellectualism as a blind alley, which demonstrated itself in a resurgence of fantasy, occultism, and mysticism and in a willingness to sacrifice the universities to end the war in Vietnam, to trade the classroom and the book for the experience, to seek answers in drugs and meditation rather than in study and experiment, to put together new groupings rather than improve old ones. "I think therefore I am" became "I feel therefore I am," and this shift from rationalism to sensationalism found its way into science fiction first in England through Michael Moorcock's state-subsidized *New Worlds* and the writings of J. G. Ballard, Brian Aldiss, and in part of John Brunner and Moorcock himself; and was picked up in the United States by Harlan Ellison, Norman Spinrad, Thomas Disch, and a host of younger writers.

Tom Godwin's "The Cold Equations" ends:

> A cold equation had been balanced and he was alone on the ship. Something shapeless and ugly was hurrying ahead of him, going to Woden where its brother was waiting through the night, but the empty ship still lived for a little while with the presence of the girl who had not known about the forces that killed with neither hatred nor malice. It seemed, almost, that she still sat small and bewildered and frightened on the metal box beside him, her words echoing hauntingly clear in the void she had left behind her:

J. G. Ballard's "Terminal Beach" also is about death, but death which is not caused but casual and dealt with not directly but symbolically through the wanderings of a man named Traven among the sterile, incomprehensible structures remaining on deserted Eniwetok, site of a post-war hydrogen bomb test. The story is evocative and its meaning comes, elusively, through descriptions of a psychological numbness to death and a premonition of atomic catastrophe. Traven's wife and six-year-old son were killed in an automobile accident, but this seems to Traven only part of what he calls the pre-Third—the two decades between 1945 and 1965 "suspended from the quivering volcano's lip of World War III." Now Traven has come to Eniwetok for a purpose he does not understand and he moves aimlessly around the island. Ballard's story ends:

> As the next days passed into weeks, the dignified figure of the (dead) Japanese sat in his chair fifty yards from him, guarding Traven from the blocks. Their magic still filled Traven's reveries, but he now had sufficient strength to rouse himself and forage for food. In the hot sunlight the skin of the Japanese became more and more bleached, and sometimes Traven would wake at night to find the white sepulchral figure sitting there, arms resting at its sides, in the shadows that crossed the concrete floor. At these moments he would often see his wife and son watching him from the dunes. As time passed they came closer, and he would sometimes turn to find them only a few yards behind him.
>
> Patiently Traven waited for them to speak to him, thinking of the great blocks whose entrance was guarded by the seated figure of the dead archangel, as the waves broke on the distant shore and the burning bombers fell through his dreams.

Stories like "Terminal Beach" partake more of the mainstream than of science fiction in its traditional form, and some traditional writers and readers of science fiction objected to what they considered their inconclusiveness, willful obscurity, pointlessness, and aping of mainstream experimental techniques at the expense of content. But the deeper objections of the traditionalists were stirred, I believe, by the mainstream attitudes New Wave writers adopted. In general, New Wave stories have traded the viewpoints of detachment for identification with the individual, and their viewpoint on reality has been subjective.

Professor Arthur Mizener believes that contemporary fiction draws upon four main traditions: realistic, romantic, subjective, and southern (the last falls outside the framework of the other three, and we will ignore it). The three traditions can be distinguished, Mizener says, by their attitude toward objective common sense: the realistic story makes us feel that objective common sense will not only be correct about how things will turn out, but right and wise and understanding that they must turn out that way; the romantic story makes us feel that objective common sense is likely to be correct about how things will turn out, but will miss the real meaning of things because it will not take into account the feelings of the central character; and the subjective story makes us feel that what men dream is so important, and therefore so real, that the objective world of common sense, however resistant to men's desires, does not finally count.

Science fiction, in the tradition established and nourished by John Campbell in the magazine first called *Astounding* and then *Analog,* is primarily realistic; science fiction in the tradition of the scientific romance of the early pulp magazines was primarily romantic. The writers of the New Wave seem primarily subjectivists—a thoroughly respectable literary position but one which is foreign not only to main-current science fiction but to science itself. It is not alien, however, to fantasy, which always has been subjective. Science fiction is a public vision; fantasy is a private vision. As a consequence, writers of fantasy always have been more acceptable to the mainstream than writers of science fiction. Ray Bradbury, for instance, was welcomed into the mainstream early in his career; Asimov and Heinlein never were—although Heinlein's least characteristic and most private science fiction novel, *Stranger in a Strange Land,* achieved some recognition. Professor Gary K. Wolfe, writing in *Extrapolation,* responded to Sam Lundwall's criticism of Bradbury's Mars as a fantasy world—or rather "the nostalgic Middle West of Bradbury's dreams"—with the statement that "the 'weakness' of Bradbury's Mars being a transplanted Middle West is what ultimately gives the book its strength because it argues that values are transmitted by individuals rather than society and that man tries to remake the natural world in his own image."

But the New Wave did more than insinuate a mainstream viewpoint into science fiction; it also brought in a greater concern for technique, for stream of consciousness and interior monologue, for shifting viewpoints and symbols and metaphors, for complex characters conducting their lives on a treadmill of meaningless days, for little people or strange people caught up in the innumerable folds of an inexplicable world, for lives that are static, trapped, or doomed. . . .

"I Have No Mouth and I Must Scream," writes Harlan Ellison, and Tom Disch writes "The Squirrel Cage."

Some of the younger writers have picked up, or reinvented, Heinlein's 1947 suggestion that science fiction be renamed "speculative fiction" on the grounds that "science fiction" is too narrow a term to cover the various kinds of fiction that qualify under any reasonable definition but include no science. The motivations of these writers of speculative fiction probably are a bit more complex: the term "science fiction" is not broad enough to cover the kind of fiction they wish to write, and a new name suggests new possibilities, new directions, and a break with old pulp origins.

By now the waves have quieted. Writers who want to do new things, experimental things, are doing them; writers who want to say new things, difficult things, outrageous things, are saying them. Many of these new voices are finding new audiences; young people, particularly, are finding the new subjective writers appealing. The net result has been, in spite of the outcries of the traditionalists, an increase in the audience for science fiction; the dividing line between the traditional and the new is blurring, and the differences may be striking to the informed but the similarities are greater to the reader looking for something different in reading matter that recognizes the pressing importance, both objective and subjective, of external problems.

A side effect of the new wave has been an increased freedom within the field to experiment, to use unfamiliar techniques and unusual subject matter—in other words to liberate still further what has always prided itself on being the freest medium for fiction. The final shape of science fiction—or speculative fiction —is still unclear. Some observers fear the dominance of the New Wave, of style to the detriment of content. If the decision were up to mainstream critics alone, this fear might be realized, for they find many familiar and valued elements in New Wave fiction, and their close analysis can be rewarding. But New Wave fiction, no matter how *avant-garde* the style (and much of it is no more *avant-garde* than *Ulysses* (1922) and *U.S.A. (Manhattan Transfer,* 1925)), still is about *something,* which is not the usual situation in mainstream fiction.

What we may expect in science fiction is a gradual return by New Wave writers to the basic principle that style grows out of and informs content, and a growing concern by more traditional writers with language, character, and subjective reality; and by both wilder journeys into the outer reaches of experiment. Already such trends are apparent. Greater variety is being tolerated, even encouraged, in subject, approach, and style. An increasing number of writers will be difficult or impossible to categorize. The goal will be the goal of the mainstream: each writer with his individual vision, his individual voice.

Meanwhile, mainstream vigor, where it exists, seems to derive from its contacts with popular culture: motion pictures, folk heroes, commercials, radio, television, comic strips, advertisements, modern myths, rock music and musicians, detective stories, science fiction. . . .

We live in a pop culture—is there any other kind?—where soup cans are art and commercials are the most skillful art forms on television; literature is just beginning to recognize these facts. Contemporary fiction may have gone as far as it can go in the examination of character, even of abnormal character, and now its major prospect, as Stanley Elkin has predicted, may be the exploration of language. One alternative is to tap the source of energy in our culture—the myths and concerns that shape men's lives—and to consider them fictionally, to turn them into story.

Mainstream writers increasingly are turning to the themes and concepts of science fiction: Barth, Borges, Boulle, Burgess, Burroughs, Golding, Hersey, Lessing, Nabokov, Rand, Vercors, Vonnegut, Voznesensky, John Williams, Colin Wilson, Wouk. . . . What they are finding are not only the vitality of popular culture and the excitement of unexplored territory (unexplored, that is, by mainstream writers) but also subjects relevant to the times in which we live and not tracked over with literary footprints, subjects with the evocative power of a freshly minted metaphor. And although these writers now may be dealing with science fiction themes at arm's length rather than in hand-to-hand engagement, as time passes they may be expected to become as knowledgeable about content and ideas as they are about technique, if they can shed the prejudices of the literary culture.

As the drunken hero of *God Bless You, Mr. Rosewater* says to a convention of science fiction writers:

> I love you sons of bitches. You're all I read any more. You're the only ones who'll talk about the *really* terrific changes going on, the only ones crazy enough to know that life is a space voyage, and not a short one, either, but one that'll last for billions of years. You're the only ones with guts to *really* care about the future, who *really* notice what machines do to us, what wars do to us, what cities do to us, what tremendous misunderstandings, mistakes, accidents and catastrophes do to us. You're the only ones zany enough to agonize over time and distances without limit, over mysteries that will never die, over the fact that we are right now determining whether the space voyage for the next billion years or so is going to Heaven or Hell.

The author of that passage, Kurt Vonnegut, Jr., obtained his first recognition in science fiction magazines and books, although he later insisted that he not be labeled a science fiction writer and made his reputation in the mainstream.

Other science fiction writers are being read outside the category, and if they have not exactly been welcomed into the mainstream they have not been systematically excluded as they have been in the past. First, of course, comes the broader readership—major success in the science fiction field today depends upon hundreds of thousands of sales to occasional or infrequent science fiction readers—and then comes the recognition. Robert Heinlein's *Stranger in a Strange Land* (1961) has sold phenomenally well to the new youth culture, as has Frank Herbert's *Dune* (1965). *Time* magazine called them "good examples of how public concerns and infatuations catch up with the science fiction imagination." Older books such as Isaac Asimov's *Foundation* trilogy (1951) and Frederik Pohl and Cyril Kornbluth's *The Space Merchants* (1953) have almost never been out of print, and Arthur C. Clarke's *Childhood's End* (1953) had gone through eighteen printings by 1971. "Walter M. Miller Jr.'s *A Canticle for Leibowitz* (1960), an extraordinary novel even by literary standards, has flourished by word of mouth for a dozen years," *Time* noted. More recent books may achieve similar success and status as the years provide them with the opportunity to achieve a reputation through some circuitous or underground route.

The new academic interest in science fiction—the first college course was taught by Professor Mark Hillegas at Colgate in 1962—has infiltrated most of the nation's colleges and universities and now is percolating down to high schools and even junior high schools. Such courses will have the effects of lending science fiction some respectability, probably of increasing the potential audience, possibly of misdirecting or petrifying the genre.

Some science fiction books will be brought to general public attention by an understanding reviewer in the mainstream, just as more mainstream writers will be turning to science fiction for material and inspiration—until science fiction and the mainstream will meet somewhere to the right of science fiction and to the left of the mainstream and where the works drew their tradition will be impossible to determine.

This process of reunion will be enhanced by the diminishing influence of the magazines, which like oak leaves have stubbornly clung to their small branches after the rest of their fellow pulps have moldered back to the condition from which they came. The old science fiction unity, the brotherhood of writers and editors and readers who learned only from each other and built upon each other's concepts, is dwindling as alternate methods of publication—original anthologies, paperbacks, even hard-covers have become more numerous and more important. The ghetto walls are demolished; the "us against the rest of the world" mentality is fading. The consensus future and the philosophical position on which it was built is beginning to fall apart as science fiction splinters into a hundred markets, into a thousand disparate, individual visions.

Science fiction will bring nothing to the mainstream if it surrenders to mainstream philosophies and mainstream values. Both science fiction and the mainstream will be stronger if science fiction retains its unique concepts, narrative strengths, idea orientation, detached viewpoints, and commitments that it developed over the long years of isolation.

FOOTNOTES:
1. *The Many Worlds of Leo Rosten*, New York: Harper & Row, 1964, pp. 328–329
2. *The Kenyon Review*, Autumn, 1962, p.733.

James E. Gunn

Born in Kansas City, Missouri, in 1923, James E. Gunn received his B.S. degree in journalism in 1947, after three years in the U.S. Navy during World War II, and his M.A. in English from the University of Kansas in 1951. He has worked as an editor for a publisher of paperback reprints, as assistant director of Civil Defense in Kansas City, as managing editor of K.U. alumni publications, as administrative assistant to the Chancellor for University Relations at the University of Kansas, and now serves the University as a lecturer in English and Journalism. He teaches courses in fiction writing and science fiction. He has served as chairman of the Mid-America District of the American College Public Relations Association, and member of the Information Committee of the National Association of State Universities and Land Grant Colleges. He has won national awards for his work as an editor and a director of public relations. He was President of the Science Fiction Writers of America for 1971–1972.

He has written plays, screenplays, radio scripts, articles, verse, and criticism, but most of his publications have been science fiction. He started writing science fiction in 1948, was a full-time freelance writer for four years and has had more than sixty stories published in magazines; eight of his novels have been published, and his master's thesis (about science fiction) was serialized in a pulp magazine. Four of his stories were dramatized over NBC radio, one, "The Cave of Night," was dramatized on television's Desilu Playhouse under the title of "Man in Orbit," and *The Immortals* was dramatized as an ABC-TV "Movie of the Week" during the 1969–1970 season and became an hour series, *The Immortal*, in the fall of 1970. His story and screenplay, "The Reluctant Witch," is scheduled for production.

This Fortress World, 1955 (Gnome and Ace)
Star Bridge, 1955 (Gnome and Ace); with Jack Williamson
Station in Space, 1958 (Bantam)
The Joy Makers, 1961 and 1971 (Bantam)
The Immortals, 1962 and 1968 (Bantam)
Future Imperfect, 1964 (Bantam)

Man and the Future: The Intercentury Seminar at the University of Kansas, editor, 1968 (The University Press of Kansas)
The Witching Hour, 1970 (Dell)
The Immortals, 1970 (Bantam)
The Burning, 1972 (Dell)
Breaking Point, 1972 (Walker)
The Listeners, 1972 (Scribner's)
Alternate Worlds, An Illustrated History of Science Fiction, 1973 (Prentice-Hall)

Alexei and Cory Panshin

Science Fiction: New Trends and Old

What are trends? Perhaps we can say that trends are the small-scale movements, evolutions, progressions, and fashions that are perceived by those living within one moment and stretching to anticipate the next. Trends are arbitrary. Their background interconnections are fuzzy. Trends are cosmic twitches.

There are people who have to anticipate trends, who have to be finely tuned to trends. Dress designers. Also boutique proprietors. Or, living on rock music, as so many of us do, we might be aware that rock music has passed through a country-influenced phase, then an art song period, and now is experimenting with decadence. We might care about trends in rock music. Or those who are interested in publishing might care about the trends that affect *Newsweek* and the trends that affect *Amazing*.

Is this the right scale? We do agree that these are trends. And, if we look at what sf criticism has managed until now, we would have to admit that until now sf criticism has lived in the moment. It has questioned the meanings of individual books—as in Damon Knight's *In Search of Wonder*, the first major book of sf criticism. Or, as in James Blish's several books, it has questioned the professional competence presently apparent in sf. It has fitted shapes over the careers of various writers, as those careers have lengthened—as in several books by Sam Moskowitz, and in *Heinlein in Dimension*. It has begun to track its past, as in de Camp's *Science-Fiction Handbook,* and again in books by Sam Moskowitz. At its most universalizing, sf has attempted to make sense of the present in terms of the immediate past, as in Kingsley Amis's *New Maps of Hell,* which would have remade the sf of 1960 in the shape of the sf of 1954, only more so.

You would have to say, then, yes, sf criticism at its best has dealt in trend-snatching.

All right, if we are dealing in trends, what are the trends of the moment that seem significant?

In the past ten years, sf has played at the adaptation of myth to sf, as in stories by Roger Zelazny, Thomas Burnett Swann, Samuel R. Delany, and Emil Petaja. In the late Sixties, the most notable sf seemed to be experiments in styles copied from mainstream models, as in stories by Brian Aldiss, John Brunner, and Philip José Farmer. Most recently, the sf that demands attention is into decadence, as in stories by Robert Silverberg, Norman Spinrad and Barry Malzberg. Almost all stories at this moment are at least a bit into decadence.

If these are trends, how do we make sense of them, let alone predict what everybody will be expressing next year? Now that Robert Silverberg has slowed his writing pace, are we to assume that the phase of decadence will soon be over? Who is to be the next Writer of the Moment?

That's one kind of trend. Here's another: the often-declared and long-cherished division between science fiction and fantasy is becoming harder and harder to maintain. Independently of the year-to-year lurches of sf given above, the symbols of traditional fantasy are being accepted in modern sf stories.

Here's another: the audience for modern sf has grown ever since Hugo Gernsback founded *Amazing Stories* in 1926. In a time when the audience for mimetic fiction is becoming steadily smaller, sf is the one literature in the Western world whose audience is steadily growing.

Here's one last trend. Since 1926, the course of modern sf has never run smooth. Sf has had its good periods and its bad ones. As examples, sf was having a remarkably bad period when John Campbell assumed the editorship of *Astounding* in 1937, and was in another period of stagnation in 1960 when Earl Kemp won a Hugo for his fan publication, a symposium entitled "Who Killed Science Fiction?" But there have been other years when nobody would have been inclined to ask that question. For instance, the early years of the Forties, when Heinlein, van Vogt, de Camp, Sturgeon, and Asimov were establishing themselves, were fruitful times. So were the middle Sixties. The 1967 year's best anthology, edited by Donald Wollheim and Terry Carr, is enough to make you smile. That isn't true of the work being written at the moment. We are getting ready to trot the 1960 question out again.

These are trends enough for anyone. If it were sufficient to talk about science fiction—new trends and old—we could pick these trends up one at a time and hash them out.

But if we did, we would not know any more than we do now. We would have a handful of well-analyzed trends, but still have no complete idea of the overall significance of science fiction.

Until now, we have always looked at sf in the most present and immediate way. We have wondered about books. We have judged contemporary standards of craftsmanship. We have added up careers as totals of and-then-he-wrote. We have taken the current temperature and pulse of the field. And we have marveled at how very marvelous this marvelous and unpredictable science fiction has been.

If we try to understand trends in terms of trends, we will be unable to see the underlying unity that explains all the trends of sf that bewilder us. We suspect that until now sf criticism has been too much in the middle of an immense and radically changing thing to do more than take present bearings.

However, for the first time now it seems possible that one might view sf from a new plane and see how it can accommodate all these very different twitches, these trends. Since it seems possible, we want to try—with the editor's permission, and your indulgence—a bit of foolery.

Here is an assumption. Any unifying explanation of sf will lie in a dimension in which we are not used to looking when we think about sf. That is, any unifying explanation of sf will look *strange* at first. It will not be easy for some to accept at first, whatever it is, because it is strange.

With your indulgence, we will attempt a strange unifying answer. Take it as deadly serious, or take it as a joke—but consider that any unifying explanation of sf will look at least as strange as this.

Let us suppose:

It seems that if there is one conclusion made by modern psychology—Freud and all his legitimate and illegitimate heirs —that can stand as proven beyond challenge, it is this: we are in large part enigmas to ourselves.

Will we all accept this? It hasn't been a current idea for very long. The *Oxford Universal Dictionary* dates the first use of the word *unconscious*—meaning not available to the conscious mind—as an adjective to 1909, and as a noun to 1920. But now it does seem indisputably true that the unconscious exists.

None of us sees himself complete and whole. Whatever we may know about ourselves that others do not, none of us is able to see himself as others may. We may think that the way we are is just the natural way we are, and never realize that it is unusual. We may tick like a clock and never realize it; we may pulse visibly. We are able to see virtues and defects in others that we are blind to in ourselves. Ask us to explain ourselves, and we will rationalize as best we can. But some things we won't be able to talk about, some we'll forget or leave out.

We know as much as we consciously know, but our unconscious knowledge is unavailable to us. This is not willful intent to ignore what is writ plain. At least, it is not merely that. We are separated from our unconscious and we don't know how to learn to know it better.

We may try to know ourselves by self-inspection, but it doesn't work. Conscious inspection inspects the conscious. We tote up what we know of our behavior. We find reasons for the behavior. We call the conscious and the reasons "I." But we are still separated from the unconscious. We cannot know the whole of our minds.

It may be that by means of education and training, it would be possible to circumvent our inability to know ourselves. But that kind of subtle instruction is not generally available. In spite of whatever hopes we might have had, it was missing for all of us in the schools and universities.

One of the ways in which we look to discover the full range of our minds is art. If we cannot discern our minds by direct inspection, we can see them indirectly—mirrored in art. Fiction is a form of the artistic mirror. In the symbol patterns of fiction we can see our minds reflected.

We believe that our minds are the sum of our knowledge of the universe. In a story, knowledge is symbolized and committed to paper. The universe of any story is a symbol of the entire mind. Our conscious knowledge is symbolized by known things. Our unconscious is symbolized by unknown things.

This is an unusual construction of fiction. We are saying that a straight chair in a story is a symbol of consciously known things. And we are saying that an invading alien in a story who lands on the White House lawn and craves present audience with the administrator of the land is a symbol of the unconscious. If this is strange enough to move you to object, please hold your objections for a moment and see how the fit grows.

We may call the kind of story that insists on the primacy of known things "mimetic fiction." This is the product of writers like Jane Austen, Charles Dickens, Mark Twain, Norman Mailer, John D. MacDonald, and even James Joyce and Zane Grey. In these stories, everything, no matter how strange, can or should be reduced by confrontation to the status of known things. That is, no matter how strange Joyce may get, what happens can ultimately be explained as dream, or the flow of thought, or madness.

Mimetic fiction is explainable in daylight terms. It might equally be called social fiction, because it deals in the world of consensus, or rational fiction, because it deals in rational explanations. This is fiction of a conscious world. Its ultimate loyalties are to the power of the conscious mind, just as the loyalties of your conscious mind are to itself.

The purpose of mimetic fiction is consciousness-raising.

Through inventory, the interconnections of the known are traced. The known gets to know itself. So might Charles Dickens acquaint you with society, Mark Twain with life on the Mississippi, and James Joyce with conscious phrasings of the existence of the unconscious.

On the other hand, the kind of story that insists on the primacy of symbols of the unknown is fantasy. Symbols of the unknown are such things as magics, or strange powerful spirits and beings, all that no ordinary power can successfully oppose. Magic can defeat an ordinary armed knight. It wouldn't be magic if it couldn't. Telekinesis can defeat an atomic bomb by mentally separating atoms.

Modern sf is fantasy. Its magics are various "scientific" powers that are stronger than any known to existing science. Its spirits and beings are robots and aliens.

Fantasy is fiction of the unconscious mind. It acts out unconscious knowledge. In the reflection of the universe presented in contemporary sf, our unconscious becomes more apparent than in any other fiction.

The purpose of fantasy is consciousness-expanding. The existence of unconsciousness, and the existence of unknown things in the world around us, forces us to expand the borders of the known. Consciousness expands itself by forays into the unconscious. Then consciousness makes a new inventory of itself—the act of consciousness-raising.

In the universe and in stories, the unconscious includes the conscious. And also, in the mind. If we accept the similarity of the three—the universe of experience, the universe symbolized in stories, and the human mind—we can demonstrate this in terms of story symbols.

An sf story may include any known symbol. In the farthest reaches of time and space, in the World Beyond the Hill, an sf story may still refer to anything presently known. Moreover, any sf story may be set in the most familiar of familiar places— Greenwich Village, for instance. And into that familiar place, an unknown power or alien will be able to intrude. Such an sf story exists—Chester Anderson's novel *The Butterfly Kid*. The unknown includes the known. The unconscious includes the conscious.

It we take this contention in terms of mimetic fiction—fiction of the conscious mind and the known universe—we discover that mimetic fiction cannot set foot in the farthest reaches of time and space. That isn't the known universe—the experienced universe has only gotten as far as the Moon. And in a known place like Greenwich Village, the most unknownlike things that mimetic fiction can produce are a flock of Brazilian sailors, or a mad poet, or the gurgle of a stream of consciousness. But the sailors are reducible to fun-loving, sex-mad Brazilians; the poet is mad, but then Village poets are inclined to be like that, and we understand; and the stream of consciousness is the ear of the conscious listening for hints. The known excludes the unknown.

But if the unconscious were to break through into consciousness, if the truly unknown and possibly not knowable did appear in the heart of the known—if the Brazilians are from Betelgeuse, if the mad poet speaks words that take form and go capering down the streets of the Village to annoy us, if we are asked to take symbols of the unconscious as the most, not the least, serious thing—then our story must be sf. Mimetic fiction, conscious fiction, won't have it, because an item in it has not been rationalized. In a mimetic story, a character might kiss a lamppost, the homeliest of known things, in gratitude that he does not have to take his fantasies seriously.

In order to write fully effective stories, stories of the whole mind, fantasists need two things. First, they need a conception of the universe in which the unknown includes the known. If the conception is compromised, the effectiveness of the stories is compromised. As in the universe of experience, so in the mind. As in the mind, so in the universe of a story. And the reverse, of course.

Second, fantasists must have a sensitive symbolic vocabulary that can be generally understood and that is capable of representing all aspects of the unconscious. Without this vocabulary, it would be difficult to represent some of what must be represented, and communication of it would be altogether impossible.

For a period of five thousand years or more, both necessary conditions existed. Representation of the whole mind was possible. In this assumed universe, the known world was Middle-earth. Middle-earth lay between the heavens, the unknown home of the gods above, and the underworld, the lower sky, the unknown home of the demons below. The juncture of worlds is the point where the two celestial hemispheres and the horizon meet. The known world is surrounded by the unknown.

In a universe like this, the unconscious and the full mind may be represented. Moreover, a sensitive symbolic vocabulary that could be read by anyone also existed. There were magics of every sort. There were strange gods, spirits, and beings. There were endless countries.

The assumption of these stories was that in a past Golden Age, access between the known world and the unknown realms had been easy. The gods had visited Earth and men had visited the gods. But even in these later times, ghosts or spirits might wander onto our Earth in search of victims or at the call of sorcerers. Interconnections between the known and unknown worlds did exist. Subtleties could be expressed.

In this universe of ours, we do learn. The unknown lures the known. The known changes by accumulation. As the known world changes, the unknown world must change to contain it.

A shift in the conception of the universe must be traumatic for the people involved. As in the story universe, so in the mind. As in the mind, so in the world of experience.

In the sixteenth and seventeenth centuries, the shape of the known world changed. Copernicus, Galileo, Kepler, and Newton revised the shape of the universe for us. They made the earth into a sphere in orbit about the sun. They made the planets into other spheres like the earth, also in orbit about the sun. They made the two celestial hemispheres into a single thing. They made the stars into other suns. In this new universe, earth was no longer Middle-earth. At best, the underworld might be found in the vitals of the earth. And the heavens were to be found nowhere.

The known had changed so radically that a new universe had to be conceived. The unknown world was seemingly turned into the known, or the knowable. In a time like this, it would be impossible to express anything but rationality. It was no accident that the eighteenth century was self-proclaimedly rational. It was no accident that the eighteenth century should have invented the mimetic novel. They could not do anything else. They made a virtue out of a limitation.

In a time when the World Beyond the Hill seems untenable, you will see sunlit excuses for midnight acts. In a century like that it will be impossible to see the entirety of the mind. The unconscious will be feared, doubted, and denied, as it has been since the eighteenth century.

In the time of disintegration of the old universe, fantasists suddenly began to live in a conscious world. This world allowed the World Beyond the Hill no place. If that were true, the end of the universe would truly be at hand. If the universe becomes totally conscious, all change will end. Stasis will have been achieved.

So fantasists reserved exception. One of the ways in which they did this was to conceive of a temporary corner of this earth in which the symbols of the unknown might claim to hold existence. The explorers of the fifteenth and sixteenth centuries had glimpsed a variety of strange countries. Fantasists placed the source of some of their unknowns in these countries, or in others like them beyond the present reach of exploration.

Exploration always proved these fairy lands false, but they were the described locations of many of the fantasies of the rational world—More's *Utopia* (1516), *Gulliver's Travels* (1726), and the lost race stories so common from 1870 to 1930. These stories were placed in the last crannies of the Global Village—in spring-heated valleys in the Antarctic, in subterranean caverns, in narrow wonderlands in the Himalayas. The last creditable example of this sort of compromise fantasy may have been James Hilton's *Lost Horizon* (1933). In this final statement of the relationship of the unknown to the known in the known world, we are told when the immortals of the fabulous land of Shangri-la are exposed at last to the light of the mimetic world, they must wither and die of old age, dissolving "like all too lovely things, at the first touch of reality."

During these past centuries of exploration, men have demonstrated in very real terms just how far they can extend the bounds of the known. They have shown they can extinguish every possible preserve of the World Beyond the Hill on this earth. And if that were all there were to the universe, the end of the universe would be at hand.

Consciousness is really very arrogant. It looms over the last delicate bit of unknown fluff in this world and, knowingly and brutally, it touches the thing, and *laughs* while the unknown fluff withers into a known thing.

Many fantasy symbols were never comfortable in this vulnerable unknown province in the hinterlands of earth. For instance, Gulliver may have found Lilliput at the ends of the earth, but no one ever found Witchland there. Many of the most powerful fantasy symbols took refuge in other unknown worlds —chiefly Never-never land.

Never-never land, in essence, is the old World Beyond the Hill. Because it was the old unknown, it could only include the old known. It must exclude much of the modern world, and hence no one was ever able to take it seriously, even in the hands of William Morris, Lord Dunsany, or J. R. R. Tolkien.

However, during these same past centuries, fantasists did locate a new true home for the World Beyond the Hill that incorporates Never-never land. They reconceived the universe. In order to do this, it was necessary that the known be extended to its fullest, as conscious busy-beavers, explorers, encyclopedists, novelists, and scientists have seen that it has been in these past three centuries of consciousness-raising. We retire from the Moon. We strain at the limits of our conscious vision. The results of investment in monumental conscious projects like cyclotrons are less while our expense grows greater. Consciousness is such a burden that we are turning as much of it over to computers as we can. Our new conscious limits are now available to fantasists.

During the nineteenth century—or, shall we say more properly, in the bit more than a hundred years between *Franken-*

stein (1818) and the founding of *Amazing Stories*—a new picture of the universe was adapted from science by writers like Poe, Verne, Wells, Burroughs, and Merritt. They presented this picture in pieces, but it was complete and established by implication prior to Gernsback. The publication of *Amazing Stories* confirmed the new universe. The name of the new fantasy —*scientifiction* or *science fiction*—indicated its nineteenth-century origin. *Amazing* assumed an audience that had made the conclusions of Poe, Verne, and Wells their premises.

This new universe, as we have come to discover it, is one so vast that the Global Village, circling its little sun in the suburbs of its galaxy, lost among many galaxies, can easily be lost. And likewise, this new universe contains reaches of time so extended that Earth could be forgotten.

A universe like this has room for the unknown. Our known world is surrounded by unknown again beyond our ability to explore.

In this new universe, the heavens and the underworld have become space and other dimensions. The Golden Age of the past is replaced by a vision of future perfection. Spirits become alien beings. Magic is replaced by science-beyond-science. Sorcerers become scientists.

The writers of the first hundred years of modern speculative fantasy established the existence of the new World Beyond the Hill. They demonstrated powers beyond the known. They showed that aliens might interact with us in a variety of ways. They showed that stories might be set in the future or on Mars, and that they might encounter the unknown there.

In the period since 1926, the period in which sf has been called "science fiction", modern fantasists have mentally explored the dimensions of their new universe. Science has played so much less a role in this process that apologists have had to strain to justify the name of science fiction. If speculative fantasy was "science fiction" prior to 1926, then sf from 1926–1957 was "idea fiction."

In these mental explorations can be found the meaning of some of the early "trends" of the field. For instance, inventors in stories built strange devices in their basements, including machines to travel in time and space. This was seen as a trend to gadget stories. Then, in the time-ships and space-machines, explorers leaped to the planets, to the stars, outside the galaxy. They scouted, mapped, and circumnavigated large portions of space and time. They saw the beginning and end of the universe. This was seen as a vogue for what the early Thirties called "thought variant" stories. Then, behind the explorers came all conditions of men—patrolmen, miners, pirates, pioneers—proving that men could survive in tents or domes here. That was a trend to adventure stories—space opera.

Behind them came the engineers, the planners, the bureaucrats, the empire-builders. In the 'Forties, space was structured into possible political units of every size, from earth in the future, to Terra and her colonies, to Galactic Empires. Time was structured into epochs in which things could change and change again from the presently known.

It was a joy and a tumble to invent this. The void was filled consistently, vividly, and plausibly with transportation, communication, government, economics, and sociology. The arguments were made over and over. The best ones were rehearsed until they became accepted justifications. The worst ones were improved or discarded. So many arguments were made that it became clear that *any* situation could be plausibly justified in a variety of ways. And what we saw of all this was the Golden Age of *Astounding*. The surly little stories of the 'Fifties were the nit-picking end of all the arguments over symbols.

In other words, we suggest that most of the trends in science fiction from 1926 to 1957, including the stories and the careers of writers like E. E. Smith, Jack Williamson, John W. Campbell, Robert Heinlein, A. E. van Vogt and Isaac Asimov, may be explained as symbol invention, the defining and testing of a symbolic vocabulary. Or, if you like, these stories put in the plumbing and engineering of the new unknown universe. People can believe in a universe with these dimensions because of these stories.

The writers of this period thought of this process of defining and testing symbolic vocabulary as "playing with ideas." James Blish, who began as an sf writer in 1940, has said, for instance:

Since at least about 1938, treatment has become steadily more important than springboard notion. Science-fiction writers borrow such notions from each other freely, to an extent that in other fields would sometimes be indistinguishable from plagiarism; this is almost never resented as long as direct quotation is avoided, and the resulting story is commonly welcomed as fresh if the borrowing writer succeeds in looking at the old idea in a new light—whether that light be dramatic, emotional, or even simply technological. Innovations of *this* kind, which are far more important in any literary field than any single germinal notion, are what make or break modern science fiction.

But what Blish is describing here is more fruitfully described as the defining and testing of symbols than as "looking at old ideas in a new light." By 1957, the symbols of sf were complete enough to sustain a wide range of imaginary activities—stories of invention, exploration, engineering, politics, economics; careers of various sorts; different life-styles. Activities as varied as the worlds of Smith, Sturgeon, Heinlein, van Vogt, Clarke, Knight, Pohl, and Kornbluth.

This range of symbols is now the common property of our culture. Children encounter the symbols of the sf of the Fifties from the time they are small. They know what a spaceship is. They know time machines. They know extraterrestrials. All these are to be found on the backs of cereal boxes. The culture as a whole is sufficiently educated in the symbols of the new World Beyond the Hill that it was able to accept and understand the TV series *Star Trek* and the movie *2001: Space Odyssey*, which were equivalent to the written sf of the Fifties. The shows had to assume an audience familiar with these symbols.

As the set of sf symbols has grown relatively complete, the symbols have been learned by a general audience. In a period when mimetic literature has been choking on its own desperation, sf has been the one consistently expanding literature in the Western world. The audience of sf has steadily grown since Gernsback. Sf has suddenly taken on interest as a subject in the academic community. The sense of this trend is apparent if we say again that a fantasist must have a sensitive symbolic vocabulary that can be generally understood and that is capable of representing all aspects of the unconscious. With the vocabulary that was established by the end of the Fifties, sf had become intelligible to a more general audience, and so attracted one.

We can assume that as these symbols continue to be used and acquire meanings and nuances through use—as our symbolic vocabulary grows more sensitive—the audience of speculative fantasy will continue to grow.

At the same time, it is clear that the symbolic vocabulary of the new reaction of the World Beyond the Hill is not as sensitive and flexible as the old vocabulary of fantasy was. Magic has subtleties that super-scientific power or even psi power do not have. Sorcerers have moral overtones that scientists do not have. There is a dimension in *Faust* that cannot be duplicated in the symbols available in *Frankenstein*.

A fantasy dragon has a wide and sensitive range of meanings as a symbol. Science fiction writers have attempted to write of alien beings that have dragonly qualities. De Camp has tried, and Jack Vance, and Robert Heinlein, and Anne McCaffrey, and Poul Anderson a number of times. All have caught at some of the essence of dragonness, but none has equaled or bettered the original.

The old symbols are useful. They were being saved in their preserve in Never-never land for a purpose. They are not going to be discarded. Instead, grounds are gradually being made for their existence in the new World Beyond the Hill.

As early as the Fifties, spacemen out on colonial survey set down on strange planets and discovered that the leprechauns had gotten there first. From that, we might have guessed that eventually it would be possible to discover all of the old symbols in the new World Beyond the Hill. If you like, the materials of our complete universe must include all that has ever been meaningful to us. Or, if you like otherwise, when the magical world discovered that the plumbing was in place, it moved into its new home.

So another trend is explained—the continuing merger of traditional fantasy into modern science fiction. The excursions into "mythology" by Zelazny, Swann, and others that marked the middle Sixties were in fact a concentration on the accommodation of potential traditional symbols to modern sf and the new World Beyond the Hill. In *Lord of Light*, Zelazny was welcoming the symbol of Buddha to the future and a distant planet. If Buddha and leprechauns can exist in the new World Beyond the Hill, what can be denied access?

A prize-winning 1971 story by Poul Anderson, "The Queen of Air and Darkness," is addressed to this process. In this story, seeming fairyland is discovered on another planet, is denied and exposed. Now, James Blish might describe this story as an acceptable variant on an old idea. Anderson himself might say that it demonstrates the pain in the exposure of cherished illusion. But we would describe the story as one testing the ability of traditional fantasy symbols to exist on far planets. And what is most interesting to us is that the fairyland was more convincing than its exposure. In fact, Anderson's characters saw a true fairyland but were too rationalistic to accept it. It was true fairyland. There is no reason that it shouldn't have been.

The problem of sf now that its full symbolic vocabulary is available is to learn to use the vocabulary, not just to extend it. To this point, we haven't found the handle on our invention. We writers haven't found our vocation yet. We don't know what we are good for. We do know that we are good for something serious, so for the past ten years we have tried our best to be serious.

We tried being mythological. But Roger Zelazny could not be serious about the Buddha. Being "mythological" didn't prove to be a serious enterprise.

Then we tried copying serious mimetic models. John Brunner tried writing like Dos Passos. And Brian Aldiss tried writing like the French antinovel and James Joyce. But the results did not justify continued serious attention after their considerable initial novelty. Aldiss's *Cryptozoic* will not be reprinted even as often as Zelazny's *The Dream Master*. We won't want to see the book again in years to come.

Most recently, like so much of the common stir in the world around us, we have been experimenting with decadence. Decadence is a very self-dramatizing way of being serious. We seem to feel serious in this way just now throughout the culture. The stories of Robert Silverberg and Barry Malzberg may be the equivalent of Alice Cooper, David Bowie, and the Rolling Stones. Or the equivalent of movies like *A Clockwork Orange* or *Last Tango in Paris*. Decadence is a mood that grips the entire culture, not just sf. It is a way of expressing frustration with the limitations of the conscious.

It isn't necessary for sf to express frustration with the limitations of the conscious. We might alternatively say that sf doesn't have to concern itself with crazy, frustrated Anglo-Saxon astronaut schlepps in the shambles of some near-future version of the Apollo program. One of us is even the author of a story like this that expressed our feelings one winter, so Barry Malzberg is not alone. If we only knew where the handle on sf was, we should have had much more to talk about than we presently do.

When we have learned how to be serious with symbols like spaceships and ray guns and telepathy and alternate dimensions, then "serious" stories like *Cryptozoic* and *Beyond Apollo* will seem symptomatic of the 1970 mind, when we didn't know what was going on and were very frustrated. Any time that we can write this narrowly and grant the possibility of only this little, while we sit amidst a wide availability of symbolic vocabulary, we must be frustrated in our seriousness.

This is true, of course, of us within our society as well. We are living narrowly and granting the possibility of little while we sit amidst a wealth of tools that have never been properly used. And all we can do is watch our friends make sick nasty criticisms in parody before the eyes of the conscious world. As in our minds, so in the world of our experience. As in our stories, so in the world of our experience.

Because, you see, if you really *believed* in the unknown world that surrounds the known, which you will do if and when writers begin to find out how to write about it seriously again, then you would look around at the contemporary multiplicity—and isn't there a lot of it—and you would put it together in new ways that you can't think of now because your unconscious is unavailable to you now. Whatever television ultimately is, it isn't anything like the purposes for which it has been used so far. But you haven't yet found the connective that makes sense of television and all the other trends of modern life. You will be more likely to as your unconscious becomes available to you.

We expect the next trend, when our period of acting out the end of the old line is over after perhaps another two years, to be a period of fragmentation of a further three or four years— lasting to about 1978 or 1979. It will be a period of private search, private experimentation, and personal solution much more markedly than it is now, behind the facade of decadence. Audiences will be smaller. Tastes will be more personal. But, particularly in retrospect, we will be able to see that among all the apparent experimentation for experimentation's sake, much of which will have seemed awfully goddamned frivolous, some was in fact serious. Truly serious.

In 1978 or 1979, we'll pause to think about this. Things will be less varied and lively for a while. The experiments will seem to have come to an end. And we will have run the old stuff to its very last breath. But then, we will look back over the experiments of 1976 and decide that some of them look pretty good. And, if we were to take their conclusions as premises, what then?

What then will prove to be another creative explosion, beginning perhaps around 1980. This creative explosion will be much greater in impact than the creative explosions that occurred in 1939–1941 and again in 1964–1968.

Everything in this description should be true of sf as it is of the culture as a whole. Once again.

After 1980, traditional fantasy will have become comfortably integrated in modern sf—speculative fantasy. The audience for speculative fantasy will be multiplied larger than its present size. Speculative fantasy itself will be radically altered in character. It will be something new and truly serious, and more enjoyable than it has ever been.

Alexei and Cory Panshin

Alexei Panshin was born in Lansing, Michigan, in 1940. He has attended schools in Michigan, Massachusetts and Illinois, and elsewhere, and has taught at Cornell University. He began to write in 1958. In 1969, his novel *Rite of Passage* won the Science Fiction Writers of America Nebula Award. In that same year, he married Cory Panshin and their work is now done in collaboration. Cory Panshin was born in New York City in 1947 and was graduated from Radcliffe College.

Heinlein in Dimension, 1968 (Advent)
Rite of Passage, 1968 (Ace)
Star Well, 1968 (Ace)
The Thurb Revolution, 1968 (Ace)
Masque World, 1969 (Ace)

Poul Anderson

The Creation of Imaginary Worlds: The World Builder's Handbook and Pocket Companion

This is an infinitely marvelous and beautiful universe which we are privileged to inhabit. Look inward to the molecules of life and the heart of the atom, or outward to moon, sun, planets, stars, the Orion Nebula where new suns and worlds are coming into being even as you watch, the Andromeda Nebula which is actually a whole sister galaxy: it is all the same cosmos, and every part of it is part of us. The elements of our flesh, blood, bones, and breath were forged out of hydrogen in stars long vanished. The gold in a wedding ring, the uranium burning behind many a triumphantly ordinary flick of an electric light switch, came out of those gigantic upheavals we call supernovas. It is thought that inertia itself, that most fundamental property of matter, would be meaningless—nonexistent—were there no stellar background to define space, time, and motion. Man is not an accident of chaos; nor is he the sum and only significance of creation. We belong here.

Once literature recognized this simple fact. Lightnings blazed around Lear; Ahab sailed an enormous ocean and Huck Finn went down a mighty river; McAndrew saw God in the machinery which man created according to the laws of the universe. But this is seldom true any longer. Barring a few, today's fashionable writers are concerned exclusively with Man, capitalized and isolated—who usually turns out to be a hypersensitive intellectual, capitalized and isolated among his own hangups. This is not necessarily bad, but may it not be a little bit limited?

In science fiction, whatever its faults, we have a medium which still allows exploration of a wider, more varied field. Of course, the story with a highly detailed extraterrestrial background is by no means the sole kind of science fiction. It is not even in the majority. Nor should it be. Too much of any one theme would put the reader right back into the monotony from which he hoped to escape.

However, when a story does take its characters beyond Earth, he is entitled to more than what he so often gets. This is either a world exactly like our own except for having neither geography nor history, or else it is an unbelievable mishmash which merely shows us that still another writer couldn't be bothered to do his homework.

As an example of the latter category, John Campbell once cited the awful example of a planet circling a blue-white sun and possessing an atmosphere of hydrogen and fluorine. This is simply a chemical impossibility. Those two substances, under the impetus of that radiation, would unite promptly and explosively. Another case is that of a world which is nothing but sterile desert, devoid of plant life, yet has animals and air that men can breathe. Where does the food chain begin? What maintains an equilibrium of free oxygen?

At the very least, a well-thought-out setting goes far toward adding artistic verisimilitude to an otherwise bald and unconvincing narrative. By bringing in this detail and that, tightly linked, the writer makes his imaginary globe seem real. Furthermore, the details are interesting in their own right. They may reveal something of the possibilities in their own right.

They may reveal something of the possibilities in these light-years that surround us, thereby awakening the much-desired sense of wonder. Finally, many of them will suggest important parts of the plot.

In the most highly developed cases, they practically *become* the story. Hal Clement's *Mission of Gravity* is a classic of this kind. But enchanting though it is, that sort of thing is reserved for writers who have the necessary scientific training.

What I wish to show here is that others can do likewise, in a more modest but nevertheless astonishingly thorough fashion. It doesn't take a degree in physics. It simply takes the basic knowledge of current scientific fact and theory which any person must have before he can properly—in this day and age—call himself educated. In addition, it requires imagination and a willingness to work; but these are qualities that every writer worth his salt already possesses. Anyhow, "work" is the wrong word, if that suggests drudgery. The designing of a planet is fascinating—sheer fun.

Because it is, I believe most readers would also enjoy seeing a few of the principles spelled out.

They involve mathematics, and equations are their natural form of expression. But too many people are unreasonably puzzled, even frightened, by equations. Those who aren't will already know the natural laws I refer to; or they can be trusted to look them up. So instead I shall offer a few graphs.[1] With their help, and just the tiniest bit of arithmetic, anyone should be able to start world-building on his own.

Needless to say, any serious effort of this kind demands more information than can possibly be squeezed into the present essay. Two reference books that are especially well suited to science fiction purposes and are, in addition, a joy to read are: *Intelligent Life in the Universe* by I. S. Shklovskii and Carl Sagan (Holden Day, 1966) and *Habitable Planets for Man* by Stephen H. Dole (Elsevier, rev. ed., 1970). Of course, there are numerous other good works available.

Like every living science, astronomy today is in a state of

1. Drafted by Karen Anderson

continuous revolution. Any book is virtually certain to contain outdated material; and "facts" are always subject to change without notice. (Indeed, as I write, the whole set of methods by which the distances and thus the properties of other galaxies have been obtained, is being called into question.) I have no desire to be dogmatic. If I sometimes appear that way in what follows, it is merely to save space. Take for granted that every statement bears a qualifier like: "This is my limited understanding of what the best contemporary thought on the subject seems to be."

Yet let us never forget that it is the best thought available. If we don't use it, we will have no basis whatsoever on which to reason.

Therefore, onward! Mainly we'll consider some of the possibilities regarding planets which, without being copies of Earth, are not as absolutely different from it as are the other members of our own Solar System. Anything more exotic, à la Hal Clement, would take us too far afield. Besides, more often than not, a writer wants a world where his humans can survive without overly many artificial aids.

A number of parameters determine what such a globe will be like. They include the kind of sun and orbit it has, the size and mass, axial tilt and rotation, satellites—to name a few of the more obvious. Doubtless there are several more which science has thus far not identified. Our knowledge of these things is less than complete. But simply by varying those parameters we do know about, we can produce a huge variety of environments for stories to happen in. We can also gain, and give to our readers, some feeling for the subtlety and interrelatedness of nature and her laws.

Normally we begin by picking a star, real or imaginary. In earlier days, science fiction customarily put planets around the familiar ones like Sirius, Vega, Antares, or Mira. It was then legitimate enough, if a trifle repetitious. But today we know, or believe we know, that few of the naked-eye stars will serve.

Mostly they are giants, visible to us only because they are so brilliant that we can pick them out across immense gulfs of space. (Sol would no longer be discernible without instruments at a distance of about 55 light-years.) Now the red giants like Antares, the variables like Mira, are dying stars, well on their way to the dim, ultra-dense white-dwarf condition. If ever they had planets—their mass makes that unlikely, as we will see in a minute—the inner attendants have been seared or even consumed, as these suns expanded. If outer globes have been warmed up, this won't last long enough to do biological evolution any good.

Probably the majority of stars in the universe are still enjoying health. Their temperatures and luminosities vary enormously. The most important reason for this is the difference in their masses. The more massive a sun is, the more intensely compressed it becomes at its core, and thus the more fierce and rapid are the thermonuclear reactions which cause it to shine. This dependence of output on mass is a highly sensitive one, so that the latter covers a much smaller range than the former.

These stars form a well-defined series, from the largest and brightest to the smallest and dimmest, which is called the main sequence. For historical reasons, spectrographers label the types O, B, A, F, G, K, M. (The mnemonic is "*Oh, be a fine girl, kiss me.*") The series being continuous, a number is added to place each star more exactly on the curve. For example, the F types begin with F_0; then we get F_1, F_2, and so on through F_9, which is followed by G_0. That last, G_0, was formerly the classification of our own sun; but more recent information has gotten Sol to be labeled G_2.

Figure 1 shows a large part of the main sequence. It omits the extremes, because they really are too extreme to diagram very well. That is, the main sequence runs from the hottest Type O blue giants, some as much as a million times the strength of Sol, on through the yellowish F and G stars, to the red dwarfs of Class M, the dimmest of which may be less than a thousandth as intense as our daystar. Types are indicated along the bottom of the graph, with corresponding masses. Luminosities—necessarily on a logarithmic scale—are shown going up the left-hand side.

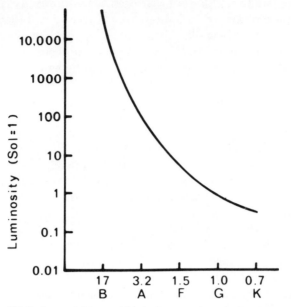

FIG. 1   Mass (Sol:1) and spectral type

From this, you can find the mass corresponding to a given brightness. It will only be a rough estimate; but then, the real values don't lie neatly on an infinitely thin curve. They vary by a fair amount, depending on such factors as the age and exact chemical composition of the individual star.

More is involved than just the total radiation. As everyone knows who has ever heated a piece of metal in a fire, temperature affects color. The hottest stars are called blue giants because they are not only giants in output, but also their light contains a distinctly larger proportion of blue than does that of Sol. They also emit a higher percentage, as well as absolute amount, of ultraviolet and X-ray wavelengths; and no doubt the solar winds streaming from them are something terrific. All these quantities drop off as temperature does, until we get to the cool, ultraviolet-poor red dwarfs. (However, the weaker ones among these last are not mere embers. Sometimes they spit out monstrous flares which may temporarily double the total brightness—a fact which I used in a story once but on which I have no copyright.)

Well, shall we put our imaginary world in orbit around one of the spectacular giants?

Sorry. Because they burn at such a prodigal rate, these great stars are short-lived. Once they have condensed from interstellar dust and gas, Type O suns spend a bare few million years on the main sequence; then they apparently go out in the supernal violence of supernova explosions. Their ultimate fate, and the precise death throes of their somewhat lesser brethren, are too complicated to discuss here. But even an A_0 star like Sirius is good for no more than about four hundred million years of steady shining—not much in terms of geology and evolution.

Furthermore, the evidence is that giants don't have planets in the first place. There is a most suggestive sharp drop in the rotation rate, just about when one gets to the earlier Type Fs. From then on, down through Type M, suns appear to spin so slowly that it is quite reasonable to suppose the "extra" has gone into planets.

Giants are rare, anyway. They are far outnumbered by the less showy yellow dwarfs like Sol—which, in turn, are outnumbered by the inconspicuous red dwarfs. (There are about ten times as many M as G stars.) And this great majority also has the longevity we need. For instance, an F_5 spends a total of six billion years on the main sequence before it begins to swell, redden, and die. Sol, G_2, has a ten-billion-year life expectancy, and is about halfway through it at the present day, making a comfortingly long future. The K stars live for several times that figure, the weakest M stars for hundreds of billions of years. Even if life, in the biological sense, is slow to get generated and slow to evolve on a planet so feebly irradiated, it will have—or will have had—a vast time in which to develop. That may or may not make a significant difference; and thereby hangs many a tale.

So let's take a star of Type F or later. If we want to give it a planet habitable to man, probably it must be somewhere between, say, F_5 and K_5. Earlier in the sequence, the system will presumably be too young for photosynthesis to have started, releasing oxygen into the air. Later, the sun will be too cool, too dull, too niggardly with ultraviolet, to support the kind of ecology on which humans depend.

Granted, a planet of a red dwarf may bear life of another sort than ours. Or it may orbit close enough that the total radiation it gets is sufficient for us. In the latter case, the chances are that it would rotate quite slowly, having been braked by tidal friction. The sun would appear huge and reddish, or even crimson, in the sky; one might be able to gaze straight at it, seeing spots and flares with the naked eye. Colors would look different, and shadows would have blurrier outlines than on Earth. Already, then, we see how many touches of strangeness we can get by changing a single parameter. In the superficially dry data of astronomy and physics is the potential of endless adventure.

But for our concrete example of planet-building, let's go toward the other end of the scale, i.e., choosing a star brighter than Sol. The main reason for doing so is to avoid the kind of complications we have just noticed in connection with a weaker sun. We will have quite enough to think about as is!

The hypothetical planet is one that I recently had occasion to work up for a book to be edited by Roger Elwood, and is used with his kind permission. I named it Cleopatra. While tracing out the course of its construction, we'll look at a few conceivable variations, out of infinitely many.

First, where in the universe is the star? It won't be anywhere in our immediate neighborhood, because those most closely resembling Sol within quite a few light-years are somewhat dimmer—ours being, in fact, rather more luminous than average. (True, Alpha Centauri A is almost a twin, and its closer companion is not much different. However, this is a multiple system. That does not necessarily rule out its having planets; but the possibility of this is controversial, and in any event it would complicate things too much for the present essay if we had more than one sun.)

Rather than picking a real star out of an astronomical catalogue, though that is frequently a good idea, I made mine up, and arbitrarily put it about four hundred light-years off in the direction of Ursa Major. This is unspecific enough—it defines such a huge volume of space—that something corresponding is bound to be out there someplace. Seen from that location, the boreal constellations are considerably changed, though most remain recognizable. The austral constellations have suffered the least alteration, the equatorial ones are intermediately affected. But who says the celestial hemispheres of Cleopatra must be identical with those of Earth? For all we know, its axis could be at right angles to ours. Thus a writer can invent picturesque descriptions of the night sky and of the images which people see there.

Arbitrary also is the stellar type, F_7. This means it has 1.2 times the mass of Sol, twenty percent more. As we shall see, the diameter is little greater; but it has 2.05 times the total luminosity.

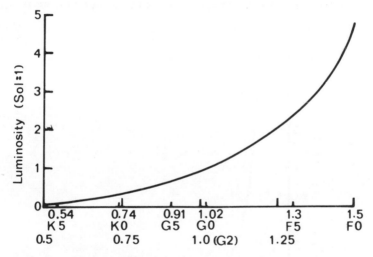

FIG. 2   Mass (Sol=1) and spectral type

Numbers this precise cannot be taken off a graph. I computed them on the basis of formulas. But you can get values close enough for most purposes from Figure 2. It charts the relevant part of the main sequence on a larger scale than Figure 1, and has no need to depict any numbers logarithmically. In other words, with the help of a ruler you can find approximately what mass corresponds to what brightness. Nor is this kind of estimating dishonest. After all, as said before, there is considerable variation in reality. If, say, you guessed that a mass of 1.1 Sol meant an energy output of 1.5, the odds are that some examples of this actually exist. You could go ahead with reasonable confidence. Anyway, it's unlikely that the actual values you picked would get into the story text. But indirectly, by making the writer understand his own creation in detail, they can have an enormous influence for the better.

Returning to Cleopatra: an F_7 is hotter and whiter than Sol. Probably it has more spots, prominences, flares, and winds of charged particles sweeping from it. Certainly the proportion of ultraviolet to visible light is higher, though not extremely so.

It is natural to suppose that it has an entire family of planets; and a writer may well exercise his imagination on various mem-

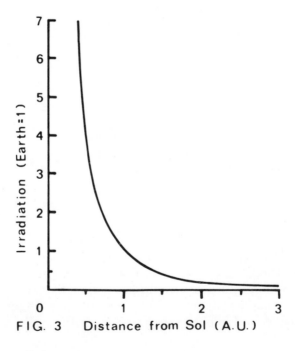

FIG. 3   Distance from Sol (A.U.)

bers of the system. Here we shall just be dealing with the habitable one. Bear in mind, however, that its nearer sisters will doubtless from time to time be conspicuous in its heavens, even as Venus, Mars, and others shine upon Earth. What names do they have—what poetic or mystical significance in the minds of natives or of long-established colonists?

For man to find it livable, a planet must be neither too near nor too far from its sun. The total amount of energy it receives in a given time is proportional to the output of that sun and inversely proportional to the square of the distance between. Figure 3 diagrams this for the inner Solar System in terms of the astronomical unit, the average separation of Sol and Earth. Thus we see that Venus, at 0.77 a.u., gets about 1.7 times the energy we do, while Mars, at 1.5 a u., gets only about 0.45 the irradiation. The same curve will work for any other star if you multiply its absolute brightness. For example, at its distance of 1.0 a.u., Earth gets 1.0 unit of irradiation from Sol; but at this remove from a sun half as bright, it would only get half as much, while at this same distance from our hypothetical sun, it would get 2.05 times as much.

That could turn it into an oven—by human standards, at any rate. We want our planet in a more comfortable orbit. What should that be? If we set it about 1.4 a.u. out, it would get almost exactly the same total energy that Earth does. No one can say this is impossible. We don't know what laws govern the spacing of orbits in a planetary system. There does appear to be a harmonic rule (associated with the names of Bode and Titius) and there are reasons to suppose this is not coincidental. Otherwise we are ignorant. Yet it would be remarkable if many stars had planets at precisely the distances most convenient for man.

Seeking to vary the parameters as much as reasonable, and assuming that the attendants of larger stars will tend to swing in larger paths, I finally put Cleopatra 1.24 a.u. out. This means that it gets 1.33 times the total irradiation of Earth—a third again as much.

Now that is an average distance. Planets and moons have elliptical orbits. We know of none which travel in perfect circles. However, some, like Venus, come close to doing so; and few have courses which are very eccentric. For present purposes, we can use a fixed value of separation between star and planet, while bearing in mind that it *is* only an average. The variations due to a moderate eccentricity will affect the seasons somewhat, but not much compared to other factors.

If you do want to play with an oddball orbit, as I have done once or twice, you had better explain how it got to be that way; and to follow the cycle of the year, you will have to use Kepler's equal-areas law, either by means of the calculus or by counting squares on graph paper. In the present exposition, we will assume that Cleopatra has a near-circular track.

Is not an added thirty-three percent of irradiation enough to make it uninhabitable?

This is another of those questions that cannot be answered for sure in the current state of knowledge. But we can make an educated guess. The theoretical ("black body") temperature of an object is proportional to the fourth root—the square root of the square root—of the rate at which it receives energy. Therefore it changes more slowly than one might think. At the same time, the actual mean temperature at the surface of Earth is considerably greater than such calculations make it out to be, largely because the atmosphere maintains a vast reservoir of heat in the well-known greenhouse effect. And air and water together protect us from such day-night extremes as Luna suffers.

The simple fourth-root principle says that our imaginary planet should be about 20°C., or roughly 40° F., warmer on the average than Earth is. That's not too bad. The tropics might not be usable by men, but the higher latitudes and uplands ought to be pretty good. Remember, though, that this bit of arithmetic has taken no account of atmosphere or hydrosphere. I think they would smooth things out considerably. On the one hand, they do trap heat; on the other hand, clouds reflect back a great deal of light, which thus never has a chance to reach the surface; and both gases and liquids blot up, or redistribute, what does get through.

My best guess is, therefore, that while Cleopatra will generally be somewhat warmer than Earth, the difference will be less than an oversimplified calculation suggests. The tropics will usually be hot, but nowhere unendurable; and parts of them, cooled by altitude or sea breezes, may well be quite balmy. There will probably be no polar ice caps, but tall mountains ought to have their eternal snows. Pleasant climates should prevail through higher latitudes than is the case on Earth.

You may disagree, in which case you have quite another story to tell. By all means, go ahead. Varying opinions make science fiction yarns as well as horse races.

Meanwhile, though, let's finish up the astronomy. How long is the planet's year? Alas for ease, this involves two factors, the mass of the sun and the size of the orbit. The year-length is inversely proportional to the square root of the former, and directly proportional to the square root of the cube of the semi-major axis. Horrors.

So here we need two graphs. Figure 4 shows the relationship of period to distance from the sun within our solar system. (The "distance" is actually the semi-major axis; but for purposes of calculations as rough as these, where orbits are supposed to be approximately circular, we can identify it with the mean separation between star and planet.) We see, for instance, that a body twice as far out as Earth is takes almost three times as long to complete a circuit. At a remove of 1.24 a.u., which we have assigned to Cleopatra, its period would equal 1.38 years.

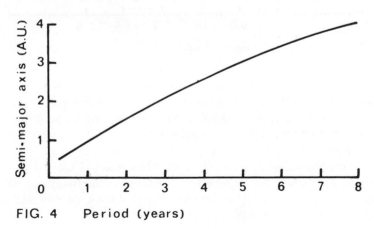

FIG. 4   Period (years)

But our imaginary sun is more massive than Sol. Therefore its gravitational grip is stronger and, other things being equal, it swings its children around faster. Figure 5 charts inverse square roots. For a mass of 1.2 Sol, this quantity is 0.915.

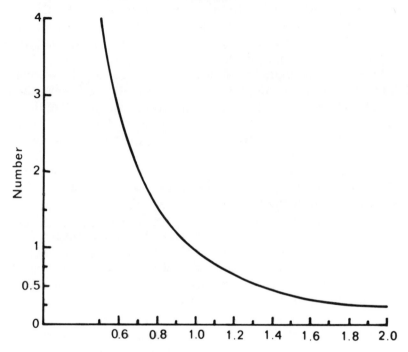

FIG. 5   Inverse square root

If we multiply together the figures taken off these two graphs —1.38 times 0.915—we come up with the number we want, 1.26. That is, our planet takes 1.26 times as long to go around its sun as Earth does to go around Sol. Its year lasts about fifteen of our months.

Again, the diagrams aren't really that exact. I used a slide rule. But for those not inclined to do likewise, the diagrams will furnish numbers which can be used to get at least a general idea of how some fictional planet will behave.

Let me point out afresh that these are nevertheless important numbers, a part of the pseudo-reality the writer hopes to create. Only imagine: a year a fourth again as long as Earth's. What does this do to the seasons, the calendar, the entire rhythm of life? We shall need more information before we can answer such questions, but it is not too early to start thinking about them.

Although more massive than Sol, the sun of Cleopatra is not much bigger. Not only is volume a cube function of radius, which would make the diameter just six percent greater if densities were equal, but densities are not equal. The heavier stars must be more compressed by their own weight than are the lighter ones. Hence we can say that all suns which more or less resemble Sol have more or less the same size.

Now our imaginary planet and its luminary are further apart than our real ones. Therefore the sun must look smaller in the Cleopatran than in the terrestrial sky. As long as angular diameters are small (and Sol's, seen from Earth, is a mere half a degree) they are closely enough proportional to the linear diameters and inversely proportional to the distance between object and observer. That is, in the present case we have a star whose breadth, in terms of Sol, is 1, while its distance is 1.24 a.u. Therefore the apparent width is 1/1.24, or 0.87 what Sol shows to us. In other words, our imaginary sun looks a bit smaller in the heavens than does our real one.

This might be noticeable, even striking, when it was near the horizon, the common optical illusion at such times exaggerating its size. (What might the psychological effects of that be?) Otherwise it would make no particular difference—since no one could safely look near so brilliant a thing without heavy eye protection—except that shadows would tend to be more sharp-edged than on Earth. Those shadows ought also to have a more marked bluish tinge, especially on white surfaces. Indeed, all color values are subtly changed by the light upon Cleopatra. I suspect men would quickly get used to that; but perhaps not.

Most likely, so active a sun produces some auroras that put the terrestrial kind to shame, as well as occasional severe interference with radio, power lines, and the like. (By the time humans can travel that far, they may well be using apparatus that isn't affected. But there is still a possible story or two in this point.) An oxygen-containing atmosphere automatically develops an ozone layer which screens out most of the ultraviolet. Nevertheless, humans would have to be more careful about sunburn than on Earth, especially in the lower latitudes or on the seas.

Now what about the planet itself? If we have been a long time in coming to that, it simply emphasizes the fact that no body—and nobody—exists in isolation from the whole universe.

Were the globe otherwise identical with Earth, we would already have innumerable divergences. Therefore let us play with some further variations. For instance, how big or small can it be? Too small, and it won't be able to hold an adequate atmosphere. Too big, and it will keep most of its primordial hydrogen and helium, as our great outer planets have done; it will be even more alien than are Mars or Luna. On the other hand, Venus—with a mass similar to Earth's—is wrapped in gas whose pressure at the surface approaches a hundred times what we are used to. We don't know why. In such an area of mystery, the science fiction writer is free to guess.

But let us go at the problem from another angle. How much gravity—or how little—can mankind tolerate for an extended period of time? We know that both high weight, such as is experienced in a centrifuge, and zero weight, such as is experienced in an orbiting spacecraft, have harmful effects. We don't know exactly what the limits are, and no doubt they depend on how long one is exposed. However, it seems reasonable to assume that men and women can adjust to some such range as 0.75 to 1.25 Earth gravity. That is, a person who weighs 150 pounds on Earth can safely live where he weighs as little as 110 or as much as 190. Of course, he will undergo somatic changes, for instance in the muscles; but we can suppose these are adaptive, not pathological.

(The reference to women is not there as a concession to militant liberationists. It takes both sexes to keep humanity going. The Spaniards failed to colonize the Peruvian altiplano for the simple reason that, while both they and their wives could learn to breathe the thin air, the wives could not bring babies to term. So the local Indians, with untold generations of natural selection behind them, still dominate that region, racially if not politically. This is one example of the significance of changing a parameter. Science fiction writers should be able to invent many more.)

The pull of a planet at its surface depends on its mass and its size. These two quantities are not independent. Though solid bodies are much less compressible than gaseous ones like stars, still, the larger one of them is, the more it tends to squeeze itself, forming denser allotropes in its interior. Within the man-habitable range, this isn't too important, especially in view of the fact that the mean density is determined by other factors as well. If we assume the planet is perfectly spherical—it won't be, but the difference isn't enough to worry about except under the most extreme conditions—then weight is proportional to the diameter of the globe and to its overall density.

Suppose it has 0.78 the (average) Terrestrial diameter, or about 6,150 miles; and suppose it has 1.10 the (mean) Terrestrial density, or about 6.1 times that of water. Then, although its total mass is only 0.52 that of Earth, about half, its surface gravity is 0.78 times 1.10, or 0.86 that which we are accustomed to here at home. Our person who weighed 150 pounds here, weighs about 130 there.

I use these particular figures because they are the ones I chose for Cleopatra. Considering Mars, it seems most implausible that any world that small could retain a decent atmosphere; but considering Venus, it seems as if many worlds of rather less mass than it or Earth may do so. At least, nobody today can disprove the idea.

But since there is less self-compression, have I given Cleopatra an impossibly high density? No, because I am postulating a higher proportion of heavy elements in its makeup than Earth has. That is not fantastic. Stars, and presumably their planets, do vary in composition.

(Writers can of course play with innumerable other combinations, like that in the very large but very metal-poor world of Jack Vance's *Big Planet*.)

The results of changing the gravity must be far-reaching indeed. Just think how this could influence the gait, the need for systematic exercise, the habit of standing versus sitting (are people in low weight more patient about queues?), the character of sports, architecture, engineering (the lower the weight, the smaller wings your aircraft need under given conditions, but the bigger brakes your ground vehicles), and on and on. In a lesser gravity, it takes a bit longer to fall some certain distance, and one lands a bit less hard; mountains and dunes tend to be steeper; pendulums of a given length, and waves on water, move slower. The air pressure falls off less rapidly with altitude. Thus, here on Earth, at about 18,000 feet the pressure is one half that at sea level; but on Cleopatra, you must go up to 21,000 feet for this. The effects on weather, every kind of flying, and the size of life zones bear thinking about.

A higher gravity reverses these consequences, more or less in proportion.

In our present state of ignorance, we have to postulate many things that suit our story purposes but may not be true—for example, that a planet as small as Cleopatra can actually hold an Earth-type atmosphere. Other postulates—for example, that Cleopatran air is insufficient, or barely sufficient, to sustain human life—are equally legitimate, and lead to quite other stories. But whatever the writer assumes, let him realize that it will make for countless strangenesses, some radical, some subtle, but each of them all-pervasive, in the environment.

(I must admit that certain of them scarcely look important. Thus, the horizon distance—for a man standing on a flat plain —is proportional to the square root of the planet's diameter. On Earth it is about five miles, and for globes not very much bigger or smaller, the change will not be striking. Often mountains, woods, haze, or the like will blot it out entirely. . . . Yet even in this apparent triviality, some skillful writer may see a story.)

If we have a higher proportion of heavy elements, including radioactive ones, than Earth does, then we doubtless get more internal heat; and the lesser size of Cleopatra also helps pass it outward faster. Thus here we should have more than a terrestrial share of volcanoes, quakes, and related phenomena. I guess there would be plenty of high mountains, some overreaching Everest; but we still know too little about how mountains get raised for this to be much more than a guess. In some areas, local concentrations of arsenic or whatever may well make the soil dangerous to man. But on the whole, industry ought to thrive.

Conversely, and other things being equal, a metal-poor world is presumably fairly quiescent; a shortage of copper and iron might cause its natives to linger indefinitely in a Stone Age; colonists might have to emphasize a technology based on lighter elements such as aluminum.

How fast does the planet rotate? This is a crucial question, but once more, not one to which present-day science can give a definitive answer. We know that Earth is being slowed down by Luna, so maybe it once spun around far more quickly than now. *Maybe.* It isn't being braked very fast, and we can't be sure how long that rate of deceleration has prevailed in the past or will in the future. Mars, whose satellites are insignificant, turns at nearly the same angular speed, while Venus, with no satellite whatsoever, is exceedingly slow and goes widdershins to boot.

It does seem likely that big planets will, by and large, spin rapidly—such as Jupiter, with a period of about ten hours. They must pick up a lot of angular momentum as they condense, and they don't easily lose it afterward. But as for the lesser bodies, like Earth, we're still mainly in the realm of speculation.

I assumed Cleopatra has no satellites worth mentioning. Therefore it has been slowed less than Earth, its present rotation taking 17.3 hours. This makes its year equal to 639 of its own days. But I could equally well have dreamed something different.

If it did have a moon, how would that affect things? Well, first, there are certain limitations on the possibilities. A moon can't be too close in, or it will break apart because of unbalanced gravitational forces on its inner and outer sides. This boundary is called Roche's limit, after the astronomer who first examined the matter in detail. For Earthlike planets it is about 2.5 radii from the center, 1.5 from the surface. That is, for Earth itself Roche's limit is roughly six thousand miles straight up. (Of course, it doesn't apply to small bodies like spaceships, only to larger and less compact masses such as Luna.) On the other hand, a moon circling very far out would be too weakly held; in time, the tug of the sun and neighbor planets would cause it to drift elsewhere. At a quarter million miles' remove, Luna is quite solidly held. But one or two million might prove too much in the long run—and in any event, so remote, our companion would not be a very interesting feature of our skies.

(Cleopatra did have a small moon once, which got too near and disintegrated, forming a ring of dust and rocky fragments. But the calculations about this, to determine what it looks like and how that appearance varies throughout the year, are rather involved.)

Within such bounds, as far as science today can tell, we are free to put almost anything that isn't outrageously big. But if the orbit is really peculiar, the writer should be prepared to explain how this came about. A polar or near-polar track is less stable than one which isn't far off the plane of the primary's equator; it is also much less likely to occur in the first place. That is, through some such freak of nature as the capture of an asteroid under exactly the right circumstances, we might get a moon with a wildly canted orbital plane; but it probably wouldn't stay there for many million years. In general, satellites that don't pass very far north and south of the equators of their planets are more plausible.

Well, so let's take a body of some reasonable size, and set it in motion around our imaginary world at some reasonable average distance. (This is distance from the center of the planet, not its surface. For a nearby companion, the distinction is important.) How long does it take to complete a circuit and how big does it look to someone on the ground?

The same principles we used before will work again here. Take Figures 4 and 5. Instead of letting "1.0" stand for quantities like "the mass of Sol," "the mean distance of Earth from Sol," and "the period of Earth around Sol" let it stand for "the mass of Earth," "the mean distance of Luna from Earth," and "the period of Luna around Earth." Thus you find your answer in terms of months rather than years. (This is a rough-and-ready method, but it will serve fairly well provided that the satellite isn't extremely big or extremely near.) Likewise, the apparent size of the object in the sky, compared to Luna, is close-enough equal to its actual diameter compared to Luna, divided by its distance from the surface of the planet, compared to Luna.

But in this case, we aren't done yet. What we have been discussing is the sidereal period, i.e., the time for the satellite to complete an orbit as seen from out among the stars. Now the planet is rotating while the moon revolves around it. Most likely both move in the same direction; retrograde orbits, like polar ones, are improbable though not altogether impossible. Unless the moon is quite remote, this will have a very marked effect. For instance, Luna, as seen from Earth, rises about fifty minutes later every day than on the previous day—while an artificial satellite not far aloft comes up in the west, not the east, and virtually flies through the heavens, undergoing eclipse in the middle of its course.

I would offer you another graph at this point, but unfortunately can't think of any that would be much help. You shall have to subtract revolution from rotation, and visualize how the phases of the moon(s) proceed and how they show in the skies. Bear in mind, too, that very close satellites probably won't be visible everywhere on the planet. Algebra and trigonometry are the best tools for jobs of this kind. But failing them, scale diagrams drawn on graph paper will usually give results sufficiently accurate for storytelling purposes.

The closer and bigger a moon is, the more tidal effect it has. For that matter, the solar tides aren't generally negligible; on Earth they amount to a third of the total. There is no simple formula. We know how tides can vary, from the nearly unmoved Mediterranean to those great bores which come roaring up the Bay of Fundy. Still, the writer can get a rough idea from this fact: that the tide-raising power is proportional to the mass of the moon or sun, and inversely proportional to the *cube* of its distance. That is, if Luna were twice as massive at its present remove, the tides it creates would be roughly twice what they really are. If Luna kept the same mass but were at twice its present distance, its tides would be $1/2^3$ or one-eighth as strong as now, while if it were half as far off as it is, they would be 2^3

or eight times as great. In addition, the theoretical height of a deepwater tide is proportional to the diameter and inversely proportional to the density of the planet being pulled upon. That is, the larger and/or less dense it happens to be, the higher its oceans are lifted.

As said, there is such tremendous local variation that these formulas are only good for making an overall estimate of the situation. But it is crucial for the writer to do that much. How do the waters behave? (Two or more moons could make sailing mighty complicated, not to speak of more important things like ocean currents.) Great tides, long continued, will slow down the rotation—though the amount of friction they make depends also on the pattern of land distribution, with most energy being dissipated when narrow channels like Bering Strait are in existence. We must simply guess at the effects on weather or on life, but they are almost certainly enormous. For instance, if Earth had weaker tides than it does, would life have been delayed in moving from the seas onto dry ground?

One clear-cut, if indirect, influence of tides on weather is through the spin of the planet. The more rapidly it rotates, the stronger the cyclone-breeding Coriolis forces. In the case of Cleopatra, we have not only this factor, but also the more powerful irradiaton—and, maybe, the greater distance upward from surface to stratosphere, together with the lesser separation of poles and tropics—to generate more violent and changeable weather than is common on Earth.

Insofar as the matter is understood by contemporary geophysicists, we can predict that Cleopatra, having a hotter molten core and a greater rate of rotation, possesses a respectable magnetic field, quite likely stronger than the terrestrial. This will have helped preserve its atmosphere, in spite of the higher temperatures and lower gravity. Solar particles, which might otherwise have kicked gas molecules into space, have generally been warded off. To be sure, some get through to the uppermost thin layers of air, creating secondary cosmic rays, electrical disturbances, and showy auroras.

The weather is likewise affected by axial tilt. Earth does not ride upright in its orbit; no member of the Solar System does.

Our axis of rotation slants about 23½° off the vertical. From this we get our seasons, with everything that that implies. We cannot tell how often Earthlike worlds elsewhere have radically different orientations. My guess is that this is a rarity and that, if anything, Earth may lean a bit more rakishly than most. But it's merely another guess. Whatever value the writer chooses, let him ponder how it will determine the course of the year, the size and character of climatic zones, the development of life and civilizations.

If Earth did travel upright, thus having no seasons, we would probably never see migratory birds across the sky. One suspects there would be no clear cycle of the birth and death of vegetation either. Then what form would agriculture have taken? Society? Religion?

It is questions like these that science fiction is uniquely well fitted to ask. Simple permutations of natural law, such as we have been considering here, raise amazingly many of them, and suggest tentative answers.

True, this kind of backgrounding work is the barest beginning. The writer must then go on to topography, living creatures both nonhuman and human, problems and dreams, the story itself—ultimately, to those words which are to appear on a printed page. Yet if he has given some thought and, yes, some love to his setting, that will show in the words. Only by making it real to himself can he make it, and the events which happen within its framework, seem real to the reader.

The undertaking isn't unduly hard. It is mind-expanding in the best sense of that phrase. Or may I end by repeating myself and saying that, for writer and reader alike, it's fun?

Poul Anderson

Poul Anderson was born in Pennsylvania in 1926, of Scandinavian parents (hence the spelling of the first name), and was raised in Texas and on a Minnesota farm, with intervals in Europe and the Washington, D.C., area. He graduated from the University of Minnesota in physics, with distinction, but having already sold some stories while in college (first significant publication in 1947), decided to become a writer. Now a long-time resident, with wife and daughter, of San Francisco Bay area; wife, Karen, occasionally writes, too.

He is the author of more than fifty books and two hundred-odd short pieces. Besides science fiction, they include fantasy, mystery, historical, juvenile, and here-and-now fiction; nonfiction; poetry, essays, translations, criticism, etc. Short stories and articles have appeared in places as various as the science fiction magazines, *Boys' Life, Playboy,* the Toronto *Star Weekly, National Review, Ellery Queen's,* and the defunct *Jack London's* magazine. Novels, nonfiction books, and short stories have appeared in fifteen foreign languages.

Former regional vice-president of Mystery Writers of America and former president of Science Fiction Writers of America.

Honors include: Guest of honor, world science fiction convention of 1959, and several regional conventions; four Hugo awards and two Nebula awards for best sf novelette of the year; "Forry" Award of Los Angeles Science Fantasy Society; special issue (April, 1972) of *The Magazine of Fantasy and Science Fiction;* Macmillan Cock Robin Award for best mystery novel; investiture in The Baker Street Irregulars, and twice winner of the Morley-Montgomery Prize for scholarship in Sherlock Holmes; Knight of Mark Twain. In the nonliterary field, knighthood in the Society for Creative Anachronism, for prowess in medieval combat.

Among Poul Anderson's more popular books are *Brain Wave, The High Crusade, The Enemy Stars, Three Hearts and Three Lions, The Broken Sword, Tau Zero.* Most recent novels are, as of now: *There Will Be Time* and *The People of the Wind.*

Hal Clement

The Creation of Imaginary Beings

The unheard-of creature and the unhuman character have been part of the storyteller's ammunition since long before the invention of writing, it seems safe to claim. Angel and demon, ghost and vampire, dragon and *rukh*, Homer's Cyclopes and Mandeville's headless men are all part of the basic human heritage. Telling how to create such beings might almost be taken as an insult to normal human imagination.

In science fiction, however, we do try to maintain standards of realism (or at least believability) for a rather more knowledgeable and technically sophisticated audience than Homer faced. This is not to say that we have *higher* standards in these respects; Homer's gods and Sinbad's island-whale were as believable in their day as moon flight and atomic energy are now. Our standards are simply based on a better knowledge of the physical universe.

Also, there is no intended suggestion that the ghost and his nonmaterial kin either have vanished or should vanish from the inventory. It is perfectly possible for a competent, informed, educated materialist of the late twentieth century to enjoy the works of Sheridan le Fanu or Lyman Frank Baum, not only with the full knowledge that they are not true histories but also safely above the need to prove his open-mindedness by saying that such things *might* be possible. However, I am confining my remarks to the rather narrow limits of "hard" science fiction, where I am qualified to hold a professional opinion. It has been charged that in restricting ourselves to "scientific accuracy" my colleagues and I are narrowing the scope of usable story ideas available to us. My answer, mathematically rather horrible but defensible under literary standards, is that the square root of infinity is not really that much smaller than infinity as far as resource material goes. Our main point is that for many modern readers, a violation of the laws of thermodynamics by the author can spoil a story just as effectively as having Abraham Lincoln changing a set of spark plugs in a historical novel.

Therefore, if we travel to Mars in a story, the vehicle must operate either along physical laws we currently think we know, or at least on more or less convincing extrapolations of those laws. Furthermore, when we get there the Martians, not to mention their lapdogs, saddle horses, dinner steaks, and rheumatism, must not strike too jarring a set of notes against the background which author and reader are, it is to be hoped, visualizing together. It is permissible and even desirable to take the reader by surprise with some of these details, of course. However, his reaction to the surprise should be the urge to kick himself for failing to foresee the item, rather than resentment at the author's ringing in a new theme.

It follows that the "hard" science fiction writer must have at least an informed layman's grasp of biochemistry and ecology.

Even in this narrowed realm, there would seem to be two basic lines of procedure for the storyteller who needs nonhuman characters and other extraterrestrial life forms. The two are not mutually exclusive; they overlap heavily in many ways. Nevertheless they represent different directions of attack on the problem, one of which is more useful if the basic story is already well set up in the author's mind, while the other is of more use in creating and developing the story possibilities themselves.

In the first case, the qualities of the various life forms have to a considerable extent already been determined; they are demanded by the story events. Excellent recent examples occur in some of Keith Laumer's "Retief" novels, such as the wheeled metallic natives of Quopp in *Retief's War* and the even more peculiar Lumbagans in *Retief's Ransom.*

In other words, if the savages of Fomalhaut VII are going to kidnap the heroine by air, they must be able to fly with the weight of a human being. If the hero is going to escape from a welded-shut steel safe with the aid of his friend from Regulus IV, the friend must be able either to break or dissolve the steel, or perhaps get into and out of such spaces via the fourth dimension. These are part of the starting situation for the author, who must assume that the creations of his intellect do have the requisite powers. If he is really conscientious (or worries greatly about being laughed at by scientific purists) he will also have in the background an ecological system where these powers are of general use and which contains other creatures whose behavior and abilities fit into the same picture.

Flying must be easier on Fomalhaut VII than on Earth. Perhaps the air is denser, or the gravity weaker, or native muscle more efficient and powerful. Ordinary evolution will have been affected by the fact that flight by larger animals is possible, so there will be a much wider range of large flying organisms than we know on Earth. There will be carnivores, herbivores, and omnivores. There will be a wide range of attack and defense systems among these beings. In short, there will be more ecological niches available to large flyers, and it may be confidently expected that evolution will fill them.

Of course there will be limits, just as on Earth. Vertebrates have been flying for nearly two hundred million years, which for most of the forms involved means about the same number of generations; but we have no supersonic birds on this planet. Even the insects, which have been flying a good deal longer, haven't gotten anywhere near Mach 1; the eight-hundred-mile-per-hour deer-bot fly which appeared in the literature during the 1930s was very definitely a mistaken observation. It would seem that our biochemistry can't handle energy at the rates needed for supersonic flight. It is the evident existence of these limits which forces the author to assume a different set of conditions on the Fomalhaut planet.

Similarly, fourth-dimensional extrusion will have to be general on Regulus IV, and the local ecology will reflect the fact. There will be hide-and-seek techniques among predators and prey essentially incomprehensible to human beings, and therefore a tremendous challenge to the imagination and verbal skill of the writer.

If fourth-dimensional extrusion is not the answer chosen, then the ability to dissolve iron may have developed—which implies that free iron exists on the planet under circumstances that make the ability to dissolve it a useful one. Or . . .

There is, of course, a limit to the time any author can spend working out such details. Even I, a spare-time writer who seldom saddles himself with deadlines, spend some of that spare time writing the story itself. In any kind of story whatever, a certain amount of the background has to be filled in by the reader's/listener's imagination. It is neither possible nor desirable to do everything for him. In this first line of attack, the time and effort to be spent on detail work are reasonably limited.

Even the second line, which is my favored technique, has its limits in this respect. However, it does encourage the author to spend longer in the beginning at the straight slide-rule work. As it happens, I get most of the fun out of working out the physical and chemical nature of a planet or solar system, and then dreaming up life forms which might reasonably evolve under such conditions. The story (obviously, as some critics have been known to remark) comes afterward. My excuse for using this general technique, if one is needed, is twofold.

First, I find it more fun. This will carry smaller weight for the author who is writing for a living.

Second, it is not unusual for the nature of the planet and its life forms, once worked out, to suggest story events or even an entire plot line which would never otherwise have occurred to me. This fact should carry some weight even with the more fantasy-oriented writer, who cares less about "realism."

I do have to admit that realism, or at least consistency, is a prime consideration with me; and as I implied some pages back with the Abraham Lincoln metaphor, even the most fantastic story can jar the most tolerant reader if the inconsistency is crude enough—anachronism is only one form of inconsistency.

This sort of realism in life design has to be on at least two levels: biochemical and mechanical.

It is true that we do not yet know all the details of how even the simplest life forms work. It is still defensible to build for story purposes a creature that drinks hydrazine, and say that no one can prove this impossible. Beyond a certain point, however, I have to dismiss this as ducking out the easy way—sometimes justifiable for storytelling purposes, but jarring on the scientific sensibility. Some facts of life are very well known indeed, and to contradict them, a very good excuse and very convincing logic are needed.

For example, any life form converts energy from one form to another. On our own planet, the strongest and most active creatures use the oxygen in the atmosphere to convert food materials to carbon dioxide and water. The chemical reactions supply the needed energy. Obviously, the available oxygen would be quickly used up if there were not some other set of reactions to break down the water and carbon dioxide (actually it's the water, on this planet) to replace what is exhausted. It takes as much energy (actually more must be supplied, since no reaction is completely efficient) to break up a molecule into its elements as is released by forming it from these elements, and any ecological system must have a long-term energy base. On this planet, as is common knowledge, the base is sunlight. There seems no need here to go into the very complicated details; few people get through high school these days (I'd like to believe) without at least a general idea of photosynthesis.

In passing, some people have the idea that fish violate this basic rule, and are some sort of perpetual motion machine, because they "breathe water." Not so; fish use the elemental O_2 gas supplied as usual by photosynthesis and *dissolved* in water, not the O in the H_2O. Aquarium suppliers are perfectly justified in selling air pumps; they are not exploiting the innocent fish-fanciers.

Substitutes for free oxygen in energy-releasing reactions are perfectly possible chemically, and as far as anyone can tell should be possible biologically (indeed, some Earthly life forms do use other reactions). There is no chemical need for these substitutes even to be gases; but if the story calls for a nonhuman character to be drowned or strangled, obvious gaseous candidates are fluorine and chlorine. The former can run much more energetic reactions than even oxygen, while chlorine compares favorably with the gas we are *all* hooked on. (That last seems a justified assumption about the present readers. If it is wrong, please come and introduce yourself!)

Neither chlorine nor fluorine occurs free on this planet; but, as pointed out already, neither would oxygen if earthly life were not constantly replenishing it by photosynthesis. It has been pointed out that both these gases are odd-numbered elements and therefore in shorter universal supply than oxygen. This may well be true; but if some mad scientist were to develop a microorganism able to photosynthesize free chlorine from the chloride ion in Earth's ocean, it wouldn't have to do a very complete job to release as much of this gas as we now have of oxygen. Breaking down ten percent or so of the ocean salt would do the trick. Present-day biological engineering is probably not quite up to this job yet, but if you want to use the idea in a story be my guest. I don't plan to use it myself; the crazy-scientist story is old hat now except in frankly political literature, and even the germ-from-space has been pretty well worked to death in the last forty years.

As mentioned, there is no chemical reason why the energy-producing reactants have to include gases at all. Oxidizing a pound of sugar with nitric acid will yield more energy than oxidizing the same pound with oxygen (if this seems improbable at first glance, remember the bond energy of the N_2 molecule which is one of the products of the first reaction). True, raw concentrated nitric acid is rather hard on most if not all Terrestrial tissues; but we do handle hydrochloric acid—admittedly in rather dilute form in spite of the antacid-tablet ads—in our own digestive systems. I see little difficulty in dreaming up a being able to store and utilize strong oxidizers in its system. The protective mucus our own stomachs use is only one of the possibilities.

Many chemical sources of energy are therefore possible in principle for our life forms; but one should be reasonably aware of the chemistry involved. Water or iron oxide would not be good fuels under any reasonable circumstances; there are admittedly some energy-yielding reactions involving these, but they call for special and unlikely reactants like sodium or fluorine—and if those reactants are around, we could get much more energy by using them on other substances.

To get more fundamental, sunlight is not the only conceivable energy base for an ecological pyramid. It is, however, by far the most likely, assuming the planet in question has a sun. Remember, the energy source must not only be quantitatively large enough; it must be widely available in both space and time, so that life can originate and evolve to complex forms. Radioactivity and raw volcanic heat are both imaginable, but the first demands rather unusual conditions if much of it is to be on hand. Vulcanism, if Earth is a fair example, tends to be restricted in space at any one time and in time at any one location, a discouraging combination. Also, radioactive energy in its most direct form comes in high-energy quanta, furnishing an additional complication to the molecular architecture problem to be considered next.

It seems pretty certain that life, as well as needing energy, must be of complex structure. It has to do too many things for a simple machine. An organism must be able to absorb the chemicals needed for its energy, and carry out at the desired rate the reactions which they undergo. It must develop and repair its own structure (immortal, invulnerable, specially created beings are conceivable, but definitely outside the realm of this discussion). It must *reproduce* its own structure, and therefore keep on file a complete set of specifications—which must itself be reproducible.

Whatever mystical, symbolic, and figurate resemblances there may be between a candle flame and a living creature, the concrete *differences* between them seem to me to constitute a non-negotiable demand for extreme complexity in the latter.

On Earth, this complexity involves the phosphate-sugar-base polymers called popularly DNA and RNA for specifications, polypeptide and polysaccharide structures for most of the machinery, and—perhaps most fundamentally—the hydrogen bond to provide structural links which can be changed around as needed without the need for temperatures high enough to ruin the main framework.

I see no reason why other carbon compounds could not do the jobs of most of these, though I cannot offhand draw formulas for the alternates. The jobs in general depend on the shapes of the molecules, or perhaps more honestly the shapes of the force fields around them; these could presumably be duplicated closely enough by other substances.

I am rather doubtful that the cruder substitutions suggested by various writers, such as that of silicon for carbon, would actually work, though of course I cannot be sure that they wouldn't. We have the fact that on Earth, with silicon many times more plentiful than carbon, life uses the latter. The explanations which can be advanced for this fact seem to me to be explanations as well of why silicon won't work in life forms. (To be more specific: silicon atoms are large enough to four-coordinate with oxygen, and hence wind up in hard, crystalline, insoluble macromolecular structures—the usual run of silicate minerals. The smaller carbon atom, able to react with not more than three oxygens at once, was left free to form the water-reactive carbon dioxide gas.) True, some Earthly life such as scouring rushes, basket sponges, and foraminifera use silicon compounds in skeletal parts; but not, except in trace amounts, in active life machinery.

I also doubt that any other element could do the job of hydrogen, which I am inclined to regard as "the" essential life element, rather than the more popular carbon. Life machinery is complex, but it must have what might be called "moving parts" —structures which have to be altered in shape, or connected now one way and now another. A chemical bond weak enough to be changed without affecting the rest of the machine seems a necessity—a gasoline engine would be hard to design if springs didn't exist and a cutting torch were needed to open the valves each cycle. The hydrogen bond (I don't propose to explain what this is; if you don't know, consult any beginning chemistry text) is the only thing I know of which meets this need on the molecular level.

This, however, is not much of a science fiction problem. Something like 999 out of every 1000 atoms in the universe are hydrogen atoms; even Earth, which seems to be one of the most thoroughly dehydrogenated objects in the observable part of space, has all it needs for an extensive collection of life forms. I suspect it will generally be easier for an author to use hydrogen in his homemade life forms than to work out a credible substitute.

To finish with the fundamental-structure level, one must admit that very complex electric and magnetic field structures other than those supplied ready-formed by atoms and molecules are conceivable. At this point, it really is necessary to fall back on the "we can't say it's impossible" excuse. Personally I would develop such life forms only if my story demanded of them some ability incompatible with ordinary matter, such as traveling through a telephone wire or existing without protection both in the solar photosphere and a cave on Pluto. At this point, simple scientific realism fades away, and I must bow out as an expert. It's not that I'm above doing it; it's just that practically anyone else could do it equally well.

The other principal basis for believability of life forms lies in the field of simple mechanics, much more common sense than biochemistry. For example, in spite of Edgar Rice Burroughs's calots, a fast-running creature is far more likely to have a few long legs than a lot of short ones. Whether muscle tissue on Planet X is stronger or weaker than on Earth, muscular effort will be more efficiently applied by fewer, longer strokes. Even if the evolutionary background for some reason started off with the ten legs (e.g., high gravity), I would expect an organism specializing in speed to develop two, or perhaps four, of them to greater length and either have the others degenerate or put them to other uses as the generations rolled on.

On the same general principle, if the creature lives on grass or the local ecological equivalent, it will probably not have much of a brain. If it doesn't have to catch food or climb trees, it will lack any equivalent of a hand—in short, any anatomical part an organism has should either be useful to that creature in its current life, or be the degenerate remnant of something useful to its remote ancestors. Exceptions to this rule among Earthly life forms are hard to find, and may be only apparent; we simply don't know the purpose of the organ in question. A former example was the "sail"on the backs of some Permian reptiles, now believed to be a temperature control device.

In addition to being useful itself, a structure must have been at least slightly useful through its early stages of development; it is hard to believe that a single mutation would produce a completely developed ear, but any ability to sense pressure variations would clearly be useful to an animal. Creatures must have existed showing development all the way from a slightly refined sense of touch to the present organ capable of detecting and recognizing a tiger's footfall in a windy forest—or an out-of-tune flute in an orchestra.

Similarly with the eye. There are now alive on Earth creatures with light-sensitive organs ranging from the simple red spot of the single-celled Euglena, through pinhole cameras with complex retinas (some cephalopods), to the lens-and-iris-equipped diffraction-limited organ of most mammals and birds, complete with automatic focusing. There are also examples of parallel evolution which were good enough to help their owners survive all the way along the route: the compound mosaic-lens eyes of arthropods and, I have heard, at least one organism that scans the image of a single lens by moving a single retinal nerve over the field.

But eyes and ears are hardly original enough for a really imaginative science fiction story. What other long-range senses might an organism evolve? Could an intelligent species develop without any such sense? If so, what would be that creature's conception of the universe? How, if at all, could sighted and hearing human beings communicate with it?

The first question at least can be partially answered without recourse to mysticism. Magnetic fields do exist, as do electric ones. Certainly some creatures can sense the latter directly (you can yourself, for that matter; bring your hand close to a highly charged object and feel what happens to the fine hairs on your skin). There is some evidence that certain species of birds can detect the earth's magnetic field. Sound is already used in accordance with its limitations, as is scent. A gravity-sense other than the one we now use for orientation would probably not be discriminating enough, though I could certainly be wrong (read up on lunar mascons if you don't see what I mean by lack of discrimination).

It is a little hard to envision what could be detected by a magnetic sense, and how its possessor would imagine the universe. Most substances on this planet have practically no effect on a magnetic field, and this is what makes me a little doubtful about the birds mentioned above. I can see the use of such a sense in navigation for a migratory species, but I have trouble thinking through its evolutionary development. Perhaps on a planet with widely distributed ferromagnetic material, the location of which is of life-and-death importance to the life forms, it would happen; maybe our Regulus IV character who can dissolve iron needs it for biochemical reasons.

The important point, from which we may have been wandering a trifle, is not whether I can envision such a situation in detail, but whether the author of the story can do so, and thereby avoid having to invent *ad hoc* a goose which lays golden eggs. If the life form in question has hearing but no sight, all right; but it should not be able to thread a needle with the aid of sonic perception. Sound waves short enough to have that kind of resolving power would demand a good deal of energy to produce, would have very poor range in air, and would incidentally be decidedly dangerous to human explorers. Of course, a story could be built on the unfortunate consequences of the men who were mowed down by what they thought must be a death ray, when the welcoming committee was merely trying to take a good look. . . .

Sound does have the advantage of being able to diffract around obstacles, so that straight-line connection is not needed; light (that is, light visible to human beings) is of such short wavelength that diffraction effects are minor. This means that the precise direction of origin of a sound ray cannot be well determined, while a good eye can measure light's direction to a small fraction of a degree. On Earth, we both eat and keep this particular piece of cake, since we have evolved both sight and hearing.

Scent seems to have all the disadvantages and none of the advantages, as a long-range sense. However, under special circumstances even a modified nose may fill the need. In a story of my own some years ago ("Uncommon Sense," *Astounding Science Fiction*, September 1945), I assumed an airless planet, so that molecules could diffuse in nearly straight lines. The local sense organs were basically pinhole cameras, with the retinal mosaic formed of olfactory cells. Since the beings in question were not intelligent, the question of what sort of universe they believed in did not arise.

Granting the intelligence, it would have been—would still be, indeed—interesting to work out their cosmology. Naturally, the first few hours are spent wondering whether and how they could fill the intellectual gaps imposed by their lack of sight and hearing. Then, of course, the intelligent speculator starts wondering what essential details are missing from *our* concept of the universe, because of our lack of the sense of (you name it). This, for what my opinion is worth, is one of the best philosophical excuses for the practice of science fiction—if an excuse is needed. The molecule-seers presumably lack all astronomical data; what are *we* missing? This question, I hope I needn't add, is not an excuse to go off on a mystical kick, though it is one which the mystics are quite reasonably fond of asking (and then answering with their own version of Truth). The human species has, as a matter of fact, done a rather impressive job of overcoming its sensory limitations, though I see no way of ever being sure when the job is done.

Philosophy aside, there are many more details of shape to be considered for nonhuman beings. Many of the pertinent factors have been pointed out by other writers, such as L. Sprague deCamp ("Design for Life," *Astounding Science Fiction*, May–June, 1939). DeCamp reached the conclusion that an intelligent life form would have to wind up not grossly different in structure from a human being—carrying its sense organs high and close to the brain, having a limited number of limbs with a minimum number of these specialized for locomotion and the others for manipulation, having a rigid skeleton, and being somewhere between an Irish terrier and a grizzly bear in size. The lower size limits was set by the number of cells needed for a good brain, and the upper one by the bulk of body which could be handled by a brain without overspecialization. Sprague admitted both his estimates to be guesses, but I have seen no more convincing ones since. Whenever I have departed greatly from his strictures in my own stories, I have always felt the moral need to supply an excuse, at least to myself.

The need for an internal skeleton stems largely from the nature of muscle tissue, which can exert force only by contracting and is therefore much more effective with a good lever system to work with. I belittle neither the intelligence nor the strength of the octopus; but in spite of Victor Hugo and most other writers of undersea adventure, the creature's boneless tentacles are not all that effective as handling organs. I don't mean that the octopus and his kin are helpless hunks of meat; but if I had my choice of animals I was required to duel to the death, I would pick one of this tribe rather than one of their bonier rivals, the barracuda or the moray eel, even though neither of the latter have any prehensile organs but their jaws. (If any experienced scuba divers wish to dispute this matter of taste, go right ahead. I admit that so far, thank goodness, I am working from theory on this specific matter.)

This leads to a point which should be raised in any science fiction essay. I have made a number of quite definite statements in the preceding pages, and will make several more before finishing this chapter. Anyone with the slightest trace of intelligent critical power can find a way around most of these dicta by setting up appropriate situations. I wouldn't dream of objecting; most of my own stories have developed from attempts to work out situations in which someone who has laid down the law within my hearing would be wrong. The Hunter in *Needle* was a deliberate attempt to get around Sprague's minimum-size rule. *Mission of Gravity* complicated the size and speed issue by variable gravity.

And so on. If no one has the urge, imagination, and knowledge to kick specific holes in the things I say here, my favorite form of relaxation is in danger of going out with a whimper. If someone takes exception to the statement that muscles can only pull, by all means do something about it. We know a good deal about Earthly muscle chemistry these days; maybe a pushing cell *could* be worked out. I suspect it would need a very strong cell wall, but why not? Have fun with the idea. If you can make it plausible, you will have destroyed at a stroke many of the currently plausible engineering limitations to the shapes and power of animals. I could list examples for the rest of my available pages, but you should have more fun doing it yourself.

There is a natural temptation to make one's artificial organisms as weird as possible in looks and behavior. Most authors seem to have learned that it is extremely hard to invent anything stranger than some of the life forms already on our planet, and many writers as a result have taken to using either these creatures as they are, or modifying them in size and habit, or mixing them together. The last, in particular, is not a new trick; the sphinx and hippogriff have been with us for some time.

With our present knowledge, though, we have to be careful about the changes and mixtures we make. Pegasus, for example, will have to remain mythological. Even if we could persuade a horse to grow wings (feathered or not), Earthly muscle tissue simply won't fly a horse (assuming, of course, that the muscle is going along for the ride). Also, the horse would have to extract a great deal more energy than it does from its hay diet to power the flight muscles even if it could find room for them in an equine anatomy.

Actually, the realization that body engineering and life-style are closely connected is far from new. There is a story about Baron Cuvier, a naturalist of the late eighteenth and early nineteenth centuries. It seems that one night his students decided to play a practical joke, and one of them dressed up in a conglomeration of animal skins, including that of a deer. The disguised youth then crept into the baron's bedroom and aroused him by growling, "Cuvier, wake up! I am going to eat you!"

The baron is supposed to have opened his eyes, looked over his visitor briefly, closed his eyes again and rolled over muttering, "Impossible! You have horns and hooves." A large body of information, it would seem, tends to produce opinions in its possessor's mind, if not always correct ones.

The trick of magnifying a normal creature to menacing size is all too common. The giant amoeba is a familar example; monster insects (or whole populations of them) even more so. It might pay an author with this particular urge to ask himself why we don't actually have such creatures around. There is likely to be a good reason, and if he doesn't know it perhaps he should do some research.

In the case of both amoeba and insect, the so-called "square-cube" law is the trouble. Things like strength of muscle and rate of chemical and heat exchange with the environment depend on surface or cross-section area, and change with the square of linear size; Swift's Brobdingnagians would therefore have a hundred times the strength and oxygen intake rate of poor Gulliver. Unfortunately the mass of tissue to be supported and fed goes up with the cube of linear dimension, so the giants would have had a thousand times Gulliver's weight. It seems unlikely that they could have stood, much less walked (can *you* support ten times your present weight?). This is why a whale, though an air breather, suffocates if he runs ashore; he lacks the muscular strength to expand his chest cavity against its own weight. An ant magnified to six-foot length would be in even worse trouble, since she doesn't have a mammal's supercharger system in the first place, but merely a set of air pipes running through her system. Even if the mad scientist provided his giant ants with oxygen masks, I wouldn't be afraid of them.

It is only because they are so small, and their weight has decreased even faster than their strength, that insects can perform the "miraculous" feats of carrying dozens of times their own weight or jumping hundreds of times their own length. This would have favored Swift's Lilliputians, who would have been able to make some remarkable athletic records if judged on a strictly linear scale. That is, unless they had to spend too much time in eating to offset their excessive losses of body heat. . . .

Really small creatures, strong as they may seem, either have structures that don't seem to mind change in temperature too much (insects, small reptiles), or are extremely well insulated (small birds), or have to eat something like their own weight in food each day (shrew, hummingbird). There seems reason to believe that at least with Earthly biochemistry, the first and last of these weaknesses do not favor intelligence.

A rather similar factor operates against the idea of having a manlike creature get all his energy from sunlight, plant style. This was covered years ago by V. A. Eulach ("Those Impossible Autotrophic Men," *Astounding Science Fiction,* October 1956), who pointed out that a man who tries to live like a tree is going to wind up looking much like one. He will have to increase his sunlight-intercepting area without greatly increasing his mass (in other words, grow leaves), cut down his energy demands to what leaves can supply from sunlight's one-and-a-half-horse-power-per-square-yard (become sessile), and provide himself with mineral nutrients directly from the soil, since he can't catch food any more (grow roots!).

Of course, we can get around some of this by hypothesizing a hotter, closer sun, with all the attendant complications of higher planet temperature. This is fun to work out, and some of us do it, but remember that a really basic change of this sort affects everything in the ecological pyramid sitting on that particular energy base—in other words, *all* the life on the planet.

It may look from all this as though a really careful and conscientious science fiction writer has to be a junior edition of the Almighty. Things are not really this bad. I mentioned one way out a few pages ago in admitting there is a limit to the detail really needed. The limit is set not wholly by time, but by the fact that too much detail results in a Ph.D. thesis—perhaps a fascinating one to some people, but still a thesis rather than a story. I must admit that some of us do have this failing, which has to be sharply controlled by editors.

Perhaps the most nearly happy-medium advice that can be given is this:

Work out your world and its creatures as long as it remains fun; then write your story, making use of any of the details you have worked out which *help the story*. Write off the rest of the development work as something which built your own background picture—the stage setting, if you like—whose presence in your mind will tend to save you from the more jarring inconsistencies (I use this word, very carefully, rather than *errors*).

Remember, though, that among your readers there will be some who enjoy carrying your work farther than you did. They will find inconsistencies which you missed; depend on it. Part of human nature is the urge to let the world know how right you were, so you can expect to hear from these people either directly or through fanzine pages. Don't let it worry you.

Even if he is right and you are wrong, he has demonstrated unequivocally that you succeeded as a storyteller. You gave your audience a good time.

Hal Clement (Harry Clement Stubbs)

Born in Somerville, Massachusetts, in 1922, Hal Clement attended public schools in Arlington and Cambridge, and received a B.S. in astronomy from Harvard in 1943. He served with 8th AAF in World War II, flying thirty-five missions over German-occupied Europe as copilot and pilot in B-24 bombers, and after the war obtained his M.Ed. at Boston University. He then taught high school science and math for four years, until recalled with his Air Force Reserve unit for two years in 1951—but he did not go overseas this time. He returned to his teaching position at Milton Academy, Massachusetts, in 1953; and is still there, but has since acquired an M.S. in chemistry. He is still in the Air Force Reserve, working in an information unit, with the rank of colonel.

Sold first story to *Astounding Science Fiction* magazine while a sophomore at Harvard, and has produced a small but fairly steady flow of science fiction ever since. He has also done a number of scientific articles in various publications, generally under his real name (Harry C. Stubbs).

He is a member or has been of such scientific organizations as AAAS, New England Association of Chemistry Teachers, Bond Astronomical Society, and the Meteoritical Society. He was a charter member of New England Science Fiction Association, and for two years has served on the Nebula Awards Committee of Science Fiction Writers of America.

Married since 1952 to the former Mary Myers of Atlantic City, N. J., he has one son in college, one about to go to college, and one junior-high-school-age daughter.

Iceworld, 1953 (Gnome)
Needle, 1953 (Doubleday)
Mission of Gravity, 1954 (Doubleday)
Cycle of Fire, 1957 (Ballantine)
Close to Critical, 1959 (Ballantine)

Natives of Space, 1965 (Ballantine) 3 novelettes
Small Changes, 1969 (Doubleday)
First Flights to the Moon, 1970 (Doubleday)
Star Light, 1971 (Ballantine)

Anne McCaffrey

Hitch Your Dragon to a Star: Romance and Glamour in Science Fiction

Romance and glamour in science fiction? Don't be ridiculous! What's romantic about bug-eyed monsters chasing (but never catching) bosomy, terrified females around weird machines and moon rockets? (Moon rockets? How absurd! Man will never get off earth.) And what's glamorous about space suits, and Buck Rogers's gimmickry, or exploring a dust-dry planet with five other guys? Sex and emotion are nonexistent in sf! Everyone knows that![1]

If you apply the *popular* definitions of romance and glamour, sf does indeed lack these qualities—with good reasons.

In the beginning, and start with the classics of Jules Verne and H. G. Wells, sf stories were written for a predominantly male audience; the premise being that the female mind was unequipped to

1. Indeed, in the January 1973 *Analog,* a reader berates the editor for abandoning Mr. Campbell's sexual morality standards, and cites "Hero" by Joe Haldeman as being pornographic and "Collision Course" by S. Kye Boult as containing sexually suggestive comments which could have been removed. He does not want his teen-age son corrupted.

cope with science or extrapolations. If the male readers wanted the stimulation of a purely "sex" story, they could find that in the erotic classics, mainstream literature, or, starting around the middle of the twentieth century, in the *Playboy* category.[2] The male readership wanted certain things from their science fiction stories: exercises in extrapolation, the use to which unproven but valid scientific hypotheses could be put in the near or distant future, or plain escapist "blood-and-thunder" adventure yarns.

Science fiction, then and to a great extent now, is more cerebral than gonadal. The perspicacious sf editor gives his readers what they want to read or watches his circulation figures drop. The four top sf magazines *(Analog, Fantasy & Science Fiction, Galaxy,* and *Worlds of If)* have survived because their editors were shrewd enough to choose the type of story their readers craved. Emotion, other than courageous fortitude in the face of alien monsters or patriotism (for the Cause, the Ship, the Society, the Planet, the Galaxy, or the Universe—depending on the theme and scope) was unwarranted. Sweating out the result of experiments is nonemotional. Romance—the starry-eyed, deep-sighing, hand-holding variety—was *verboten* as unnecessary. Sf had to cater to a narrow, highly specialized, fact-conscious, emotion-eschewing group. Much of the sf written in the '30s and '40s, though solidly based on sound scientific speculation, was duller than a laundry list and very often written, s'help me God, by the "practicing scientist in the laboratory who had a good idea for a story and actually wrote it." (I've forgotten John Campbell's exact alphabetization of this category of writer). Isaac Asimov is the most spectacular exception of the trained scientist turned science fiction writer. Sir Fred Hoyle is another. Then there is Hal Clement who teaches math and sciences. Alan E. Nourse, T. J. Bass, Roy Meyers and Michael Crichton, and C. Davis Belcher all rate an M.D. after their names. M. R. Anver and Jesse Bone are veterinary surgeons. Joe Hensley, Ted Thomas, and Walter F. Moudy are lawyers; Larry Niven and Greg (who talks to computers) Benford have ad-

2. Paradoxically, some very fine sf stories have been published in *Playboy.*

vanced degrees in pure science; Burt Filer holds a dozen patents; Keith Laumer's an architect, etcetera, etcetera. The secondary point of this is that the scientist-*cum*-writer does not have to sound scientifically sterile and dull.

You will also quickly perceive that, with one sex-pseudonymous exception, all the above mentioned are men. Even before the equal-opportunity campaigns of the '50s and '60s, there were women writers of science fiction. Some found it wiser[3] to use ambiguous pen names so as not to prejudice the male readers against a story by a blatantly feminine author. C. L. Moore nevertheless managed to inject a good deal of the tenderer sentiments in her books; Leigh Brackett's well-rounded characterizations and plots are/were a delight, and Andre Norton remains the mistress of superb fantasy.[4] Marion (in some parts of the world that is the masculine spelling) Zimmer Bradley tends to write sf from the male viewpoint as does Lee Hoffman. Judith Merril determinedly wrote from the women's viewpoint —diaper stories they were nicknamed. But the staunchly female writers include Miriam Allen de Ford, Mildred Clingerman, Margaret St. Clair (under several pseudonyms), Katherine Maclean, and Doris Pitkin Buck. By the late fifties this chosen few was joined by Evelyn S. Smith, Kate Wilhelm, Rachel Payes, J. Hunter Holly, Jacob Transue, the late Rosel George Brown, Carol Emshwiller, Sonya Dorman, and me. There are still a few who prefer the masculine disguise: M. R. Anver, A. M. Hopf, Sydney van Scyoc and D. C. Fontana.[5] By the late '60s, and thanks to the Clarion State College Sf Workshop and the various universities and colleges now offering courses in science fiction and sf creative writing, more women are turning to this rewarding and stimulating field.

Not entirely because they were forced to write more from the viewpoint of the opposite sex, women sf authors are more adept

3. I.e., the editor suggested, recommended, or insisted on the change.
4. I remember a heated argument with one young fan in 1965. He categorically refused to believe that Andre Norton could be a woman. He may still not believe me.
5. When I joined the Science Fiction Writers of America in 1965, there were 30 women members of the total 275. By 1970, in a total membership of 425, there were 52.

in their characterizations and portrayals. Again I cite Leigh Brackett, Lee Hoffman, Andre Norton, and Marion Zimmer Bradley, and add Kate Wilhelm and Ursula K. Le Guin.

On the other hand, Robert Heinlein's women are horrors: excuseless caricatures of "females." Alexei Panshin in *Rite of Passage,* his novel à la Heinlein, created a most believable and likable female protagonist, thus surpassing the Master. Personally, I've always found James Schmitz's women people I would like to know. His Telzey, the teeny-bopper with a telepathic whammy, is a delightful brat, in direct contrast to the travesty of Heinlein's Podkane of Mars. One top-flight writer of sf has been chided for using only one type of heroine: the sort of earnest, if attractive, females who joined the Communist party in the '30s, the Army in the '40s, did social work in the '50s, and started communes in the '60s. A girl who would "die" for a principle. Great, but girls don't "die" for principles. Men do. A girl marries the clunk and converts him to her way of thinking later. In bed.

While I've never encountered Harlan Ellison's females—our social spheres have been vastly different—they are recognizable as members of my sex.

Not only was the female viewpoint unappreciated in most of the '20s, '30s, and '40s, but also women were generally relegated to the position of "things," window dressing, or forced to assume attitudes in the corner, out of the way. Woman as a valid character or, heaven forfend, protagonist was a *rara avis*[6] (in the Latin, as in modern English, "bird" was slang for "girl"). The female often existed in the story as the straight "stupid" off whom the Hero or the Good Scientist could bounce enough theory so that the dumbest male reader would understand the story's science rationale. I don't know of any woman worth her nylon tights who'd wring her hands in a corner while her boyfriend (can't use the term "lover" in sf, you know) is getting clobbered by something hideous or dangerous. I'd have been in there swinging with *something* helpful.

Come to think of it, most sf story heroes were pretty dull

6. One notable exception occurred in H. Beam Piper's "Omnilingual"—Dr. Martha Dane.

tools. Me, I'd have left them preening over the moral or scientific coups and gone off with the villains. Evil *is* sexually exciting. And too much nobility of spirit and high purpose leads to dissatisfied wives.

Until just recently, those writers who were also female and persisted in expressing themselves, not only found it expedient to masculinize their names but to "rephrase" their stories for "better reader response."

I came broadside against this requisite. No one had told me that women were not supposed to write sf and that few read it. After seven years of voracious reading in the field, I'd had it up to the eyeteeth with vapid women. I rebelled. I wrote *Restoree* as a tongue-in-cheek protest, utilizing as many of the standard "thud and blunder" clichés as possible with one new twist—the heroine was the viewpoint character and *she* is always Johanna-on-the-spot. The science in the yarn came from the gleeful mind of a pure research scientist in Dupont. The gentleman was an avid escapist reader of sf and used to chortle over flaws in the science of *Analog* stories.

Naturally the male readership didn't like *Restoree*. The book was reamed by fanzine critics, a blackballing which worked to my advantage because everyone had to read the book to see if it was as bad as all that. Very few male readers tumbled to the fact that I had deliberately written a space gothic.

My second notable encounter with the male-orientation problem was with "A Womanly Talent," published in *Analog*. The story deals with the attempts of parapsychics to get professional immunity for their registered members in the practice of their particular variety of psi (telepathy, teleportation, telekinesis, and clairvoyance). Ruth Horvath, although she has tested as "psi-positive," has an unidentifiable Talent; her husband, Lajos, works for a local insurance company, directing his precognitive faculty towards fire. I wanted Ruth to be a "liberated woman." John Campbell asked me to define Ruth in terms of a customary womanly role to cater to his readership. Essentially, he told me, man still explores new territory and guards the hearth; woman minds that hearth whether or not she programs a computer to dust, cook, and rock the cradle. I felt I could go along with

John's request—in my inimitable fashion. Sam Lundwall, the Swedish sf expert, took me to task for this concession and chided me for espousing such anti-liberation notions. He failed to appreciate the underlying facetiousness of my treatment. Because Ruth did, during the course of the story, what the men could never have done, and she did it in the traditional role of mother-mistress-healer. Actually, I was two up on the *Analog* readership: the woman not only bests the men in the story *but* there was an explicit sex scene in *Analog*'s virtuous pages. Not, mind you, that I snuck that in on John Campbell. Oh, no, to the contrary. As he told me later, that scene was an integral part of the plot development and could not have been omitted without destroying the story. He did indeed see no need of s.e.x. as a shock device. Nor did I.

Nor do I apologize for the fact that all my sf stories are basically love-oriented. Helva in "The Ship Who Sang" is a surgically stunted woman, her body encased in a titanium shell, her brain synapses connected to her ship body's control so that she *is* the ship. She loves, deeply, humanly, and the title story evoked tears from many readers—or so I've been told. Helva loves, loses her lover, and finds another.

Then I hitched my dragon to a star, won two awards, and no one has complained about sex, love, or the emotional content in my stories. A basic theme in *Dragonflight* and *Dragonquest* is the symbiotic love relationship between humans and their dragon companions. Love in several facets is the main theme of both novels. Emotional content and personal involvement are *expected* in stories written by me. In fact, I've had stories returned to me by editors because they lacked these elements: a case of "I'm damned if I do, and damned if I don't."

Prior to the '60s, stories with any sort of a love interest were very rare. True, it was implied in many stories of the '30s and '40s that the guy married the girl whom he had rescued/encountered/discovered during the course of his adventure. But no real pulse-pounding, tender, gut-reacting scenes. The girl was still a "thing," to be "used" to perpetuate the hero's magnificent chromosomes. Or perhaps, to prove that the guy wasn't "queer." I mean, all those men locked away on a spaceship for months/years at a time. I mean . . . and you know what I mean even if I couldn't mention it in the sf of the '30s and '40s. Did you ever *see* Flash Gordon kiss Dale Arden or hold her hand loverly-like? And Tarzan only *admits* that Jane is his woman.

Love did occasionally get a chance to rear its lovely head in the antiseptic atmosphere of sf. The most extraordinary example of love dominating an sf story will be dealt with at length later. The examples which I personally remember with a sigh are: Alfred Bester's hero, Lincoln Powell, falls in love with Barbara in *The Demolished Man.* James Schmitz wrote a real good love story in "Space Fear," one of his Lanni, Agent of Vega yarns; Lanni is *very* feminine despite square eyeballs and silver hair. There were three very moving love stories, appearing in *Fantastic Universe* in the mid-fifties, about telepaths on Mars: the author's name is beyond my research facilities in Ireland and I suspect that it was a pseudonym for there were never any other stories under that author's name. In *Mars Child,* Cyril M. Judd (Judith Merril and Cyril Kornbluth) wove a tender love story about Anna who blew glass because the "noise" from other people's thoughts distressed her too much. I fondly recall the love interest in J. T. Macintosh's *Born Leader* and Wilson Tucker's "Wild Talent."

On the odd side of the blanket, Theodore Sturgeon was the first author daring enough to tackle the question of homosexual love in a short story, "Affair with a Green Monkey," *(Venture,* May 1957). Ursula K. Le Guin deservedly won both 1970 Hugo and Nebula Awards for her magnificent novel *The Left Hand of Darkness.* Her understatement of the attraction-love-empathy between a member of her one-sexed species and the heterosexually inclined protagonist makes it more powerful!

Not all science fiction was dryly written or sterile as far as imagery was concerned, or humanness. To cut the aridness, there was Avram Davidson's gentle charm, Grendel Briarton's outrageous punster, Ferdinard Feghoot, the ofttimes unnerving whimsy of Doris Pitkin Buck and H. Beam Piper, or Miriam Allen de Ford, Damon Knight's incisive satire—to name a few of the grace notes around the sterner melodies played (unheard) in outer space. What was basically lacking in the general story menu was any intense emotional involvement. You couldn't care less about the characters in the stories after you'd closed the book. The "adventure" had been fun, or the scientific twist made you murmur, "Well, I'd never have thought of doing that with this," or the gimmick amused you. I remember a story from *Analog* in which Mr. A (or was it General A?) has to get the scientists off their unthinking rumps and develop an anti-grav unit. He provokes them by showing a film of a man actually defying gravity,[7] a clumsy power pack strapped to his shoulders. Unfortunately, the film ends as the inventor comes crashing to the earth. Mr. (or General) A says that the man is dead, his secret died with him, but if *he* could develop an anti-grav unit, so could they. They do. Then Mr. (or General) A presents them to the "actor" who confesses that he had "died" to shake up their inflexible notion that gravity couldn't be neutralized simply because it hadn't yet been done. It's years since that story came out but all I can remember is the scientific gimmick and the philosophy.

Fortunately for the maturity of sf, newcomers wiggled into the pages of *Fantasy and Science Fiction, Analog, Galaxy,* and *If.* Keyes published a quiet story entitled "Flowers for Algernon" which was later screened as *Charley.* In 1952, in *F. and S.F.,* Zenna Henderson introduced the People: tender stories with a high emotional content about a race of parapsychic people who are forced to flee their world (the sun went nova), and their problems blending into the multitude on Earth. Her two books, *The Anything Box* and *The People, No Different Flesh* (Doubleday), compel the reader to share the tremendous sadness of the People for the loss of their beautiful homeworld; one appreciates the gallantry of their exodus and the sacrifice of the ones too old to make the terrible journey. The aura projected by Miss Henderson stays with the reader like a benediction.

New lyrical writers started publishing and were acclaimed by the fans: Roger Zelazny and Samuel R. Delany were notable among the men. Carol Emshwiller paints her canvases with a

7. This story predates the James Bond movie use of a power-pack Buck Rogersian one-man flight unit although, as I recall the cover illustration, the two had striking similarities.

delicate brush and an economy of word, delineating some portion of intensely experienced personal conflict: i.e., "Pelt." Sonya Dorman's wry sense of humor and the macabre lends her writing unusual color. The late Rosel George Brown humorously depicted Future Woman's domestic problems with aliens to baby-sit and she created the inimitable Sybil Sue Blue, galactic policewoman.

Not all emotional "shouts" came from the distaff side. The incredible Harlan Ellison writes as if an inner fuse is about to blow before he can get all the words on his pages. ("Pretty Maggie Moneyeyes," "I Have No Mouth and I Must Scream," "Try It with a Dull Knife" can be cited as particular examples of high emotional content.) I've never been more terrified than I was scurrying through Norman Spinrad's "The Big Flash" because it was so awfully possible.[8] Keith Laumer's simple statement of courage in the "Last Command" has no equal in the field. And Poul Anderson's poignant timeless love story "Kyrie" is another subtle masterpiece.

On the other hand, real humor in sf is at the highest premium. Humor is as much an emotional involvement as tragedy—but rarer. Jack Wodhams is a very funny man; so is Harry Harrison. And Avram Davidson, Randall Garrett, dear Grendel Briarton, and Damon Knight. But not often enough. Keith Laumer pokes fun at diplomacy in all of his Retief yarns, and David Gerrold in combination with Larry Niven is a good gag team. Theodore Cogswell once did an elaborate story, caricaturing (all in good fun) sf writers and editors. Personally, I think Carol Carr outdid them all in her absurd story—"Look, You Think You Got Problems?"—a Jewish (would you believe?) sf story. Feh!

In passing I note that two of the most powerfully emotional scripts written for *Star Trek* were "Journey to Babel" by D (orothy) C. Fontana and "The Empath" by Joyce Muskat. First-rate seat-clutching panic-watching was provided by Norman Spinrad's "The Doomsday Machine," and David Gerrold's

8. In fact, because of the immense possibility that Norman Spinrad's story *might* come true, the Milford SF Writers' Conference at which it was first read debated long over whether it should be published at all.

"The Trouble with Tribbles" bags the honors for the funniest episode of that much lamented series.

These writers are modern, as far as sf goes. The oldest fans may beat their breasts for the good ol' days of thud blunder and *real* science in *Astounding, Fantastic,* and *Amazing* magazines, but if sf were still driving the star trails with sawdust heroes and cardboard villains—more translated from westerns than integrated in the space age—sf would have been trapped in a Möbius Strip.

With the injection of emotional involvement, a sexual jolt to the Romance and Glamour, science fiction rose out of pulp and into literature.

Notwithstanding the facts (1) that originally science fiction was predominately male-authored and written for a specifically science-trained male readership, (2) that the women writers of sf had to go along with that prerequisite until the '50s, (3) that Love was the unmentionable and emotional involvement unwanted, there is more Romance and Glamour in science fiction than in any other form of literature, classic or contemporary.

Mr. Webster is the first witness for the defense of that statement.

> *Romance:* (1) formerly a long narrative in verse or prose, originally written in one of the Romance dialects, about the adventures of knights and other chivalric heroes.[9] (2) later, a fictitious tale of wonderful and extraordinary events, characterized by much imagination and idealization. [10]

> *Glamour:* to cast the glamour, an enchantment, seemingly mysterious; elusive fascination or allure.

By these definitions, any science fiction or fantasy tale abounds with Romance and Glamour: The Romance of man with the products of his agile and inventive mind, with his mechanical miracles. The Glamour of the glittering possibilities

9. Examples to the point: Conan the Warrior, Doc Savage, Tarzan, Buck Rogers, John Carter, Captain Nemo, Orcott-Morey-Wade-Fuller (of the early John Campbell novels); Richard Seton, "Skylark," Grey Mouser, Retief, Nicolas van Rhyn, to name a few of the best known.
10. What could be more descriptive of science fiction and fantasy?

of the Future, or of Better Planets under Other Stars, has cast an enchantment over the dogmatic reader. It strikes me as utterly romantic that a reader, otherwise pragmatic to the point of boredom, could be carried by another man's or woman's whimsical flight of imagination through the tallest possible tales, based on some minor, if valid, scientific hypothesis. Or in the realm of fantasy, William Hope Hodgson, James Branch Cabell, Robert S. Howard, L. Sprague deCamp, Poul Anderson, Avram Davidson, Andre Norton, and Thomas Burnett Swann (to name a few personal favorites) can so "cast the glamour" that the otherwise sanguine reader is compelled to suspend belief while the book remains open.

What could be more romantic even to world-weary modern readers than Rostand's seven ways to get to the Moon as expounded by Cyrano de Bergerac? Or more glamorous than Captain Nemo's incredible Nautilus? Even the harsh satire of Zamyatin's *We*, Huxley's *Brave New World*, Bradbury's *Fahrenheit 451*, and Brunner's *Stand on Zanzibar* has a fascination that is inescapable.

Ultimately, however, the standard of Romance and Glamour —even using Webster as a basic redefinition—is set by the individual's concept of romance and glamour. "Everyone to his own taste," said the old lady as she kissed her cow. And Damon Knight once joshingly suggested that the clever sf writer could make his reader "queer for skunks"—at least for the purpose and duration of his story.[11]

Since we are dealing with science fiction, it would be nice if we could reduce Webster's definitions to equations. However, most "hard" science fiction aficionados would probably quarrel with our algebra, so we can content ourselves with simply trying the notion of such equations on those stories which, in our own estimation, don't quite come off, each of us formulating his or her own. Of course, Reader 1 will disagree with Reader 2. The possibilities for satisfying any individual requirements are

11. As a corollary to this, read Mr. Knight's "The Great Cow Pat Hoax," fortunately well anthologized. And commemorated by the Faithful with a plasticized cow pat, complete with fly, which reposed on the organ in the Knights' home.

all the science fiction, thus far written and to be written to the cube. Within science fiction, you will—eventually—find exactly what suits you. For the war buffs, read Gordon Dickson's *Soldier Ask Not,* or *The Tactics of Mistake;* for political strategy and intrigue, John Brunner's *The Squares of the City;* historical reinterpretations in Keith Roberts's *Pavane;* the amusing diplomatic shenanigans of Keith Laumer's *Retief;* the panoramic historical canvas of Isaac Asimov's *Foundation* or Frank Herbert's *Dune;* the metaphysics of Stanislaw Lem's *Solaris;* religious conscience in James Blish's trilogy *(A Case of Conscience, Dr. Mirabilis,* and *Black Easter);* pure alien viewpoint in Hal Clement's *Ice World* and *Mission of Gravity;* enigma in Brian Aldiss's recent novels and Joanna Russ's *And Chaos Died;* mystery in Alfred Bester's *Demolished Man* and Isaac Asimov's *Caves of Steel.* Robert Silverberg speaks to today's young adults in *Tower of Glass* and *Son of Man.* The list should include most of the sf written. Which is why the casual reader of sf should not abandon the genre if his first few ventures do not satisfy him.

Sometimes the glamour is cast so compellingly that the writer is embroiled in the magic he imagined. Robert Heinlein keeps his whereabouts secret to prevent himself from being inundated by those wishing to "share water" with the author of *Stranger in a Strange Land.* L. Ron Hubbard became so involved in his own theory of Dianetics that he gave up writing science fiction and became the major exponent of this philosophy. Arthur C. Clarke is constantly being buttonholed and told what he "actually meant" by *2001: A Space Odyssey.* On a much more minor scale, I have a small problem with the supply of dragons. The line forms—in *back* of me!

Some authors—E. E. Smith and Edgar Rice Burroughs—were incredibly bad writers as style goes but the formula was so potent that the books are constantly reprinted because of the demand. Plotting and action overcame such minor considerations.

Consider, too, the tremendous fascination cast by J. R. R. Tolkien's *Lord Of The Rings* trilogy which was "honored" by a *Harvard Lampoon* "Bored of the Rings." Middle Earth *exists* for its devoted adherents.[12] You might say that Tolkein is hobbit-forming. My particular neighborhood in Ireland boasts two "Samwise" hounds, a "Bilbo Baggins" half-breed, two "Frodo" cats, and a very small child who is known to his family as "Hobbit."

With the exception of the Sherlock Holmesian Baker Street Irregulars with chapters in any parts of the world, I know of no other branch of imaginative fiction that has so strong a glamour for its readers.[13] In fact, when Conan Doyle tried to kill Holmes, there was such an uproar, the detective had to be resurrected to satisfy the outraged fans. James Blish had to blow up the galaxy to end his *Cities in Flight* series.

All readers have one or two—perhaps many more—books or stories that have affected them deeply in the course of their reading life. Speaking subjectively, I got turned on to science fiction by reading Edgar Rice Burroughs, A. Merritt, and H. Rider Haggard the summer I was twelve. But the Carnegie Library in Upper Montclair, New Jersey, had little more than the "classics." Fortunately I got another exposure to the magical equations when I was a young married woman. This time Edmund Hamilton's splendidly romantic *Star Kings,* Andre Norton's *Beast Master* and *Daybreak 2000 A.D.,* and Isaac Asimov's *Foundation* series wove the essential "glamour."

The science fictional story that has had the most influence on me personally and philosophically is Austin Tappan Wright's *Islandia.* An exceptional novel on every count, *Islandia* is surviving the test of time on sterling merits. The book was published first in 1942. I took my voyage to Islandia's shores at sixteen, and I've reread the abridged version of 1,032 pages roughly every two or three years. *Islandia* was, in 1942, termed a utopian novel but, by its scope, the novel exceeds any category. Islandia, as a place, is fully conceived, with meteorology charts, maps, detailed city plans, fables, poetry, and a history (written by one of the novel's characters). *Islandia* is also the

12. My second son has worn out five sets of the trilogy.
13. There is actually another novelist, Georgette Heyer, who exerts a tremendous fascination for her readers. But as the Regency period existed and Miss Heyer is authentically recalling that era, it is not a true exception.

exception to the rule of loveless sf stories. For *Islandia* defines and illustrates many facets of that emotion: the love of the hero, John Lang, for a country not his own, for which he had the greatest empathy and keenest affection—*alia* is the Islandian language word for this aspect of love. Islandians differentiate between *apia* (sexual lust) and *apiata* (puppy love or infatuation, soon to pass but hot and fierce while it lasts). *Ania* is the enduring, mature love between two people who desire to perpetuate their love in children, the energy and devotion of building a home together (continuing a home, actually, since love of birthplace is very strong in every Islandian). There is also *amia*, the love/affection/respect/esteem in which one can hold a group or a single person with no sexual overtones. And *linamia*, the strong friendship that occurs between members of the same sex only once or twice in a lifetime.

Good taste precluded promiscuity among Islandians yet John Lang does have a passionate love affair *(apia)* with Nattana Hytha. Lang also suffers through an intense platonic longing for Dorna, sister of his best friend, Dorn, with whom Lang exchanges *linamia*. Lang is cautioned against marrying an Islandian woman as there would always be an unbridgeable difference in outlook. He goes back to the States briefly to test his love for his adopted country, Islandia, and discovers true *ania* for a young American girl, Gladys Hunter. The two marry in Islandia and live, we hope, with reasonable felicity thereafter. Wright never suggests that life in Islandia is perfect.

Islandia is not without prostitutes, but they are not considered degenerate or classless: women seek this way of life for a variety of reasons. When they leave the protection of their family, the house in which they then abide looks after them *in loco familiae*. No shame is attached to their profession so that they are free to return to their home provinces and marry. An amazing notion when you consider that *Islandia*, although conceived by its author in his youth, was written during the '20s and '30s in Puritan American Pennsylvania.

Islandia is far more than John Lang's love stories, or his realization that Islandia is heart's home. It is a plea against the disadvantages of progress—disadvantages under which we are all suffering in this polluted world, and from which many of us take refuge in the enchanted pages of science fiction.

I have often looked longingly at the globe of the world, yearning to find Karain continent—somewhere. Mr. Wright never gives the exact longitude or latitude. I suppose that one of our astronauts may have seen it in passing—and judiciously kept silent. Islandia could not have survived her stubborn and glorious isolation in a modern world of jumbo jets and Telstar. Fortunately for us war-weary, illusion-shattered readers, she remains intact, as Mr. Wright first envisioned her, richly endowed with the glamour and romance that is the basic ingredient of all science fiction.

Anne McCaffrey

Born April 1, 1926, in Cambridge, Massachusetts, Anne McCaffrey returned there to take a B.A. cum laude degree in Slavonic Languages and Literatures at Radcliffe College. After working as an advertising copywriter, she married Wright Johnson, had three children and did freelance stage direction of opera and operetta, occasionally performing in shows herself. With conductor Clarence Snyder, she stage directed and produced the American Premiere of Carl Orff's *Ludus De Nato Infante Mirificus* in Greenville, Delaware. She began to write full-time in 1965 when her youngest child started school. From 1968–1970 she served as Secretary-Treasurer of the Science Fiction Writers of America. After her divorce in 1970, she moved to Ireland with her children where she is currently working on new novels and enjoying the amenities of the country, particularly hunting on her Irish gray, Mister Ed.

Ms. McCaffrey published her first short story in 1954 but did not publish with any regularity until the 1960s when the "Helva" stories began to attract attention. Since then she has published over thirty-five stories, eight novels, an anthology, and a cookbook. "Weyr Search" won her the Hugo Award in 1967, and "Dragonrider" (from the same series) claimed the Nebula Award in 1968 which, incidentally, made her the first woman to win both awards. She has lectured to universities, high schools, and library study groups in the States, been a Guest of Honor at conventions in the USA, Canada, and England, and has appeared on television and radio on both sides of the Atlantic.

Restoree, 1967 (Ballantine)
Dragonflight, 1968 (Ballantine and Walker & Co.)
Decision at Doona, 1969 (Ballantine)
Ship Who Sang, 1970 (Ballantine)
Alchemy & Academe, 1970 (Doubleday), editor
Dragonquest, 1971 (Ballantine)
Mark of Merlin, 1971 (Dell)
Ring of Fear, 1971 (Dell)

To Ride Pegasus, 1973 (Ballantine)
Out of This World Cookbook, 1973 (Ballantine)
Catteni & White Dragon, (Ballantine, forthcoming)
Queendom's Story & Sight Unseen, (Dell, forthcoming)

Gordon R. Dickson

Plausibility in Science Fiction

There is no question that plausibility—that writerly art of making a story worthy of belief—in science fiction makes a different and extra demand upon its author in comparison, for example, to that which an equivalent piece of historical or contemporary fiction makes upon its creator.

The large reason for this different and extra demand is that science fiction attempts, by its own definition, to give its readers something more than they would expect to receive from an equivalent piece of non-science fiction.

In all forms of story-making, imagination is required for the creation of characters, the rendering of scenes, and in the organization of the action. These three vital elements not only need to be entertaining and original, but must also convey an impression of reality, or the reader will lose faith in the story and abandon it. However, science fiction undertakes a requirement beyond these three. It contracts with its readers to provide not only these necessary elements but also to offer an experience outside of ordinary reality; and it undertakes to make this particular experience believable—however unfamiliar or bizarre—or fail as a story.

Of all other forms of fiction, only the

historical novel approaches this additional requirement in its proper form. The historical short story or novel promises in character and action all that the contemporary story does, laid in the here and now; but the historical story also attempts to do this with its scene laid in a time that is far enough in the past to be unfamiliar to the readers. Superficially, then, it might seem that the undertaking of the sf story is no greater than that of the historical story in that, as the historical story undertakes to place its scene backward in time while the sf story merely places itself forward or elsewhere, the added difficulties of both forms must be equal.

But this is literally a conclusion based on a superficial view. A little closer attention to the difference between the requirements for authenticity in the three forms shows that if the contemporary author finds the straw of reality necessary to make his literary bricks lying openly around him in observable experience, the writer of historical fiction is only required to go a step further and dig for what he requires—to research for it, in fact, among the collected evidence of history concerning the period in which he is writing.

Moreover, in neither one of these two forms are the requirements for correctness of their realistic elements vital. The reader is not usually disposed to quarrel with the even moderately entertaining writer of fiction dealing with the contemporary scene just because the furniture of that scene is not portrayed with total accuracy or correctly connected with the period of his story. Minor anachronisms can be dismissed—though the good writer of contemporary fiction will know and render his scene as scrupulously as any other artist.

Similarly, an entertaining historical writer can with some safety turn out to be either a lazy researchist, in which case his work may be peppered with historical inaccuracies, or he can with comparable safety go to the opposite extreme. If he is an overzealous researcher—in fact, a historian in writer's clothing —he may deafen the mental ear of his reader with wagonloads of recorded fact that have only a flimsy justification for being mentioned within the framework of the story.

Again, if he is a good writer of historical fiction, he commits neither sin. He will achieve the difficult task of digging up and interweaving just the right choice and amount of historical fact in just the proper place and manner in his narrative to make his outdated scene glow with life and reality. But individual artistry and success should not be allowed to cloud the very real, basic differences in technical problems between the three story forms.

If the writers of both contemporary or historical fiction may succeed in spite of either lazy or excessive handling of the straw of reality in their scenes, the sf writer has no such freedom available to him. This is because his scene, by definition, cannot call on the authority of what is, or has been, actually existent. His premise is that what he has to tell you either does not exist, or has not yet come into existence. Consequently, he cannot take refuge in the record book. The only pretension to reality in scene that he can make is to show the scene as an integral part of a narrative which *as a whole* impresses the reader as something that could actually happen. In short, the straw of a manufactured realism with which the sf writer makes his particular literary bricks must be entirely convincing to the reader in its own right, or the whole story will lose its power to convince. In sf, the matter of a realistic—i.e., plausible—scene is one of the pillars that bears the whole weight of the story. If it fails, the story crumbles.

If this much is true in science fiction with the scene, it is on the same ground true of the elements of character and action. In a contemporary or historical story, we expect to find the characters resembling people we have known in our own lives; and the more they resemble, the more we feel they are true to life. In science fiction, on the contrary, we look for and expect to find ways in which the characters are different from anyone we have known, with differences that will reassure us we are not being served the warmed-over present, dished up falsely on a science fictional plate.

In contemporary or historical action we assume that the events taking place will reassure our sense of belief by taking place in the patterns and modes that we recognize from our own practical experience of life; and the more they seem to do so, the more we feel that what we are vicariously experiencing is made of the stuff of real events. But in science fiction we look forward to seeing that which takes place happen for reasons and causes we have never ourselves encountered or suspected to exist. Otherwise, there will be no surprise, no thrill of opening a door upon the unknown, which is what we expect to feel when we take a literary venture into the undiscovered lands lying outside the realms of the real present and the real past.

So then, if the straw of apparent reality is so ultimately necessary to successful science fiction, and if that straw exists nowhere around us to be picked up or even mined for—how can plausibility in science fiction be achieved?

The answer of course is by a refinement of the method by which a historical writer makes his story real to a present-day audience. The historical writer researches for the elements of reality out of which he constructs his story. The science fiction writer must research at second remove, not directly for the elements themselves, but for the raw materials out of which to manufacture these elements. He must take the process of infusing his story with reality clear through from the equivalent of digging of iron ore to the striking of the steel nails with which he will fasten together the imaginative panels of his story's structure.

The basic principle underlying what he does is one used by all writers—contemporary, historical, and science fictional alike. Behind every art, there are laws basic to it. Just as one might say that there is a physics of music, there is a physics of painting, a physics of sculpture, a physics (and physiology) of dance, and a physics of writing. In writing the most obvious and commonly recognized laws have to do with organization, of pattern with the form—for example, the recognized limitations of time and space within the one-act play, the strictures generally observed in the successful short story. A common mistake is to believe that these laws governing literary form are arbitrary and possibly academic ones, and the mind unfettered by tradition is free to break them without penalty. No misconception was ever greater.

The fact of the matter is that these strictures were not the invention of critics, professors, editors, nor even of writers, but of the readers themselves. From the beginning of all the arts, there have been continual efforts by the artists in all fields to work toward a larger and more effective vocabulary with which to speak to their audience. Each artist wrestles with this problem in his turn and, usually at the cost of his own trial and error, discovers that a solid core of existing techniques exists simply because these techniques have been proved more effective upon the audience than the alternatives that have come to his mind and the minds of generations of artists before him. In the end, if he is a serious artist and worker, he masters these techniques and goes on to develop from there in his struggle to achieve maximum personal expression, in his turn evolving refinements of technique upon which later artists will build.

In this manner, the classic short story form evolved on the basis of the classic tale, enjoying greater success with the reader or listener simply because the short story offered a richer and more satisfying literary experience to the reader than the older form.

So with classic forms generally in all the arts. The more ancient of these bear the same order of relationship to the newer forms following them that Newtonian physics bears to Einsteinian physics. The latter is simply a more sophisticated tool than the former; but the latter does not negate the former within the former's own terms, any more than the convenience of stretching out an objective lifetime by the contraction of time at near-light speeds, in the Einsteinian universe, negates our own subjective experience of the time it takes to travel at more Newtonian speeds about the surface of contemporary Earth.

Therefore, the technique of infusing sf with plausibility finds its solution in an already observed writing principle, that of the anchor in reality.

Like most workable principles in all the arts, this particular one relates to a fact of human perception—that we physically identify other people and objects on the basis of a certain number of recognized signals. In the case of a rock, these may be such signals as color, shape, lack of motion, and the sort of position in the surrounding environment in which a rock would probably be found. In the case of more educated or familiar reading of signals, the identification could be: veined white = quartz rock; and "no rock there previously" = "must have fallen from overhanging cliff." The recognition mechanism of the reader, in his vicarious perception of the life that exists on the printed page, subconsciously demands from the story object a parallel to the signals he would get from the actual, physical object in real life. If he is merely told that it is a piece of quartz rock, his desire for identificational signals goes begging, and this puts a strain on his belief in the story. If he is allowed to see the color and veining of the rock (and if he knows quartz well enough to identify it by those signals) his signal-desire is at least partially satisfied and his belief is unimpeded.

The literary principle of giving him such anchors in reality, then, is an integral technique of the art of writing. As in actual life, there is a critical number of such signals which, once reached, carry complete conviction in the scene to which they belong. Examples of the power of these signals have been such constructions as rooms in which the laws of perspective were taken advantage of by the builder, in order to give a false appearance of distance, or to convince someone within the room that the floor was level when actually it was tilted. Even the evidence of the gravitational pull, when at odds with observed reality, has to fight hard for belief in the face of a critical number of accepted identificational signals.

The writer, then, takes advantage of that fact. He multiplies the number of his signals in any scene until he believes he has reached such a critical number. Taking the quartz rock mentioned before as one part of the scene of a firelit encampment in the woods, for example, the author might add such unarguable signals as the smell of the wood smoke from the fire, the crackle of the burning branches, the feel of the cool night wind on the backs of naked hands and necks not facing the fire. . . .

Each one of these things would be anchored in reality—in the real appearance of quartz rock, the smell of woodsmoke, and so on. The art of the writer is not so much to tell the reader a story;

but to evoke, through the medium of a highly restrictive code of black marks on white paper, the images of a story which the reader will build out of his own experiences with life. Each time the author sets out an anchor in reality by evoking a sight, sound, or smell which the reader has tucked in his own memory, he increases the plausibility of his story to the critical point where the reader will give up all resistance to belief and live it in his imagination, as fully as the author did in his while writing it.

This, then, is the operative principle in fiction with regard to plausibility; and it is common to all fiction. In science fiction, however, it has acquired an added dimension in developing to meet the needs of a story form beyond those of the past and present story, for which its original dimensions were sufficient.

The needs placing their demand on this principle originate in the lack of that straw of reality I mentioned at the very beginning. As I pointed out, with the story laid in present reality, the anchors of reality are there to be experienced firsthand. Anyone can light a fire in the woods and smell its smoke; anyone can have a piece of quartz identified to him and remember what it looks like. Similarly in the story laid in past reality, while the physical evidence may no longer be there to be experienced directly by the author, accounts and descriptions of it are often available, which can be absorbed by the author (if he has the necessary talent) to the point where he can see these in his mind's eye just as clearly as a contemporary, directly experienced evidence—and proceed to convey them to the reader with similar effectiveness.

The difficulty with this technique only emerges in the science fiction story, where the author has neither real experience directly available nor the record of it to draw upon. In spite of these lacks, the unconscious response of the reader still demands of him that he justify his extraterrestrial scene, his alien creature, and his unconventional action as if all these things had anchors in familiar, Earthly reality.

To treat the reader's demand as unreasonable, and ignore it, is not the solution. In the end, every author must come to terms with the reader's demands, or lose him, a loss which means little to the reader—he simply goes on to some other author who does come to terms with his demands—but which can destroy the writer. The answer to this situation is that if the reader wishes his story anchored in reality, he must have it so anchored, by one means if not by another.

The means which has developed to meet this demand is the anchor in reality at second remove. Briefly, this is the extraterrestrial scene, the alien form and response, anchored to a reasonable extrapolation of an existent possibility, which is itself anchored by way of research or theory to present reality. In brief, imagination is justified by an hypothesis, which is in turn justified by fact.

For example, an intelligent alien life form existing on a world at temperatures above anything a human could stand for more than a few seconds could be justified by a relatively recent discovery of miniature aquatic life existing in natural hot springs here on Earth at temperatures only a little below the boiling point.

However, plausibility in science fiction is not merely a simple matter of the author informing the reader of such a chain of justification; any more than naming rock, woodsmoke, and firecrackle was enough to give the illusion of reality to the contemporary scene of the encampment. For the chain of justification to convince the reader of what he is reading, he must experience the connection at first hand in his own imagination.

In short, the author must show him—through the eyes of one of the human characters in whom the reader's conviction has already been established—the minute Earthly organism surviving in near-boiling water, then the path by which such an organism could evolve to size and intelligence comparable to the high-temperature aliens, then the similarity-connection between the high-temperature alien and the evolved Earthly organism.

This creates a logic-chain which in effect answers the reader's desire for an anchor in reality by tying the completely fanciful alien to the sober reality of contemporary Earth. It is, of course, not easy to do. The images that make up the logic-chain must be worked into the narrative without interrupting or slowing down the action, for which they only provide the scene. To do this poses two requirements, both of which are troublesome, but can be fulfilled by the writer who is willing to work.

The two requirements are for experience and information—the experience necessary to render a scene to the reader in a series of images, rather than tell it to him in chunks of narrative where the author speaks with his own voice, and the information about such things as the minute organisms living in the water of the hot spring, which is not found in the general large-circulation trade papers and magazines. In short, continuing practice and continual research for information.

As far as experience and practice are concerned, there is little point in talking or writing at length about it. The writer either will work at his art, or he will not—the decision to do one or the other is an interior one, not amenable to outside argument. As far as research goes, however, there are some useful things to be said.

Information comes to the science fiction writer by two main channels. One is through the written word in books and those publications which specialize in information—and that channel at the present time is as wide as from the daily newspaper through the *National Geographic* magazine, to *Science Magazine, Science News-Letter,* and a host of small, specialty publications in the fields of scientific and academic research. A hallmark of the science fiction field has been that its successful practitioners are by natural inclination, apart from their writing, avid observers in many areas. Each author usually has a small number of fields in which he is particularly interested, but he will tend to take at least a passing interest in an additional and much larger number. This type of curiosity has been traditionally typical of the writer in general; but those writing in the science fiction field, with its concern for the future scene, have given the trait a special meaning. Although most of them enjoy the process of literary research for its own sake, it pays off immeasurably in the process of their writing—not only directly supplying the sort of plausibility connections of which the small organisms in the hot spring were an example, but, almost more importantly, setting the writer himself on the right track to search out the specific information he needs.

There is a second channel of information which tends to grow with time in the case of the individual writer. Over a period of years as he works, he tends to make the acquaintance of a number of people who are experts in their own fields and to whom he can turn directly with specific questions about information in their specialty. This is the other main channel by which necessary information comes as grist to the literary mill; and its existence grows out of the entirely honest interest of the writer in what the specialist is doing, apart from any writing needs.

Down these two conduits flow the raw material of plausibility in science fiction. But to begin with, it is raw material only. It remains for the writer to process it into anchors in reality for the scenes, actions, and characters of his otherwise wholly imaginary stories. This processing is an art in itself—one of the most difficult of arts, in fact, for it must take place entirely in the immaterial laboratory of the writer's thoughts. The process of creativity is an unexplainable as well as a highly individual accomplishment. All that can be said about it with certainty is that the primitive, raw elements which will make up any created work are fed into some particular mental furnace, where a melting together and a transmutation of their basic natures take place, so that they emerge from the furnace combined, transformed, and solidified into an ingot of value in some way greater than the total of their original worths. This transformation, however, is only the unconscious end-part of the process. In preparation, there is the necessary selection of just the correct raw elements and materials—the real and invented facts of the story which the writer will need to justify the actions of his imagination; and the marshaling of these facts until they strike enough sparks from each other to kindle a unique and special life of their own.

The words *unique* and *special* are the operative ones in this context. Plausibility in a story—any story—depends upon the inevitability of its action, and this inevitability must derive from one of two sources: either the inevitability of circumstance—as when the rope by which a man is climbing down a cliff breaks, so that he has no choice but to fall; or the inevitability of character—in which, say, the nature of the climbing man is such that, although he knows the rope will probably break, he chooses to try the climb down, regardless.

Because inevitability finds its reason either in event or character, and because event and character are necessarily bound together in any competent story—the event determining the choice which the character must make, and the character determining by his choice what event will follow upon his choosing—these two elements must share this unique and special life. They must be related together by it, or the imaginary world (in sf, the imaginary universe) that they share will not be able to put out the signals of reality necessary to convince the reader that his literary experience is the true counterpart of life. Without that conviction, the story will fail in its effect.

Therefore, in the preparation that goes before the writing, during the process of assembling the elements of the story, all necessary parts must be brought into contact, until they spark off their own creative fire. For the alien life form to be real, it must have a point of view, which almost necessitates an alien character. For the reader to be convinced of the roots of extrapolative logic that lead from the hot spring on Earth to the high-temperature alien world, a point of view must be established which surveys that connection. This almost necessitates a human character. But behind the alien, and behind the human point-of-view character are those other characteristics of their races that make them the unique individuals they are. Therefore, other characters, both human and alien, may be needed. Finally, human and alien must interact in the logical chain of events that spring from their point of first contact in the story, and proceed through the developments that make the story itself something more than an anecdote. When they do interact, their interactions must come inevitably and realistically out of what the characters are in their own human and alien terms.

In the end, inescapably, character determines action and both determine scene. So that, in the final essential, the story's plausibility depends upon the homogeneity of the resultant literary ingot, including that added and particular science fictional element of justification at second remove, for everything that will be alien or strange to the reader.

More than for an author writing in any other fictional form, there is a requirement upon the sf writer to do his homework completely in advance. Only when enough justifying factors have been worked out, only when enough speculation on the alien character and scene has been made, will the creative kindling occur. Then, if everything had been done faithfully and in full, will come a moment in which all the facts, imaginary and real, will flow together into a *gestalt* of the fictional scene, characters, and action; the whole science fictional universe of his story will have become both real and alive, so that he will no longer need to puzzle out specifically just what a particular character will do in a particular situation. The resultant action will come out of the *gestalt*, automatically, as if he had asked himself what some relative or old friend would do in such a case.

When that happens, he need only go ahead and write; because everything within the story area will now be suffused with a justification of reality. Everything will be plausible, because any implausibility now would be an intrusion on, and a violation of, a pattern already brought to three-dimensional life.

Gordon R. Dickson

Born November 1, 1923, in Edmonton, Alberta, Canada. On graduating from high school in 1939, at the age of fifteen, he entered the University of Minnesota to work toward a degree in creative writing. Left the University for military service from 1943 to 1946, but returned from California in 1947, and received a Bachelor of Arts degree in 1950. He then became a full-time writer, and has written uninterruptedly ever since. His "Soldier, Ask Not," won the science fiction Hugo Award for best shorter-than-novel-length-fiction of 1964, which was presented at the World Science Fiction Convention at London, England, in September 1965. He also won the Science Fiction Writers of America Nebula Award for best novelette: *Call Him Lord,* in 1966.

Works include: radio plays, over two hundred short stories and novelettes, thirty published novels, and four books under way but not yet published.

Gordon Dickson's novels have sold over a million and a half copies, here and abroad; and his writing has been translated into many foreign languages, appearing in twenty-three countries. He has served two terms as President of Science Fiction Writers of America, and is a member of Authors Guild and Mystery Writers of America, and a Director of the Science Fiction Writer's Speakers Bureau.

SHORT STORY COLLECTIONS

Danger—Human, 1970 (Doubleday)
Mutants, 1970 (Crowell-Collier)

NOVELS 1950 THROUGH 1960

Alien From Arcturus (Ace Books)
Mankind On the Run
*Genetic General
Time to Teleport
Delusion World
Spatial Delivery

*indicates books in the Childe (Dorsai) Cycle.

Naked to the Stars (Pyramid)
Earthman's Burden (Gnome Press) with Poul Anderson
Secret Under the Sea (Holt, Reinhart, Winston)
Necromancer (Doubleday)

NOVELS SINCE 1960

Alien Way, 1966 (Bantam)
Mission to Universe, 1967 (Berkley)
Space Swimmers, 1968
Soldier, Ask Not, 1968 (Dell)
Hour of the Horde
Wolfling, 1969
Secret Under Antarctica, 1962 (Holt, Reinhart, Winston)
Secret Under the Caribbean, 1963
Space Winners, 1965
Planet Run, 1968 (Doubleday) with Keith Laumer
None But Man, 1969
Five Fates, 1970, with Keith Laumer, Harlan Ellison, Poul Anderson, Frank Herbert
Tactics of Mistake, 1970
The Pritcher Mass
The Ice Knives—to be published
Spacepaw, 1969 (Putnam)
Alien Art (Dell)
Retribution Seven
Sleepwalker's World, 1971 (Lippincott)
Outposter
Hour of the Horde, (Putnam/Berkley)
Pilgrim and Professional (to be published) with Poul Anderson
Star Prince Charlie (to be published) with Poul Anderson

Jack Williamson

Science Fiction, Teaching and Criticism*

I still recall the wonders of Hawthorne and Poe when I first happened on them long ago in the dusty cupboard that held our rural school library. Later I came upon Mark Twain's *A Connecticut Yankee in King Arthur's Court* and even a yellow-paged copy of Bulwer-Lytton's *The Coming Race*. But Burroughs and Merritt and their exciting kind were absent from the shelves and not yet known to me, though they were running in the pulps for sale on the newsstands I hadn't learned about. Pulp science fiction was forbidden trash, morally doubtful and, so my teacher-father feared, unhealthy for the mind.

Things are different now. The George Arents Research Library at Syracuse proudly houses the papers of science fiction people ranging from Forrest J. Ackerman to Roger Zelazny. Scores of other schools have built up major science fiction collections. Even in my own hometown, Eastern New Mexico University is preserving the papers of Leigh Bracket and Edmond Hamilton, as well as my own.

In the past decade, science fiction has made a sudden invasion of the classroom. Though a few special lectures had been

*Note: This essay borrows a few passages from other papers of mine.

given earlier, the first officially scheduled college course called science fiction seems to have been the one Mark Hillegas taught at Colgate in 1962. His beachhead has grown. In *Teaching SF*, I have listed more than 250 science fiction and fantasy courses offered in American colleges during the past two or three years; James Gunn estimates an actual total nearer one thousand.

This sudden conquest is still far from complete. Tradition-bound department heads and curriculum committees still veto proposed new courses, and the would-be teacher has to be persuasive. In a brief for her course at Monroe Community College in Rochester, Carylyn Wendell announces that "science fiction has grown up and become respectable," and quotes good witnesses in its defense. Insofar as it reflects our common humanity, our common tasks, and common dangers, Isaac Asimov testifies, it "serves the world well, and America particularly well."

Sheila Schwartz finds value in its attention to "the shared outer space which is the same for all men and dwarfs such traditional concerns as sex and religion. The focus of science fiction is the illumination of the technological society in which science and technology must be understood and rationally controlled by man lest he risk complete destruction both as individual and as species."

The most eloquent witness is Kurt Vonnegut's Eliot, in *God Bless You, Mr. Rosewater*, who tells a group of science fiction writers: "I love you sons of bitches. You're all I read any more. You're the only ones who'll talk about the *really* terrific changes going on . . . the only ones with guts enough to *really* care about the future, who *really* notice what machines do to us, what wars do to us, what tremendous misunderstandings, mistakes, accidents, and catastrophes do to us."

Braced with such appeals, academic science fiction is gaining ground. The number of reported courses continues to double each year. Most of those I know about are fresh and pertinent, enlivened with films, guest lecturers, and all sorts of unorthodox innovations. They're fun to teach. Many students like their focus on the urgent issues and tomorrow. In spite of the skeptics, I think they're here to stay.

Looking in this essay at the teaching and the criticism of science fiction, we must take the critic first. He defines and evaluates what is to be taught. Here is where our problems begin, because—beyond James Blish and Damon Knight—certified critics scarcely exist. The mainstream critics have seldom made much sense about science fiction when they happened to notice it at all, and the amateurs are often in violent disagreement.

The very nature of science fiction is in bitter dispute. The chief issue is what might be called the futurological aspect, the claim of future possibility expressed by Hugo Gernsback's old slogan for *Amazing Stories:* "The magazine of prophetic fiction." To many readers, including most of the students who enroll for my own course, this sense of prophecy defines science fiction. To many contemporary critics and writers, it is naive nonsense. The quarrel is due partly to the way all fiction works, I think, and partly to those conflicting attitudes toward science that have troubled Sir Charles Snow.

The predictive gift of science fiction is a principle of popular mythology. Everybody knows how Jules Verne forecast the airplane and the submarine and flight to the moon, how H. G. Wells forecast atomic bombs. We're all looking for the impact of newer technologies, more wonderful or dreadful. The average writer, however, is more stage magician then scientist or prophet. His business is the creation of illusions good enough to win a momentary suspension of the reader's unbelief. Most of his devices are common to all sorts of literature—empathic characters, dramatic action, emotive atmosphere, meaningful theme, evocative language. The distinctive feature of science fiction—the special device that sets it off from other sorts of fantasy—is the claim that it could come true. This is important to the man in the street, even though he may be pretty ignorant about the actual limits of science and pretty tolerant about story logic. It is less important to the literary artisan who places greater faith in those other hard-learned devices of his trade. With no serious prophetic intention at all, the writer in search of story interest often opts for the least probable event, rather than the most probable, simply because he needs the unexpected. He usually knows what Wells discovered, that serious social forecasts mix poorly with fiction.

Yet, for all that, a few writers have been competent scientists genuinely concerned with things to come. Wells had learned biology from T. H. Huxley, Darwin's great champion, and his *Time Machine* grew out of a very sober extrapolation of the future evolution of life on earth. Polishing his techniques of technological and social prediction in story after story, he became the first futurologist. He announced his "discovery of the future" in 1902 and turned away from science fiction to begin his long campaign for the world state he projected as a refuge from the frightening future he had foreseen.

Wells was of course not quite the inventor of modern science fiction—credit for that must be shared with Verne and Poe and Mary Shelley, perhaps even with Defoe or Swift or Plato. But he crystallized the genre and established its techniques—his method was to limit each story to a single new assumption, surrounded with everyday detail, and developed with a strictly consistent internal logic.

The Wellsian method has shaped most science fiction since. Hugo Gernsback reprinted the best of Wells in *Amazing Stories* —the original science fiction magazine, launched in 1926. John W. Campbell edited *Astounding*, which in time became *Analog*, with the same respect for at least an illusion of scientific probability. (He also used Wells's recipe for the fiction in *Unknown*, his magazine of fantasy.) Ben Bova, his editorial successor, is renovating the same tradition, and *Analog* still leads the field in circulation.

Even though most science fiction may be produced and read for sheer entertainment, there have always been a handful of writers who shared Wells's command of the scientific method and his concern about the fate of man. Aldous Huxley and Arthur C. Clarke and Isaac Asimov and Robert A. Heinlein are examples. Their sometimes serious futurology has kept life in the popular myth that science fiction does foresee the wonders and the terrors of the future.

Not that the bulk of published science fiction has ever owed any great debt to science. Wells himself was often more concerned with illusion than reality—as witness his own *Invisible Man.* But open defiance of the Wellsian convention is a rather recent thing. The slogan of revolt was "the New Wave," shouted a few years ago by Judith Merril and J. G. Ballard.

The rebellion sprang from an ignorance of science and a terror of technology. Slanted against the idea of progress and all the works of private enterprise, New Wave fiction magnified all the ugliness around us: of war and racism, of filth and crime and drugs and pollution. Its forecast futures were nightmares of overpopulation, mechanized oppression, and universal frustration, its gloating pessimism only thinly garnished with "new" stylistic devices too often borrowed from the literary experimenters of Joyce's generation, all this raucously merchandised as the wave of the future.

It's old now. Though it did wash up occasional bits of power and beauty, it failed to move most readers. Such able writers as Chip Delany and Harlan Ellison and Brian Aldiss, who once seemed to be swimming with it, have now gone their own brilliant and individual ways. Subsiding, it has I think left us all enriched with a sharpened awareness of language and a quickened interest in literary experiment—but still split with the old division from which it sprang, a quarrel now grown wider and more savage than ever, with the culture of science often breaking into retreat before the rearmed leaders of tradition.

I wonder how far science fiction itself has been a cause of this crisis of faith in our science and ourselves, how far only a symptom. At least since Swift, it has been debating our nature and our future. Several of Wells's great early novels were deliberately written as later voyages of Gulliver, borrowing Swift's black pessimism to criticize our smug belief in progress. Though it may seem ironic, I suspect that Wells and his anti-utopian heirs helped ignite the panic mistrust of technology that is now stifling our space programs, choking off funds for all research, even stalling efforts to cope with the energy crisis.

A glance at its critical history is enough to show that science fiction has never been noticed so much for purely literary values as for the dangerous inventions that keep escaping off its pages into reality. Before World War II, it was commonly regarded as crude pulp stuff, beneath criticism. My own early searches for scholarly discussions of "pseudo-scientific fiction" generally failed. There were a few bright bits—Wells's prefaces to his own "scientific romances," Haggard's comments on his writing methods, Coleridge's famous saying about "that willing suspension of disbelief for the moment, which constitutes poetic faith"—but even those precious bits were left from an older generation.

The atomic bombs and the V-2 rockets not only vindicated the prophetic power of science fiction in the minds of the faithful, but also awoke an uneasy public interest in whatever more dangerous device might be the next to escape. A small boom was born from that apprehension. Fans began setting up their own little firms to reprint the old pulp stories in book form. When Fantasy Press and Gnome Press and Arkham House and the others had established a market, the large publishers followed. Dressed now in hard covers, science fiction began getting its first serious critical attention since the world lost its first great faith in H. G. Wells.

One early book was *Of Worlds Beyond* (1947), a symposium on writing science fiction edited by Lloyd Arthur Eshbach, with essays by Campbell, Heinlein, van Vogt, de Camp, and other old hands. J. O. Bailey's *Pilgrims Through Space and Time*, published the same year, was a more significant critical beginning. Perhaps the first major academic study, it traces early use of the theme of travel in time and space, with emphasis on fiction written in the period 1870 to 1915. Recently reprinted, it is a rich mine of bibliographical and plot information about rare early titles—evidence that science fiction, under whatever name, was already a very sturdy infant even before the arrival of Verne and Wells.

Before the end of that postwar boomlet, two more major books came out. L. Sprague de Camp's *Science-Fiction Handbook* (1953) was slanted for the writer, and the market tips are now long out of date; de Camp is a scholar, however, who both knows and writes science fiction, and the book is still useful for his historical and biographical and critical comment. *Modern Science Fiction*, an anthology of essays edited the same year by

Reginald Bretnor, became a standard critical text. But the bubble was already bursting. Of some thirty-odd magazines, only half a dozen survived. Though Basil Davenport's brief *Inquiry into Science Fiction* came from Longmans, Green as late as 1955, the major publishers were warily turning science fiction back to the fans.

Damon Knight's *In Search of Wonder* (1956) was published by Advent, a small firm set up by a group of Chicago fans. Knight's achievement, to paraphrase Anthony Boucher's introduction, was simply to take science fiction seriously as a field of literature, to apply ordinary critical standards, and to make the result meaningful. Exposing "chuckleheads" and "cosmic jerrybuilders," dissecting "half-bad" writers, he brought a sharp mind and a new sense of value into the field. The book was reissued in 1967, with new essays added. Meanwhile, in 1964, Advent had also published *The Issue at Hand*, by "William Atheling"—who writes fine fiction as James Blish. Equals in wit and insight and contempt for chuckleheads, Knight and Blish have produced what is still perhaps the best science fiction criticism at hand.

Most of the other Advent titles have been more fannish than critical—among them Alva Rogers's *Requiem for Astounding* (1964), Ron Ellik and Bill Evans's *The Universes of E. E. Smith* (1966), and Harry Warner's *All Our Yesterdays* (1969). But *The Science Fiction Novel* (1959), introduced by Basil Davenport, collects critical essays by Robert Heinlein, C. M. Kornbluth, Alfred Bester, and Robert Bloch. Alexei Panshin's *Heinlein in Dimension* (1968) is notable as the first full-length study of Heinlein—who can still be defended as the foremost American science fiction writer.

Academic researchers were meanwhile following up Bailey's explorations of earlier science fiction. Marjory Hope Nicolson's *Voyages to the Moon* (1948) is a study of imaginary moon trips in books published through the years 1493 to 1784. Roger Lancelyn Green carries his survey of such old dreams out to other planets and down to the twentieth century in *Into Other Worlds: Space Flight from Lucian to Lewis* (1958), brightening his findings with lively summaries of many novels now forgotten. In 1960, the domain of science fiction was recharted for the literary community by the popular British novelist Kingsley Amis. His *New Maps of Hell* reflects enthusiasm for the satire and contemporary social comment that he finds in such writers as Frederik Pohl, but he shows little concern for the futurological probing that I think gives science fiction its basic appeal.

The brightest achievement of science fiction criticism seems to have been the restoration of H. G. Wells—a just debt paid, I think, to the chief inventor of the genre. Once immensely respected, Wells had been misunderstood by a whole generation of critics, who considered him a hack journalist or a "crass materialist" or a hollow-headed utopian, or more commonly ignored him altogether. His son Anthony West began the rediscovery with an article in 1957 that pointed out the dark philosophic pessimism beneath the life and wit and rich invention of Wells's great fiction. Bernard Bergonzi followed in 1961 with the *The Early H. G. Wells,* a detailed study of the "scientific romances" that emphasizes their ambivalence and skepticism. My own dissertation, interpreting this early fiction as Swiftian criticism of the idea of progress, was finished in 1964 and more recently rewritten for book publication. Mark Hillegas, in *The Future as Nightmare: H. G. Wells and the Anti-Utopians* (1967), traces the influence of Wells's early work on Evgenii Zamyatin's *We*, on Aldous Huxley's *Brave New World*, and George Orwell's *1984*, on down to contemporary science fiction, documenting the use of Wells's own ideas and images to attack the utopianism of his later career. This later Wells, the world-planner, the world-educator, the would-be world-saver, is the subject of W. Warren Wager's *H. G. Wells and the World State*, a study that shows Wells to have been somewhat wiser than his critics. The Wells papers are now at the University of Illinois, and a stream of books has come from scholars there, on Wells and George Gissing, Wells and Henry James, Wells and Arnold Bennett. Lovatt Dickson's *H. G. Wells: His Turbulent Life and Times* (1969) continues the story of his private life, which Wells himself had begun so ably in his own *Experiment in Autobiography*. Although no complete life and works has yet appeared, Wells research is still in progress. Recent studies have appeared in Russia and France. When Professor Darko Suvin gathered an international group at McGill University in 1971 for a symposium on "H. G. Wells and Modern Science Fiction," critics came from Europe and Japan.

Such critical activities have been encouraged by a new climate of respect for science fiction, more pervasive and enduring than the postwar flash of interest but probably rising from similar concerns—with new ecological alarms now added to the old fears of war and space and the atom. Since the major publishers are turning friendly again, more people are entering the critical arena. One popular authority is Sam Moskowitz, an old-time fan and collector who was editor of Gernsback's last, short-lived science fiction magazine in 1953. In *Explorers of the Infinite* (1963) and *Seekers of Tomorrow* (1966), Moskowitz profiles the creators of science fiction. His lives of the writers are interesting, but his efforts at criticism seldom go beyond the game of tracing story origins through seeming similarities of plot. His more recent volumes, *Science Fiction by Gaslight* (1968) and *Under the Moons of Mars* (1970), are useful histories and anthologies of science fiction in the popular magazines, 1891–1911, and 1912–1920.

Richard A. Lupoff's *Edgar Rice Burroughs: Master of Adventure* (1965: revised and enlarged for the paperback edition, 1968) is a scholarly—and entertaining—study of the most popular science fiction writer of all. Donald A. Wollheim's *The Universe Makers* (1971) deserves mention as an inside view of contemporary science fiction by a man who helped to shape the genre. As a long-time editor for Ace Books and now as an important paperback publisher himself, Wollheim has doubtless bought and printed more science fiction than anybody else. His book is intensely personal and very readable, marred I think by his limited knowledge of other literature and by occasional unfairness to some of his rival editors, but still fascinating for its view of science fiction as a sort of faith in man and his science, and particularly for its sketch of man's imagined future in space —of the rise and fall of the coming Galactic Empire that has been the background of so much "space opera."

The new academic approval of science fiction is already swelling the flow of scholarly comment—some of it excellent, some seemingly born from the logic of publish or perish. *Into the Unknown* (1970) by Robert Philmus is a survey of "the evolution of science fiction from Francis Godwin to H. G. Wells," erudite but slightly dry. Robert C. Elliott's *The Shape of Utopia* (1970) traces the idea of the ambiguous "good place" or "no place" from the golden age of the ancients to the nightmares of today. David C. Goldsmith's *Kurt Vonnegut: Fantasist of Fire and Ice* is a useful booklet in a promising new critical series from Bowling Green University Press. Robert Silverberg's *Mirror of Infinity* (1970) spans the period from Wells to Harlan Ellison with fine stories selected and discussed by a baker's dozen of current critics. In *A Spectrum of Worlds* (1972), Thomas Clareson has chosen another set of stories, ranging from Ambrose Bierce to Silverberg, introducing and annotating them in a way that relates science fiction to the main traditions of modern literature.

Clareson's *SF: The Other Side of Realism* (1971) is a thick anthology of mostly recent critical essays, some of them excellent. His *Science Fiction Criticism: An Annotated Checklist* (1972) classifies and describes some eight hundred items, of widely varied value. Another listing—more than a hundred items, many not noted by Clareson—is Advent's *SF Bibliographies* (1972) by Robert Briney and Edward Wood.

With such exceptions as Jules Verne, science fiction used to be pretty much a British-American phenomenon, with America offering the richest markets and England many of the more literate writers, but now, with its swelling popularity in every industrial country, the criticism has become an international conversation. Though cut off from us by censorship, Russian science fiction seems to share our debt to Wells. Isaac Asimov has edited *Soviet Science Fiction* and *More Soviet Science Fiction* (1962), collections that reveal no hint of any New Wave. In a more scholarly work, *Other Worlds, Other Seas* (1970), Darko Suvin discusses and anthologizes socialist science fiction from Poland, Rumania, Czechoslovakia, and Bulgaria, as well as from the USSR. His Marxist dialectic may offer a narrow standard of value, but the stories are often brilliant.

But all this scholarship has had very little to do, I suspect, with making a place for science fiction in American high schools and colleges. Most of the credit for this new wave of recognition, as for the postwar wavelet, must be due to fear—to the contagious fear of the future that has brought our old faith in science to a crisis. All the dilemmas of accelerating change are suddenly too near to be ignored any longer. We see ourselves trapped in a frightening paradox. Terrifying as technology may seem, our own survival is bound up with it. Hence science fiction in the classroom. Pro or con, it can speak about our world predicament with far more force than the statistical predictions of the computer futurologists. Though it does offer other and maybe higher values, this relevance is what most college courses stress. The readings for my own are selected to review this ever-new debate about the nature and stature and future of man, with Swift and Wells and Huxley and Ellison challenging the optimism in Asimov and Clarke and Heinlein.

As some sort of referee in this conflict, what credentials should the critic show? First of all, I think, an awareness of other literature, along with some knowledge of the traditions of criticism and humanism and an ear for language. Sam Moskowitz does poorly on this first test, as Blish points out. Knowing only science fiction, he has a limited view of even that.

Beyond this general cultural background, the critic should also understand the conventions of science fiction. This implies a sensitivity to social change and a grasp of the scientific method. Here we must disqualify most of the well-known mainstream critics—Northrup Frye and Leslie Fiedler are the only ones I have seen at science fiction gatherings. Amis, in *New Maps of Hell*, seems widely read in the genre, yet so little aware of real change that he tends to reduce science fiction to disguised satire on the present.

Finally, the critic should not belong entirely to either of Snow's two cultures. He must see the limits of progress that Wells explored so tellingly and the genuine danger that unguided technology might desolate our planet. But he must also perceive that same technology as the essential instrument of our own survival, must learn to discount the indiscriminate attacks upon it that have recently become an automatic reflex of Snow's traditional academics.

This last point disqualifies the New Wave critics—and also, I think, the naive Marxists who are equally at war with technology and capitalism. The motivation seems to be a sort of romantic individualism in revolt against all social control. The common error is the failure to see that the continued benefits of a technological civilization are going to require an increasingly fine division of labor and an increasingly firm social discipline. The critical platform of the party-line Marxist—whose one criterion of literary excellence is simply "correctness"—is narrow enough to suggest that the ironic outcome of all these romantic thrusts for absolute individual independence may be only to hasten the New Wave nightmare of total slavery to a mechanized state. This crucial problem of the Age of Science can't be solved by mere emotion, but I think our whole world culture can be endangered by it.

Personally, I keep reconsidering where I stand. Hillegas identifies my best fiction as anti-utopian, but I am still optimist enough to feel cheered by Edwin Land's faith that we can solve any problem we can state. In a novel, *Bright New Universe*, I tried to write a utopian reply to Huxley's *Brave New World*—only to discover that the need to get dramatic conflict into the story had led me to make the traditional opponents to progress so powerful that the actual establishment of the better world required an unlikely intervention from outside the earth. I suspect that the popularity of the nightmare school of science fiction is at least partly due to the fact that dramas of universal disaster are far more exciting than plans for universal happiness. Compare the attention value of a city burning and a city growing. More and more I agree with Stuart Chase that technology is worth at least two cheers. For all our ecological apprehensions, the majority of mankind still seems to feel that technological progress is worth whatever it may cost. We won't willingly give up antibiotics or electricity or even the ominous power of the atom.

If critics had to face the tests outlined above, not all would pass. But science fiction is many things to many people—nowadays that it is often speculative fantasy with no science at all. The total flow of comment has become vast and various enough to carry every sort of interest. The general magazines and journals print frequent articles, often better informed and less satiric than they used to be. The fiction magazines *Galaxy* and *If* and *Fantasy and Science Fiction* run critical columns by such perceptive people as Joanna Russ and Theodore Sturgeon and Lester del Rey. With Ted White as editor, *Amazing* and *Fantastic* have found space for criticism, most notably for an ambitious series by Alexei and Cory Panshin. *Analog's* P. Schuyler Miller has become the dean of science fiction reviewers, the notes in his monthly column genially descriptive rather than critical.

Extrapolation, edited by Thomas Clareson at the College of Wooster, is the oldest academic journal, launched in the late 1950s as the newsletter of the MLA seminar on science fiction. *Science Fiction Studies* is coming now from the department of English at Indiana University, Terre Haute. In England, *Foundation* is the journal of the Science Fiction Foundation. Elsewhere, criticism has become multilingual. *Helikon,* for example, is an impressive Hungarian journal that recently devoted a whole issue to science fiction, with a list of contributors that includes Darko Suvin—who is a Yugoslav Marxist—the Polish novelist Stanislaw Lem, the Soviet Wellsian Julius Kagarlitsky, and other critics from other nations, including the Americans Frederik Pohl and Donald Wollheim.

Everywhere, the fan magazines offer the most copious source of science fiction criticism, seldom very scholarly but now and then excellent—the Atheling-Blish essays in *The Issue at Hand* appeared originally in *Skyhook, Axe, Warhoon,* and *Xero.* These fan magazines are commonly one-man labors of love, brief of life, erratic in intention, and frustrating to the collector. Not always interested in formal criticism or general literature, the writers usually do know science fiction. Recent useful comment has appeared in *Algol, Riverside Quarterly, Speculation, SF Commentator,* and assorted others. *The Alien Critic* is the individual voice of Richard Geis. *Locus* features timely news; *Luna* is chiefly a bibliographic record of current fiction and comment. Takumi Shibano's *Uchujin* is the organ of Japanese fandom. Ugo Malaguti's *Nova SF* is a beautifully printed Italian review that carries critical essays and such fannish features as letters to the editor along with translations of classic science fiction. The international reach of fandom and fan criticism is more striking, perhaps, in a recent issue of *SF Commentary.* Published in Australia, it features contributions from the United States, Canada, England, France, Austria, and Poland. (The French student enjoys Bradbury, Simak, Ballard, and Ellison. The Pole is Stanislaw Lem, author of *Solaris.* The Austrian is Franz Rottensteiner, a caustic Marxist, scornful of most Western science fiction.)

Turning now from the critics to the teachers of science fiction, we find their points of view equally diverse. Though most commonly harbored in departments of English, they are also in history, religion, social studies, communications, humanities, history of science, chemistry, physics, design, theater and speech, popular culture, and honors—at every level from junior high to graduate school. Course titles show emphasis variously on social criticism, on the shape of the future, on science itself, on utopian thought, on literary fantasy, on science fiction as a vehicle for religion and philosophy.

John Campbell—a strong partisan of the culture of science— was distressed when he saw a preliminary breakdown of the required reading lists. He was featuring "hard" science fiction in *Analog,* and he felt sure the readers preferred it, because his magazine was selling about as many copies as all three of his chief competitors, which were devoted mostly to "soft" science fiction or fantasy. Bewildered by the lack of hard science fiction on the required lists—except for a few books by Wells, Hal Clement, and Asimov—he asked why the colleges were "teaching *non*-science fiction courses labeled science fiction."

When I suggested that perhaps most of the teachers belonged to Snow's traditional culture, he seemed to agree. "I think the basic separation of the two cultures is somewhat like the late unlamented angry debates over science versus religion—based on the two different kinds of truth, with the academics insisting angrily that the only True Truths are the truths of human realization, of human consensus." He added, with Campbellian irony, "The scientific 'facts' are no more than opinions anyway, and scientists are arrogant, nasty fellows claiming a special authority with no more reason than anybody else for their opinions. And their opinions are unpleasant, unkind, inhumane, and arbitrary things such as 'You can't get something for nothing,' and 'Things always run downhill,' and other arbitrary impediments they put in the way of fine and noble ideas."

Impossible to classify as the courses may be, I think most of them might be placed somewhere on a broad spectrum that ranges from futurology to fantasy. At the pole of futurology, the emphasis is on technological and sociological extrapolations in the real world; at the pole of fantasy, on symbolic myth or "transcendence" or stylistic value or sometimes pure escape. Campbell preferred stories that probe alternative futures in somewhat the same way that good historical fiction reconstructs the probable past. But the defenders of fantasy point out that mythic fiction can make even profounder statements about our human predicament.

Courses in the nonfictional future have been growing as fast as science fiction. Yet, according to Professor Dennis Livingston of Case Western Reserve, "there is not much overlap between the futurists and the sf people. Some people now engaged in forecasting for fun and profit do have sf backgrounds (Joe Martino, Don Fabun, Harry Stine), while some sf writers are called on from time to time to lend their talents to exploratory projects (Asimov, Anderson, Pohl)." Livingston sees himself as a middleman between the two disciplines.

Classroom methods vary as widely as the cultural slants. In Livingston's utopian course, teams of students studied present-day radical groups that claimed to have "a handle on the future." In a course on "Religious Dimensions of Science Fiction," Andrew J. Burgess, also at Case, had students working out ways to communicate religious concepts to the insect inhabitants of a planet in the constellation Scorpio. Richard Doxtator has brought Ray Bradbury and other writers to his class at Wisconsin State by conference telephone. Arlen Ray Zander, at East Texas State, has bridged the cultural gap by combining a physicist, a psychologist, and two English professors into a teaching team. James Gunn, at Kansas, is not only teaching, but also filming a science fiction course available for rental from the Audio-Visual Center at Lawrence.

The science fiction virus reached the high schools a few years ago, and it is spreading fast there. Teachers often report multi-section courses with several hundred students enrolled. Special high-school texts are already appearing, such as Harry Harrison's *Science Fiction Reader* and Sprague and Catherine de Camp's *3000 Years of Fantasy and Science Fiction*.

The trickle of college texts that began with Silverberg's *Mirror of Infinity* and Allen's *SF: The Future* is swelling toward a paperback flood that includes Harrison's *The Light Fantastic*, Clareson's *Spectrum of Worlds*, Ofshe's *Sociology of the Possible*, McNelly and Stover's *Above the Human Landscape*. More are out or on the way. Most of these are "quality" paperbacks, priced at five or six dollars. Though they seem to be selling well, reading lists show that most instructors still use the low-cost newsstand paperbacks that come from Ace, Avon, Award, Ballantine, Bantam, Berkley, DAW, Dell, Fantasy House, Lancer, Paperback Library, Popular, and Signet.

The total output is currently about one a day, including reissues. Average print printings are fifty to one hundred thousand copies, but the wasteful newsstand distribution system destroys perhaps half the copies unsold—and often makes particular titles hard for college bookstores to obtain. This abundance may baffle the individual critic, but there are two efforts at organized criticism—the Hugo awards at the fan conventions, and the Nebulas, from the Science Fiction Writers of America. Both are under fire, because too few voters read all the stories and too many awards are won by high-pressure campaigns.

The magazines are suffering from poor distribution and paperback competition, but they are still a major source of new science fiction, especially of shorts and novelettes. Half a dozen competing anthologists currently offer the collected "best of the year." The newest rivals of the magazines are the periodic books; among them, Fred Pohl's *Star* series was followed by Damon Knight's *Orbit*, Chip Delany's *Quark*, Robert Silverberg's *New Dimensions*, Robert Hoskins's *Infinity*, Terry Carr's

Universe, and Harry Harrison's *Nova.* Roger Elwood alone is editing scores of new paperbacks. Harlan Ellison's huge *Dangerous Visions* anthologies have encouraged experimental writing. Translations of able new foreign writers are beginning to appear.

Though all this may overwhelm the critic, it offers riches for the teacher. Tabulating eighty lists of required texts, I found nearly three hundred books named at least once. The top twelve were Asimov's *I, Robot,* Bradbury's *The Martian Chronicles,* Heinlein's *The Moon Is a Harsh Mistress* and *Stranger in a Strange Land,* Herbert's *Dune,* Huxley's *Brave New World,* Le Guin's *The Left Hand of Darkness,* Miller's *A Canticle for Leibowitz,* Pohl and Kornbluth's *The Space Merchants,* Silverberg's *Science Fiction Hall of Fame* (volume I), Wells's *The Time Machine* and *The War of The Worlds.* Heinlein and Wells emerge as the most-taught writers here, with two titles each, but there is no unanimity—no title appears on more than one list out of three.

Glancing at the science fiction student, James Gunn reports a survey of the more than 150 members of his class at Kansas. Only 39 were already fans, and only 42 "wanted to know the history and the literary value of science fiction"; 106 enrolled simply "because the course sounded interesting." When they checked a list of writers they already knew, Ray Bradbury came in first, followed in order by Heinlein, Asimov, Clarke, Vonnegut, and Ellison. Speculating about why students take to science fiction, Gunn suggests "the prevailing alienation which leads young people to seek a literature of alternatives, the affluence (until the recent recession) of the young, and the availability of good juvenile science fiction."

For teacher and critic alike, the major puzzle is not this sudden academic acceptance of science fiction, but rather its earlier rejection. It wasn't always in the doghouse. Its first appeal is wonder, and the amazing tale has always been popular. Critics from Aristotle and Longinus to Tasso and Edmund Burke recognized wonder as a literary value. Verne found no special ghetto waiting for his "imaginary voyages," nor Wells for his "scientific romances." By the 1920s, however, when Gernsback was inventing such new labels as "scientifiction" and "science fiction" for the stuff in his pulp magazines, critics—and book publishers—had no use at all for the marvel tale.

The causes for this fall of wonder seem complex and not very clear. The rationalism of a scientific age was hostile to the irrational which Aristotle had seen as the chief sense of wonder—and science fiction, if not quite irrational, does test the limits of reason. The tradition of the modern novel is no friend of science fiction. *Don Quixote,* perhaps the first great novel, was begun as a satire on the wonder romance. The novel soon became the genre of the rising middle class, respecting reason more than feeling, too much absorbed with money and morality to care about the marvelous.

The history-minded critic can trace the cultural split we have seen in current science fiction back at least to the Renaissance, when modern science was born. Once upon a time—so the story goes—man lived at the center of a simple world, one created for his own comfort and maybe to test his fitness for heaven. Materially, by today's measures, he was disadvantaged. Spiritually, he wore the image of God. Shakespeare and John Donne were among the last literate inhabitants of that good world, before satanic science divided it into a sphere of knowledge and a sphere of faith. The two spheres are Snow's two cultures, still at war.

Taking an even longer perspective, we might suggest that the culture of science is simply a current phase of the utopian tradition that begins, perhaps, with Plato's *Republic*—the idea that reasonable men can create an ideal society here on earth. The tradition is Greek; it reflects the self-confidence of Homer's Odysseus. The anti-utopian tradition appears even older. Its roots are Egyptian and Hebraic, I think; its mythic anti-hero is Adam. Homer's symbol for reason is the glorious Athena, the comrade and helper of epic man. The Hebrew symbol is the snake, the betrayer. In the pattern of the culture that built the stone pyramids, the Hebrew tradition makes society dominant, visiting divine wrath on any impious individual who tries to disturb it. The Greek tradition allows more individual freedom, a more hopeful view of change. H. G. Wells, I think, was torn between those two traditions, with the Hebraic dominant in his great early fiction and the Greek in his later campaign for a modern utopia.

Such immense generalizations are very coarse nets, I know; they let most of the truth run through. History was never simple. No two people have experienced the impact of our fragmented culture in quite the same way, and nobody is likely to agree entirely with any statement about it. Yet I think it does make some sort of sense to say that Asimov and Clarke and Heinlein and a good many others are spokesmen for the Greek tradition in those optimistic moments when they choose to show men solving problems to make things better. I think it makes sense to call the New Wave writers the sons of Adam—along with all the earlier anti-utopians who show man tripping over his own intelligence, and even the producers of the science-horror films in which arrogant scientists came to grief for seeking "what man was not meant to know."

Whatever it may say about our roles as masters or victims of the machine, the wonder story is still a living voice. If it was once nearly stifled by rationalistic science and realistic fiction, it is louder now. The mainstream novel has begun to stammer. Its middle-class concerns of money and sex have lost most of their old obsessive appeal, at least on the campus. Maybe not yet dead, realistic fiction is less alive than it used to be. As a model for writer and critic, science is also losing its old charisma. Though the individual scientist may try to be as strictly rational as ever, his world seems far less so. Each new insight leads to new and unexpected bafflements—the atom is split into swarms of new enigmas, the great telescopes discover more quasars than answers. The scientist has grasped the keys to a technological utopia, but also to inferno. Faced with new dilemmas of his own invention, he finds his best computers not yet so wise as Homer's Athena. His expanding universe is it seems at least irrational enough to admit a renewed sense of wonder.

The panic fear of a technological crisis, however, has no doubt done more to get science fiction into college than any appeal to wonder. The Greeks among us are still busy building wooden horses, and the sons of Adam are alarmed by the new threats to their ancient ramparts. Pro or con, science fiction offers at least a vivid language for reporting the impending battle. At the best, it can hope to fuse the insights of new science and truths of old tradition into a better way of looking at our evolving world.

Jack Williamson

Jack Williamson was born in 1908 in Bisbee, Arizona Territory, to pioneering parents who moved first to Sonora, then to Pecos, Texas, and finally in 1915 by covered wagon to the sandhill homestead in eastern New Mexico where he grew up. The big event of his youth was the discovery of Hugo Gernsback's *Amazing Stories*, which promised an escape from dust storms and drought into more exciting worlds of the imagination. He entered college the year his first story sold, but dropped out before graduation because the courses had little to do with science fiction. For many years, he was a freelance writer. As an Army Air Forces weather forecaster, he reached the Northern Solomons in 1945. Upon his return to New Mexico, he married and settled in Portales. During the science fiction boomlet of the early 1950s, he created a comic strip, *Beyond Mars*, which ran for three years in the New York *Sunday News*.

Returning to college, he received the B.A. and M.A. from Eastern New Mexico University in 1957. A teacher there since 1960, he is now a professor of English. He received his Ph.D. from the University of Colorado in 1964 with a dissertation, which has now become a book, on the early science fiction of H. G. Wells—*H. G. Wells: Critic of Progress*. Writing more or less steadily since 1926, he has published two and a half million words of magazine science fiction and nearly thirty books, several in collaboration. His teaching fields include the modern novel, literary criticism, and science fiction. He has recently been speaking and writing to promote science fiction as an academic subject.

The Legion of Space, 1947 (Fantasy)
Darker Than You Think, 1948 (Fantasy)
The Humanoids, 1949 (Simon and Schuster)
The Green Girl, 1950 (Avon)
The Cometeers and One Against the Legion, 1950 (Fantasy)
Seetee Ship, 1951 (Gnome)
Dragon's Island, 1951 (Simon and Schuster)
The Legion of Time and After World's End, 1952 (Fantasy)

Undersea Quest, 1954 (Gnome) ; with Frederik Pohl
Dome Around America, 1955 (Ace)
Star Bridge, 1955 (Gnome); with James Gunn
Undersea Fleet, 1955 (Gnome); with Frederik Pohl
Undersea City, (Gnome); with Frederik Pohl
The Trial of Terra, 1962 (Ace)
Golden Blood, 1964 (Lancer)
The Reefs of Space, 1964 (Ballantine); with Frederik Pohl
Starchild, 1965 (Ballantine); with Frederik Pohl
The Reign of Wizardry, 1965 (Lancer)
Bright New Universe, 1967 (Ace)
The Pandora Effect, 1969 (Ace)
Rogue Star, 1969 (Ballantine); with Frederik Pohl
People Machines, 1971 (Ace)
The Moon Children, 1972 (Putnam)
H. G. Wells: Critic of Progress, 1973 (Mirage)
The Power of Blackness (Putnam—in progress)
Doomship, (Ballantine—in progress); with Frederik Pohl

A Critical Sampler

Amis, Kingsley. *New Maps of Hell: A Survey of Science Fiction.* New York: Harcourt Brace, 1960. By a mainstream novelist, who emphasized elements of satire and contemporary social comment.

Atheling, William, Jr. (James Blish). *The Issue at Hand.* Chicago: Advent, 1964. Intelligent and outspoken essays by a veteran writer.

Atheling, William, Jr. *More Issues at Hand.* Chicago: Advent 1972. Recent Blish, still wittily abrasive. Probably the best criticism at hand.

Bailey, J. O. *Pilgrims Through Space and Time: Trends and Patterns in Scientific and Utopian Fiction.* New York: Argus Books, 1947. Reprinted with new foreword by Thomas D. Clareson, Westport, Conn., Greenwood Press: 1972. Important study of the emergence of science fiction, emphasis on the period 1870–1915.

Bergonzi, Bernard. *The Early H. G. Wells: A Study of the Scientific Romances.* Manchester: Manchester University Press, 1961. The standard study of Wells's early—and great—science fiction.

Bretnor, Reginald (ed.). *Modern Science Fiction: Its Meaning and Its Future.* New York: Coward-McCann, 1953. A symposium by leading writers, editors, and critics of its time, this has been a standard reference work.

Briney, Robert, and Edward Wood. *Sf Bibliographies: An Annotated Bibliography of Bibliographical Works on Science Fiction and Fantasy Fiction.* Chicago: Advent Publishers, 1972. A valuable listing of 107 items.

Clareson, Thomas D. (ed.). *SF: The Other Side of Realism: Essays on Modern Fantasy and Science Fiction.* Bowling Green, Ohio: Bowling Green University Popular Press, 1971. A diversity of essays, mostly recent, sometimes excellent.

Clareson, Thomas D. *Science Fiction Criticism: An Annotated Checklist.* Kent, Ohio: Kent State University Press, 1972. Lists some eight hundred items, of widely varied critical value.

Clareson, Thomas D. (ed.). *A Spectrum of Worlds.* Garden City, N.Y.: Doubleday, 1972. Fourteen stories, from Ambrose Bierce to Robert Silverberg, introduced and annotated to relate science fiction to the main traditions of modern literature.

Davenport, Basil. *Inquiry into Science Fiction.* New York: Longmans, Green, 1955. A brief appreciation.

Davenport, Basil (ed.). *The Science Fiction Novel: Imagination and Social Criticism.* Chicago: Advent, 1964. Four lectures on science fiction as social criticism, by Robert A. Heinlein, C. M. Kornbluth, Alfred Bester, and Robert Bloch.

de Camp, L. Sprague. *Science-Fiction Handbook: The Writing of Imaginative Fiction.* New York: Hermitage House, 1953. An important book of its time, still a useful reference.

Elliott, Robert C. *The Shape of Utopia: Studies in a Literary Genre.* Chicago: University of Chicago Press, 1970. The idea of utopia traced from golden myth to nightmare.

Eshbach, Lloyd Arthur. *Of Worlds Beyond: The Science of Science Fiction Writing.* Chicago: Advent, 1964. Reprint of a 1947 symposium.

Franklin, H. Bruce. *Future Perfect: American Science Fiction of the Nineteenth Century.* New York: Oxford University Press, 1966. An anthology of early American science fiction with comment by a Marxist scholar.

Green, Roger Lancelyn. *Into Other Worlds: Space Flight in Fiction from Lucian to Lewis.* New York: Abelard-Schuman, 1958. A scholarly but readable survey of space flight in literature, with summaries of rare early novels.

Hillegas, Mark R. *The Future as Nightmare: H. G. Wells and the Anti-Utopians.* New York: Oxford University Press, 1967. Emphasizes the influence of the early Wells on Zamyatin, Huxley, Orwell, and more recent science fiction.

Hillegas, Mark R. (ed.). *Shadows of Imagination: The Fantasies of C. S. Lewis, J. R. R. Tolkien, and Charles Williams.* Carbondale: Southern Illinois University Press, 1969. Essays on three creators of modern fantasy.

Knight, Damon. *In Search of Wonder.* Chicago: Advent, 1956. Enlarged second edition, 1967. Collected essays by a science fiction veteran. Intelligent, sometimes devastating.

Lundwall, Sam J. *Science Fiction: What It's All About.* New York: Ace Books, 1971. A Swedish fan's view of the genre.

Lupoff, Richard A. *Edgar Rice Burroughs: Master of Adventure.* New York: Canaveral Press, 1965. Revised and enlarged edition, New York: Ace Books, 1968. An entertaining—and scholarly—study of the most popular science fiction writer of all.

Manuel, Frank E. (ed.). *Utopias and Utopian Thought*. Boston: Houghton Mifflin, 1966. Articles by scholars looking at the idea of utopia from a dozen varied points of view.

Moskowitz, Sam. *Explorers of the Infinite: Shapers of Science Fiction*. New York: World, 1963. Useful information on early writers, marred by critical myopia and too many errors of fact.

Moskowitz, Sam. *Seekers of Tomorrow: Masters of Modern Science Fiction*. New York: World, 1966. About more recent writers.

Nicolson, Marjorie Hope. *Voyages to the Moon*. New York: Macmillan, 1960. Reprint of a 1948 survey of the moon voyage as a literary theme before the nineteenth century.

Panshin, Alexei, *Heinlein in Dimension*. Chicago: Advent, 1968. A readable and useful but maybe not-quite-adequate study of the foremost American science fiction writer.

Philmus, Robert M. *Into the Unknown: The Evolution of Science Fiction from Francis Goodwin to H. G. Wells*. Berkeley: University of California Press, 1970. Highbrow scholarship, sound but sometimes dull.

Silverberg, Robert. (ed.) *The Mirror of Infinity: A Critics' Anthology of Science Fiction*. New York: Harper & Row, 1970. With a dozen fine stories, each introduced by a different critic, this book surveys science fiction from Wells to Ellison.

Suvin, Darko. *Other Worlds, Other Seas: Science Fiction Stories from Socialist Countries*. New York: Random House, 1970. Suvin, a Marxist critic now at McGill University, introduces and edits selected science fiction from five socialist nations.

Wollheim, Donald A. *The Universe Makers: Science Fiction Today*. New York: Harper & Row, 1971. A valuable "inside" view of science fiction by a veteran editor and publisher who has helped form the genre.

Index

335

74 75 76 77 10 9 8 7 6 5 4 3